Teaching Snapping Turtles How to Chew Bubblegum

By Jonathan Heatt

Teaching

Snapping Turtles

How To Chew

Bubblegum

JONATHAN HEATT

Copyright © 2014 by Jonathan Heatt

Las Vegas, NV

Dedicated to the Nutter Center sign

Prologue

Most of the Las Vegas journalists are sniveling worms. Like the rotting maggots infesting Jason Voorhees' scalp, they feast on the brains of decomposing men. Or maybe the city itself is a festering blister and the media is the pus oozing from the sore.

There's nothing new to write about. The Economy stagnates as the mogul's pay rises. The casino showrooms smell like roses while the sidewalks outside reek of underground oceans of shit. Is that the foundation of this town? If so, then no wonder the fecal flies swarm overhead, looking for another carcass to feast on.

It's a tough town to crack. Failures get raked over the coals on the front page. Even the winners sometimes get mauled by tigers. And the arthropodal peanut gallery jeers on the sidelines with twisted grins and forked tongues…the favorite hobby of invertebrates.

Those who can't do become Vegas journalists. Some of these swine are so desperate for stories that they instigate bestiality among family members just so they can write about it. For what? Posterity? For a fleeting semblance of fame inside some cramped newsroom? For a perverse fulfillment of public self-flogging?

No.

For no other reason than a simple and obvious one: Lack of Imagination. Creative talent stumped these eight-legged creatures long ago, so now they spin their webs of bitter hate – trapping their Readers in a slow death of Mediocrity.

Does this city deserve better journalism? Maybe not.

The majority of tourists who visit this neon nest of hypocritical depravity end up losing their money, and sometimes, their minds right along with it. It's only right the Locals who seek enlightened editorials should lose also…but I am here to provide readers a gonzoesque glimpse into Las Vegas and the American Dream…two ideas intertwined like crossed fingers on a bloated corpse.

I'm not a journalist, just a reporter of human nature, with no outlet available but the truth. The local Vegas mags, or what I refer to as glossy tampons, are subsidized in direct co-relation to the materialistic fervor they can incite in their readers. Rapacious Capitalistic Douche dictates the craven mundane content of its writers whose articles are dull as dishwater and tamer than dickless donkeys.

These outlets are closed to a man of my talents and modest wants. All I seek is the truth about American Society, and I wrote this book so I wouldn't be alone on my journey.

"What you have to understand is that good writing isn't necessarily saleable, and alot of people get rich writing awful bullshit. Editors are nearly always dim assholes and the American Press, in general, is a pile of hired shit."
-HST (Hunter Thompson)

Dog Days of Insanity

On a smoldering summer afternoon I headed out to Boulder Highway in search of the American Dream. If I didn't locate it there I was prepared to cut a nihilistic swath of depravity through Las Vegas until I did locate it. Emboldened by the books of my idol, Hunter Thompson, I was ready to get in serious trouble in order to find a little truth in a big town full of lies.

Much to my chagrin, I cut the journey short…not out of self-preservation, but because I'm married. Marriage is the bane of nihilism, sort of like boric acid is harmful to roaches. Marriage is a toothache of the mind. And only a bevy of booze can soothe the restless fever.

Before the alcohol mixed with the 105-degree heat and formed an intoxication of mass proportions that certainly promised ugliness, I went home. But I did come to a conclusion. The American Dream is an elusive whisper of promises seldom heard in a raucous casino…maybe because that dream has vanished. Not died, but not dreamt of anymore. What has replaced it is sleep.

The new era of our society is: *The American Sleep.*

Oil and radiation bubble the oceans. Noxious fumes swirl over the highways. Blood drips in the Middle Eastern deserts. And all Americans really care about are Big Macs and animated movies with fat green ogres that resemble the still-breathing boogers I used to wipe under my desk in 11th grade geometry class.

Unemployment sucks, but surely those people can find jobs if they really wanted to. Foreclosures suck, but those people should have checked the fine print on their mortgages. Diabetes, cancer, and heart disease all suck, but fuck it, I'll eat the McRib anyway.

The Herd Mentality has replaced the American Dream. Free-range grazing is the new lifestyle. House on house. No yard. Car on Car. Traffic jams.

Ants.

If you saw ants swarming your garden, what would your reaction be? Now picture ants swarming your planet. Is that a Dream or a Nightmare? Voltaire saw men for what they really are, insects devouring each other upon a tiny speck of dirt. I'd have more sympathy for the Human Race if it were just a bunch of flawed people trying to do the best they can. Instead, it's a bloodthirsty race beholden to bigotry and superstition, susceptible to greed, apathy, and arrogance. A thousand clans sparring over each other's land and the resources residing underneath -- digging their graves in the name of oil and natural gas.

    Americans are spoiled. Hunger pains easily satiated by a million fast food grease kitchens posted up on every block like so many drug dealers. Pocketfuls of carbs and plastic straws to suck up the empty calories. Toilet paper readily available. Even wireless Internet. Same thing. Talking shit is the same as wiping your ass after a chilidog-eating contest. Only thing we don't have is a crisis. Yeah, 9/11 was scary for about a year or two, but now: business as usual. WW II and the Cold War were different…Americans faced extinction. That type of crisis forced you to get smart fast. Maybe the threat of nuclear annihilation kept more Americans aware of their surroundings. At the very least, they were more caring, even if it was in a Klanish sort of way.

    The threat today lives within us. Apathy. Gluttony. Ignorance. A bad case of the stupid-ass. 4th of July is just another day for fireworks to explode over the sky. Some teenagers have no idea how old America is. Simple arithmetic and history elude the young; too lazy to even Google simple facts.

    You say cheeseburger. I say freedom. You say *Dancing with the Stars*. I ask what happened to Mars?

    Global Warming is passé. Junkies grace the front pages. You do drugs and you eventually die. Is that news? But our planet's dying too. A prolonged wake of ostrich policies. Death by interstate. Puff, puff, pass the planet. Unfortunately we're not Gods capable of interstellar travel – planet hopping is not an option. Instead of deitifying our fears, let's worship the planet we live on.

    You don't appreciate life unless you stare death in the face. At least glance at the ugly visage. A subtle taste of decay goes a long way. That's what I see.

Author's note: *Humans are greedy. At our basest form, we want something. At our best, we seek knowledge…which is Everything.*

Conversation is Intellectual Stimulation. A book is a conduit to the Author's mind. The Reader is expected to Interpret the message then communicate it to others…which in turn, Creates Thought. Reading is active participation. Most everything else is passive. To read is to create thought and to progress society. And so is Writing.

Too many people stare entranced at a brainless television show or violent movie. And too many people create these brainless shows for the hackish reasons of money & fame. They fancy themselves performers. And they perform to the detriment of society, creating a swollen ignorant mass of unenlightened apathetic people. A higher calling is being a communicator or storyteller. Otherwise, we're just performing, and what's the use of performing for someone who isn't able to appreciate the audacity of the performance?

1.
Diagnosis

The white race is a disease...

A chicken pox that dabbled in slavery and genocide, Crusades and Imperialism. Europeans have a long history of warfare, death, and destruction that is romanticized in fiction. The reality is that the Enlightenment is a minor footnote along the road to the morass that now passes for progress. Like any disease, it keeps mutating into a more destructive version to offset evolution, and its current manifestation of Capitalism puts the entire planet at risk.

Blacks are no better. They are the most hypocritical full-of-shit race on the planet. Blacks decry racism yet have no qualms about killing each other for a buck or for power, whether it's in Rwanda or Chicago. Beat a dog too long, the dog turns violent. Mike Vick is a witness.

The most superstitious culture on our petri dish of a planet are the Hispanics, no doubt the result of centuries of Catholicism being brutally beat into their genes. Mexicans are incapable of comfortably running their own country so they keep coming to America, and the ones that stay in Mexico are terrorized by Drug Cartels...a cannibalistic cabal of gangsters seizing on the opportunity of failed American drug & gun policies. These Cartels are the most vicious people on the planet, a baton that has eagerly been passed around throughout history.

Hispanics further south are perpetually torn between right & left wing politics...which are usually determined by the pigment of their skin. The South American continent has suffered the Spanish flu-like conquistador boorish behavior since the white man discovered it. The indigenous people are treated like dirt so the white people can extract the natural resources from the land. This has been a reoccurring theme in North & South America, and especially, Africa. Everywhere the white disease spreads it takes what it wants and has no problem destroying anything in its path.

Asians are insectile pathogens overrunning their polluted environments with massive populations resembling ant colonies. India too. Both "developing countries" embrace coal and other fossil fuels...even though they've been "developing" for the past few thousand years. Both races have the potential to overtake the white race as being the most destructive in their quest to see who can spew more CO_2 emissions. Global Warming is treated as a western myth designed to keep the East down. Once the sea level starts rising, and coastal cities become flooded, India & China will skirmish over land, drinking water, and other resources. Insects have a hard time co-existing when ecosystems radically change.

And last, but least, the Muslims are a bevy of different races still living in the stone age, intent on destroying anyone who doesn't believe in their backwards religion. Their tenuous web of ignorance could come undone with an increase in education, but as America proves, education doesn't eradicate all ignorance. The United States is the melting pot of mass shootings, and nothing is done about it. Americans cling to their guns like Muslims cling to their Koran. Which is more destructive?

Maybe it's not about race. Maybe it's Human Nature that is the Problem. We're just Animals with opposable thumbs and a nature to destroy. Instead of being failures, we're really over-achievers cursed from the beginning. Our greatest accomplishment will be the prolonged devastation of the very Earth that gives us Life. That is a perverse talent. An insistence to propagate at all costs takes narrow-minded Focus.

Mankind is all one big genetic experiment run amok...intent on making survival as difficult as possible. Too many tribes clamoring to be the number one disease. And so the Super Germ infects the planet. Earth is an interstellar AIDS victim. Other planets are shedding their atmospheres so they don't get sick.

Eleanor Roosevelt said something about lighting a candle instead of cursing the darkness, but too many people today are so blind that they don't even know darkness surrounds them. Show that darkness to them, then light a flare, a candle is too weak. Maybe my book can do both.

You may notice that my writing sometimes takes on a bitter, almost combative tone. Good. You can read. I can't be sweet to a snapping turtle. They'll just poke their head into their shell and ignore me. So I haveta shake the green beasts upside down like champagne at the Super Bowl. Force 'em to poke their head out, and then cram the bubblegum into their craw. Teachin' 'em how to chew is impossible unless you have their attention.

And that goes for all of you. Every person reading this book needs to know the journey ahead is tough. A one-way ticket through the underpass of reality. The lights are out, oncoming traffic is common, and there are no more seatbelts. So let go of your fear, it won't help you here.

The main thing to remember is that darkness IS at the end of the tunnel. But maybe we can all travel together and light the way with benevolent curiosity. No matter what happens, try to understand that there is no such thing as opposition, except for the obstacles within. Most diseases are curable, and most problems can be solved. It just takes radical ingenuity, and in our case, as human beings, this involves changing the way we think. Racial superiority isn't real. It is delusional fiction created by ignorant people.

We are all to blame, and all in this together.

Author's note: *This diagnosis may be a bit extreme, but nothing less will shake away the apathy currently afflicting the American People. A penicillin shot isn't comfortable or fun. Bend over and grit your teeth. You might even enjoy it...*

Everything is connected: Politics, Capitalism, Culture, Sports, etc. This book will be a journey through the many facets of American life. Topics may shift abruptly in order to be palatable to the contemporary ADD psychosis of instant gratification. And the only instant emotion you will feel is anger. This is intentional because anger is a worthy emotion to spur change. The only promise I can make to the reader is that I will not pander and I will not deceive. This book is the truth. If you want to be instantly gratified then go masturbate, if you want to learn something then read on...Or do I what I do, and do both.

2.
Happiness is a Warm Gun

Real Evil exists in the world. And it's up to every one of us to battle it. Even the minute portion that exists inside us, be it benign or malignant. Can't destroy evil in the world if it lurks within. The best way to do it is to love one another, and most importantly, to love ourselves.

Newtown and 9/11 were reminders that tangible Evil exists in the world. And not some diluted idea with latent thoughts of evil like you see in some hackneyed thriller. But the Beast itself. And it resides around us. Evil is Human. And most people don't know. They've been lulled into complacency by fairy tales. Lied to by egotists. And weakened by false promises.

Guns give Evil a means to expression. And I'm truly disgusted that our federal government did absolutely nothing after Newtown. Dead children are merely a political speed bump for the system.

But I'm not going to forget. Ever.
To me, Newtown isn't just some blurb on the timeline of our moral decline. It's a call to action.
To Empathy.
To Love.
To Life.

"Hey Joe, where you goin' with that gun in your hand?"

Which is worse...an NRA Republican or a cowardly Democrat who remains silent on Gun Control?
 Never a dull moment in America, the land of the free and home of the gun. We are not brave, or we would have done something, anything, after Newtown. Instead, we did nothing. We are cowards. We'd rather continue letting children die

so we can play with our guns. The entire situation disgusts me and makes me embarrassed to be an American. Every week there are new reports of people being shot by some gunman on a rampage. This past weekend there were shootings in every city you ever heard of. Gun Violence is the number one social ill currently afflicting America...a casualty rate that proves Afghanistan is a safer country to live in. It's time for the American public to wake up and combat this problem because the politicians won't.

Considering that on average over 12,000 Americans are murdered from gun violence per year, and that the sole purpose of a gun is to kill, and the main purpose of the NRA is to flood American streets with as many guns as possible and to fight any legislation that will protect Americans, it is not a stretch to label the NRA as a Terrorist Organization...who are subsidized by mercenary weapon manufacturers.

We have become a nation of domestic terrorists who mistake guns for freedom. Held hostage by fantasy. A gun is our birthright. A tool to kill.

The new Moloch is the NRA -- a Levantine God to whom children are sacrificed. Mass shootings are the best thing to ever happen to the gun industry. Sales of AR-15s shot through the roof after Newtown. A Mayan bloodlust pales in comparison to the NRA's idolatry of Guns...but we are all Moluching in the mire of perverted masculinity. In the movies the hero is the guy with the gun, but in real life my heroes are victims of gun violence: JFK, RFK, MLK, John Lennon, Harvey Milk, Malcolm X, Abraham Lincoln, and Newtown.

And nothing's changed. 32 Americans are murdered with a gun *everyday*. Violent movies still bang away on the big screen. Laws remain lax. 40% of gun sales have no background checks. I feel like a stranger in a land of ignorance. Mental Illness is the copout for the pro-gun apologists, yet the right-wingers cut mental health spending. So they really don't give two shits. The lowest mental-health spending per capita states are red states. Gun states. More guns combined with less mental health services is the hillbilly way.

Mental health is the red herring to take the attention away from the real issue: guns. Even if the right-wing politicians actually believed that mental illness was the cause of gun violence, then why would they cut mental health services? *Mother Jones* reported that states have cut $4.35 billion in public mental-health spending since 2009. Now that is really insane!

It's all a charade. Guns kill people, but we sure do love 'em like apple pie...not people, we adore weapons. What goes better with the American flag than an instrument of mayhem? Lives are cheap. And those instruments are not. There's big loot to be made from the monotony of death, and there are quite a few Senators who care more about this money than the safety & welfare of their constituents.

These Sinators would like you to believe it's about the 2nd Amendment...but it's really about a dollar sign.

The Senate failed the American People on 4/17/13 when they voted 54-46 against universal background checks that would include online gun sales and sales at gun shows. These checks had the potential to save lives. 90% of Americans supported this measure, but the Senate sided with Big Death. To his credit, Obama supported the measure, but failure only proved that the presidency of the United States is an impotent talking head position weighed down by the inferior counterbalances of ignorance & bigotry. According to *Mother Jones*, there has been a pronounced rise in mass shooting over the past five years. Let's add this statistic to the website: WhatTheFuckHasObamaDoneSoFar.com.

Why did Nevada Senator Dean Heller vote No? "Onerous paperwork." Coupled with his fear of the Federal Guvment, of which he works for, Heller is the very definition of Insane. Another NV politician is against Gun Control: Joe Heck...he thinks that sort of thing gets in the way of raising his racist son who insults women, gays, and Obama...according to the Heck family, Mr. Obama is a spear chucker. Doctor do-nothing Heck is a military man who opposes any form of gun control whatsoever...even if that means dead bodies bleeding in a naval yard.

Less than two years after the Carson City IHop shooting, Brian Sandoval, the Boobeoisie governor of Nevada, expressed condolences for the victims of gun violence yet he voted against universal background checks. According to some right-wingers, all the ills of gun violence would be easily remedied by religion...though reality proves otherwise, as Eduardo Sencion immersed himself in the Bible. He was a devout Catholic diagnosed with paranoid schizophrenia...a bit of redundancy. Too much of a good thing is drinking a twenty pack of Tecate; too much religion turns a deranged mind dangerous. For as much war & bloodshed it has caused, the Bible should come with a warning label like a pack of cigs.

Sencion was diagnosed with severe mental disorders yet a dozen years later he's wielding an AK-47 at an IHop. He killed four people, including three National Guardsmen. Sencion had two assault rifles, two handguns, 30-round mags, and 595 rounds of ammo. Sandoval did nothing. And still does nothing, but offer condolences. He prays for the Metro officers gunned down in Las Vegas by radical Tea Party gun nuts. Two hail marys and nothing. No leadership.

It's sad, Sandoval may not be to blame, but he sure is worthless when a veteran who served two tours in Afghanistan comes back home to Nevada and gets shot & killed teaching at a middle school. Tragic Irony that borders on the Absurd, this sort of mayhem is common in a country that possesses a THIRD of all the guns in the world. But more guns will make us more safe, right? Maybe we can work our way up to having half the guns in the world. Why stop there? Let's get all the guns.

Devise a Free Trade Agreement where we can trade our jobs to other countries for their guns. And if they don't give us their guns, we'll take 'em! Do it the Mao Zedong way: "Political power grows out of the barrel of a gun." The NRA would agree.

Republicans shoot down gun control because they love Amuricans dying for freedom. And Heller & Heck don't think gun control is important even after another shoot-out on the strip. Harry Reid was too busy, focused on the esoteric sequestration problem while an ongoing primal dilemma affected his constituents. And he ignored it. Of course Republicans rather lay off hundreds of people instead of raise taxes on the rich; this reality shouldn't distract a seasoned politician from a Real Problem. But maybe the problem is that Reid *is* seasoned. No surprise as the NV Legislature is a gang of emotionally and physically stultified freaks that debate Uncommon Sense every two years.

Families of the Newtown massacre were in DC during the universal background check vote. Rand Paul called them "props", proving Paul is the biggest Cunt in American politics.

The only politicians with a modicum of courage were lawmakers in NYC, Connecticut governor Dan Malloy, and the Colorado state senators who supported gun control then got recalled for their efforts. A measly 10,000 signatures on a petition is now a threat to Democracy. No more waiting for the next election, the NRA can get rid of pesky politicians like John Morse & Angela Givon through the back door weaknesses of state constitutions. I thought recalls were for inferior consumer products like Toyotas and Firestone Tires. Now admirable politicians who take a rare moral stance on guns can be recalled also.

A Big Disappointment

Maybe American Politics will be much better twenty years from now as certain websites will transmogrify the election process and take power away from lobbyists & special interests groups, and put the power back where it belongs: with the people. A shame that change has to happen so slowly...countless people suffer due to lack of political leadership.

The NRA's news conference after Newtown confirmed that some ignorant people are incapable of change...especially if it is profitable to stay the same. An Ignorant Man points the finger at everyone else for blame instead of looking in the mirror and taking responsibility. The good news is that the world is constantly evolving, and as America progresses, ignorant fossils like the NRA will get left behind and not be a part of the process.

The 2nd Amendment was adopted in 1791 when Slavery was legal. It's no longer socially acceptable to own slaves, but it's cool to have guns. America has more guns than people.

Adam Lanza fired 154 rounds in less than 5 minutes during the Newtown massacre. He had a Bushmaster assault rifle and several 30-round magazines. This horrible crime will always be a stain on America's soul, and the fact that there was a rush to gun stores to buy weapons after this massacre proves that our country is sick. Murder & violence is entertainment -- Hollywood's specialty. Movies, TV shows, and video games promoting first person shootings are still being made by despicable people. Everything is dictated by money with no moral decency or regard for human life. Americans' attitudes on guns and violence kill children. Point blank.

Instead of Gun Control we should transform Schools into prisons with barbed wire and armed guards. Get the lil' bastards ready for their future. Call it privatized progress, the teabag way.

A million Americans have been killed by guns over the past 30 years, yet the Supreme Court, mis-led by chief justice John Roberts, limits local gun bans. Is there any way to limit the Supreme Court, or ban them?

The United States' policies are also an implicit function to the Mexican madness of drugs & murders promoted by brutal cartels.

No gun laws: Weapons go South.
Weed illegal: "Drugs" go North.

Our harebrained anti-weed Volstead Act benefits the new era of Capones. Back in August of 2011, there was a Mexican casino massacre that consumed 52 lives. Obama was outraged while vacationing at Martha's Vineyard. A bit of disconnect, eh?

Guns kill both Americans and Mexicans at a tragic rate. The skin tone may be different shades, but blood bleeds the same color. The only constant is the gun. We need a new bible where Adam & Eve pick a Glock off the tree of untruth. Instead of being naked, our government god would hand us bulletproof vests to wear to church. Unfortunately, in the real world, government & god are one and the same, an indifferent entity that cares nothing about the carnage it creates. Solutions are not apples or testaments, but ideas created by us.

Here are some common sense Gun Control ideas:

-Have firm measures implemented into the acquisition and ownership of a firearm. It is easier to get a gun than a driver's license in this country! How stupid is that?

A universal background check coupled with a psychiatric evaluation and thorough training course should be required to own a gun.

-Allow only 2 firearms per household. One for protection and one for hunting. That's it.

-Put a cap on the amount of ammunition an individual is allowed to purchase. Some say this would be hard to track, but a gun ID card would be the way to go. Casinos in Vegas can track my slot play based on my player's card; I would think that we could track the amount of ammo someone is stockpiling.

-Allow cities like Philly, Chicago, NYC, Detroit, and DC to ban guns outright. Period. No guns allowed in the city. If you're caught with a gun, you go to prison. For a long time.

-Do not allow concealed weapons. This isn't the Wild West and we don't need citizens armed anymore. That is what police are for. And they are trained in the use of firearms...except for some rogue cops in Oakland.

-Change the national mindset of owning a gun. Most believe it is a birthright. An entitlement. It isn't. It's a privilege only reserved for the sane and well trained. We have an army and a police force now. It is not the late 1700's, and there is no need for a militia (...unless we can transport them to England the next time there is a newsflash regarding the Royal Family). Amend the constitution to reflect this reality.

-Implement harsh gun laws. Have penalties that reflect the crime. Petty drug users & peddlers are not the threat. Violent people who shoot other people are (and sex offenders -- there is no rehabilitation process for the genetically-defunct individual...keep them locked up).

-Ban gun shows. A no-brainer. Any hick with a pulse can pick up a weapon. Gun shows are a celebration of killing tools. Carnivals celebrating death.

-Impose a steep tax on the purchase of firearms. The money gained could be directed towards police equipment and training.

-Ban assault weapons, armor-piercing bullets, and 30 shot clips. Again, another no-brainer.

-Institute these measures on a federal basis. State gun laws are a nice gesture, but hold no significant power when guns are readily available in other states, thereby creating a lucrative black market.

 I originally wrote these ideas in a blog four years ago, fingers on a keyboard that mattered nothing. And like any virus left unattended, gun violence has only gotten worse like Chlamydia in a sleeping bag spent with a hooker on a hot night. Even though 90% of Americans want something doesn't mean anything will happen. Have you seen the new Superman movie?
 But it's no joke. These changes should have been implemented after the Virginia Tech massacre. How many more people need to die before we REALLY address this issue? If the slaughter of innocent children doesn't change anything then we're a culture of people that deserves to fade away...
 Only in an insane country FBI checks for people buying guns increase at a record rate in the same month of the Newtown massacre. The firearm makers/murder-profiteers pocket over $4 billion per year...exploiting our constitutional rights to be homicidal slayers.
 During that same month I noticed something. There are a lot of so-called Democrats who are cowards. They are quick to vocalize their displeasure on an array of political topics, but when it comes to Gun Control they remain silent. Assholes pucker up like Lifesavers. Maybe they are ninnies with nines who like to shoot shit, or are more concerned with maintaining some form of tenuous social status. They are no better than Teabaggers...the same thing actually, blinded by selfish ideology without regard to the safety & well being of Americans.
 This particular breed of egotistic Democrat only supports programs that directly benefit them. And why not? They've been selfish needy vermin since they were squirted into our presence. A suckle here and there...and they still want one...so long as they qualify for Universal Health Care with their Pre-Existing Conditions...the most common condition being a cunt. Cannibals. You are what you eat. No one explained this truth to him or her while they were being born. They care about their camel-toes, but my views on guns bore them.

 A great and true saying: All it takes for evil to flourish is for good people to do nothing.
 And this is why gun violence has flourished. If a person does nothing then they are good for nothing. And their country slowly but surely suffers as a result.

Trying to think of the right word to describe gun violence in America:
Tragic
Infuriating

Ongoing

A better way to communicate the pain might be a name: Hadiya Pendleton. A victim of gun violence has a name. A real person. Congress is bought but tries to hide it with pontification. It is time to change Everything. Congress/Government and Gun Violence.

   If you're not a part of the peaceful revolution then you're a part of the problem. And if you're not sure then get the fuck out the way and eat your Wendy's...

Author's note: *Arizona has some of the weakest gun laws in the country and Ms. Giffords was shot there along with others. Nothing was done. The fallacy of Dodge City endures. Justice is fleeting and it rarely occurs in a country controlled by guns. We live in insane times...interesting in their tragic absurdity...where Ms. Giffords goes to a gun range & gun show later to drum up support for gun control. I still believe she is a brave American, fighting for what is right. A responsible solution is to not have guns...for in a country where a physically disabled person who has been shot in the head can still wield a weapon is beyond surreal. This sort of thing enters the atmosphere of Asinine. Devolution of all reason and hope. Where we clutch a Glock along with the Bible and praise the Almighty for delivering such madness upon us. As much as I try with alcohol and other methods, I am unable to reach that height of insanity. No matter how high I get, I still am not capable of seeing that deadly logic. I open my back door and see the sky, and thankful to see it...and I don't need a gun to appreciate it.*

State historian Marshall Trimble said, "Arizona is a microcosm of the whole United States. We are you. We are everybody." Sheriff Clarence Dupnik called Arizona "the Mecca for prejudice & bigotry." Arizona is not I. And it should not be the microcosm of anything other than Arizona. We have to change. Not "we should." We have to. I have to believe that we are not evil people. And our actions should start to describe us instead of empty words.

More guns equal more chaos & more death. The more desensitized to this problem we become, the less our culture matters. A violent culture is to be loathed, not celebrated.

American

The remnants of skeletons past, discharging hate as their world dissipates.
Precipitates
Tribal warfare over the spoils of ignorance.

Past tense becomes present tense,
when the masters of the past gift-wrap the presents.

Guns, Gangs, and Drugs replace Love,
Mercy is the name of a heroin addict selling the opposite.

Blindness is the coincidence of conformity.
We all just happen to be...
on Facebook, bragging about money...
and family.

But my neighbor isn't my cousin, or brother,
just another
person who doesn't look like me.
So I don't trust my community.
But I'll tweet that I'm happy to be...

American

3.
Trayvon

Why doesn't the Black Community rally every time a young person is killed as a result of black on black crime? Why is it so much worse when a white guy kills a black guy when so many other black guys are killed by their brethren? A Black Man died. That should ignite nationwide indignation no matter the cause.

Black on black bigotry is a form of self-hate. That racial violence is the true epidemic facing the black community. Maybe it's easier to point the finger instead of lookin' in the mirror.

I've hung with plenty of Trayvons in my life. We'd have a holiday house party when my parents were gone, and they'd raid my fridge when I wasn't looking. I wouldn't trust my chocolate-covered buckeyes around them, but they are fun to kick it with...black guys in hoodies who like Skittles. No reason to provoke, get beat up by, and then shoot them.

2 Cent Penny to the Fray -- July 13, 2013

    The acquittal tonight wasn't Right. Things haven't been that way for a while -- on all accounts and both sides. This case devolved into media misdirection, taking the focus away from the bigger problem. Sure, the case stunk of racism and murder, but it's Florida and a jury of your peers is the opposite sex and race.
    George Zimmerman is the bloated face of cowardice and guns. He is us and we are he. Everyone.
    His innocent-like lard disguise fooled the jurors. Fat is the new Normal. So Zimmerman put on a fat suit to conceal his evil. And the swamp gators bought it.
    Whispers of riot float through social media, but the demands on the street are a bit louder. That's the wrong way. Riots only damage property and make the participants villains. Righteous Anger is better served productively. Injustice is an Opportunity to make a positive change in your community. For every george zimmerman there's another 30 Black Guys willing to kill another Black Guy. Basic

Observation. And that's wrong. And I shouldn't be the one making this observation, but someone has to.

Start with teaching the youngsters about the Red Summer riots of 1919, and then take it from there. Connect the dots. The best revolution of all is a revolution of the mind. Education outside of Education. Blacks were brought to this country in chains and mistreated, and turned into abused people who now direct that anger towards each other. The race riots of the 1919 Red Summer occurred in more than 3 dozen cities, and left thousands of blacks homeless. Lynchings and beatings occurred. WEB Dubois wrote, "By the God Heaven, we are cowards and jackasses if now that the war is over, we do not marshal every ounce of brain and brawn to fight a sterner, longer, more unbending battle against the forces of hell in our own land." And now the forces of hell are in the mirror. One of the most effective con jobs ever was turning the blacks from prospective socialists into soulless capitalists who fight and kill each other. The Establishment applauds Kanye! And boos George Zimmerman.

Zimmfuck may not have been convicted tonight, but his life is over. Like OJ...or Dahmer. These sorts of crimes usually have a way of sorting themselves out. He has become the face of racist cowardice. Only in America can a fat Klan-like neighborhood watchman who likes "pulling a trigger on a nigger" be found innocent. Well...maybe not only in America...but only in Florida. The ill-legal system in the panhandle penis of America let that white girl off the hook for killing her kid. Florikkka was the state that helped elect GW...and now this. A state where justice goes to take a vacation. A sewer that passes for a swamp.

The main issue being lost in the shuffle down in FLA is Gun Control. Any halfwit yokel with a pulse can purchase a gun. Stand your ground really means lose your life if you look twice at the wrong person.

Guns are turning our populace into a bunch of psychopathic pussies. Our country is obsessed with firearms. Half of the movies released feature a guy holding a gun on the movie poster. You know there's a problem when Jonah Hill is posing like a twat with 2 guns on a poster. Zimmerman probably loves *21 Jump Street*. He bought tix to *22 Jump Street*, and a loaded 22 just in case there are black people who chew their Skittles too loud. A movie theater is now a place to hold your ground.

Back to Trayvon...

Before people plan riots, they should consider travelling to Chicago and riot there first...demand answers for 47 shootings and 11 people dying this past 4th of July weekend. Those numbers are down from a year ago, where 60 people were shot and 12 killed. How come no one is rockin' hoodies, protesting this? See how the media manipulates your thoughts and takes away the emphasis of feeling? "Truth" is shook in a maraca to the left, and to the right is another bunch of beans...reinforcing paralytic hypocrisy. Shake 'em long enough and loud enough and people start to believe it. Or don't care. Or start to obsess about the obvious thing.

Back on June 11, 2012 another 8 people died and 40 were wounded by gun violence in Chicago. Add that to the 40 shot and 5 killed this past weekend: April 25 – 27, 2014. This sort of thing should cause an outrage. The police chief made excuses and concocted positive statistics. But there is nothing positive about it. Be a man and take responsibility. And that goes double for the black community. Father's day is celebrated with 40 flesh-breathing targets shot, and 7 kills.

There was not any sort of real anger about this...outside of Chi-town. Our country was too busy watching repeats of *the Walking Dead*, or playing *GTA*. A fictional outbreak on AMC numbs minds as the true disease is already happening -- 32 deaths a day. I could spend a whole book the size of War & Peace describing the separate incidences of gun violence in this country. There is no peace. Just a populace of gun fanatics at war with itself.

The media/Establishment wants the Black Community to play the outraged victim, even though the only real way to Empower Yourself is to take responsibility for your actions. Stop making excuses. Stop being the victim. And only then can you make progress and solve problems.

Racism is wrong. So is killing your own kind when so many of your own kind worked so hard to get equal rights. Maybe this was the plan all along when the cops murdered the Black Panther leaders: to make the blacks in Chi-Town a toothless pack of jackals hungry for each other's skins.

For all his political grandstanding, mayor Rahm Emanuel is an incompetent spinmeister posing as a man. In 2012 there were more than 500 deaths in Chicago, and he had the audacity to serve up a propagandized nugget that "there is a decrease in homicides." Police Superintendent Gary McCarthy queefed that compared to 2011 there was actually an 8% reduction in shootings. Chi-Iraq is not safer. The carnage continues. And where's the national attention? Focused on Florida?? Americans shooting each other continuously in Chi-town and nothing's being done but lip service. So it's no surprise that a limpdick white dude gets off shooting some black kid in Florida.

I didn't think the night could get anymore heinous...but then ...

The beer in the house ran out. I blame myself. Tonight has been not been a "tough night" for the writer because it has been really tough for everyone else. A writer may or *may* face internal doubts, but when an external shitstorm happens then it only reinforces the need to be a writer. Make some sense of the muck.

Yesterday I watched a good movie: *Chasing Mavericks*. The mentor made the protagonist write an essay about fear. What is fear? A good question. I used to fear succeeding. I thought my lifestyle would become a prison of responsibility. And now, I only get a few hours sleep and I have nothing but responsibility...so that fear was just another shitball to be flushed. My book is a real stick a big toe in the hot springs type of thing. It keeps me home writing on a Saturday night in Las Vegas because it's the safest place for a sane person. Sat nite is tourist nite -- a special party of 8 dollar beers and $30 cover charges only to be crammed into a lazer light show throbbing with warmed-over microwaved Disco. I'd rather rest up for my weekend, which starts on Monday...devoid of goons and douches.

Getting back to the beer. It's gone, and so the wine tastes even better...

Before I could sleep a couple hours the rednecks next door were bashing and booming. Clanging and scraping. Dropping pianos on a bed of cymbals every half hour. Moving out. Good. Maybe back to Winnipeg where they belong. The corpulent patriarch of the clan tried to provoke me one night while I was puffin' cheebah in my backyard. Average run of the mill shit-talk that I giggled at. Good thing I wasn't drinking.

The boll weevils have fled the scene, leaving a pile of trash stacked up like cardboard pyramids on the sidewalk. Hillbots sure do acquire a lot of disposable possessions in a short period of time. A Walmart lifestyle suited for inbred larvae; genetically defective insects that have to eat through objects in order to gain sustenance.

Bulldogging Bulldykes All Night

Even the nice neighborhoods of Las Vegas are rife with weirdos. The night of the Zimmerman verdict the albino bulldykes across the street set off fireworks. A racist celebration or ironic comment? I don't know. I didn't ask. I wasn't in the mood for either.

Those carpetbagging carpet-munchers were whipped up in a frenzied state of righteous white anger. There were four of 'em and they all spit loogies on each other, aiming for the swastika tattoos hovering over each tit. These big-girthed girls carried switchblades and soccer balls soaked in kerosene. Every five minutes they would light a ball and kick it. Another comet in the sky.

Finally they all got tired, and went inside to watch Mel Gibson movies and guzzle apricot schnapps...so I tied 200 yards of twine around their house while they slept. Then I staggered home to finish writing this chapter. Was it wrong to vandalize their home? And so what is right? 'Turn the other cheek' advice is in short supply these days. There is an electric charge that hangs in the air, a sort of aggressive aggravation that can turn a simple walk to the convenience store into a life and death matter.

Gun violence occurs everyday, but thinking about it everyday can turn a person either pessimistic or crazy. Ignoring the problem doesn't solve it. Neither does obsessing about it. The only thing that matters is Action. Start walking down that corridor and soon you find out that it is never-ending...yet it is the only one worth walking down.

It's a constant struggle between right and wrong. Perpetual politics. Why care? Why give a shit? This is how it is and always will be: Beasts of men scrapping for money. And most of the people who are exploited hate your guts & politics. Ignorant assholes that just want another Oreo and a dixie cup of Sunny D. The hedonistic lifestyle has its merits. JFK & MLK might still be alive if they fully embraced it. Instead, they sought a better society, and for what? So we can eat TV dinners while watching *Big Brother*? We elect the same assholes from the same parties who all do the same thing. Foils in a 3rd-rate sitcom who bicker & smile along with the studio-provided applause.

Religion, Politics, Sports -- all the same thing. You believe what your parents believe. Education is a nuisance to the Establishment. Keep the heathens entertained with whatever sells. And in turn, the Masses sell their souls to the God of antipathy & consumption. Some call it Moloch. I call it us.

Author's note: *The American Justice System is a horrific canal ride in a carnival haunted house. Tommy Chong was sentenced to 9 months in federal prison for selling glass bongs. Zimmerman served 0 days. Perspective.*

Twisted priorities make true justice hard to grasp here in the 50 states.

4.
Everything is Entertainment

The night of the Zimmerman "innocent" verdict, *Huffington Post* had an article about Trayvon's Dad's heartbroken tweets. To the right lower corner was a smiling Zimmerman. To the right upper corner was an advertisement for a movie: *RIPD*

Rest in Peace Department

Sort of sums up the state of affairs for the media in this country. Everything is Entertainment...even an unarmed boy getting stalked and shot by a coward. But wait...blow up bombs at the Boston Marathon and *Rolling Stone* magazine will put you on their cover like a rock star.

Everything is Entertainment. Glorifying an Islamic killer is edgy.

And so I buy a Vegas newspaper and browse the bullshit. The cover story is about a local teen awaiting a heart transplant. Below that story is a front-page article praising the return of Twinkies. Then I pick up a magazine and see an ad for a Chevy Camaro: "You could live without it...if you call that living."

And so before I commit suicide I watch television and see the NASA space shuttle being used as a prop for Toyota Tundras. Instead of killing myself, I should kill everyone else's sense of integrity and become an Ad Man. Use the Tomb of the Unknown Soldier as a backdrop to sell Trojan condoms. The tagline: Save a soldier's life, jimmy up.

The Internet is no better. MSN.com wants to customize your news based on if you are left or right. Whatever happened to just objective news? The media has no problem jerking you off with either hand...personally, I prefer left,,,just becuz I wore out the right during puberty.

This Entertainment even impedes upon my bowel movements. *Readers Digests* are compact handheld publications seemingly custom-made for shitter material. Jokes easily dismissed as shart missiles, but an article caused me to pause an ass applause: "The 100 most trusted people in America Today". Number one was Tom Hanks...yeah, I might trust him to take a number two in my bathroom, but that's it. Speaking of number two, it was Sandra Bullock. Another actor.

I can't trust a person that would trust a racist biker to smear shit mustaches on their face. Dirty Sanchez, my trust is not. The director of *Speed 2* trusted Bullock, and where did that get him? Trust is a rare commodity earned over time. *Readers Digest* makes a mockery of it. Good thing the pages come in handy when I run out of toilet paper.

Bullock is an inspiration. The next time I find myself in an embarrassing situation I'll just adopt an African baby. Maybe its blackness will wash away my white flaws.

Actors always cry about the paparazzi & media yet use that same spotlight to promote their egos. Jodie Foster wants everyone to know that her private life is Private! And the best way to convey that message is onstage with television cameras spreading her words to millions.

Show News is Bad News

Back in 1992; Barbara Walters interviewed Mark David Chapman, who claimed he killed John Lennon because he wanted to be somebody. And with Walters help, the psychopathic killer got his mug on television. Anything for ratings. Bob Costas would agree. He interviewed a renowned pederast on television, all for the coveted ratings. It's all about the Benjamins, baby. And so, simple moral decency is neglected. Paddy Chayefsky is smiling somewhere.

Bob Costas gave Jerry Sandusky the spotlight on primetime TV. What does that say about Costas? Or American culture? Our celebrity culture has mutated to include child rapists, and Cuntstas had the scoop. Definition of a Cuntstas: A male or female who takes advantage of tragedies to further their career without interest in the truth.

Being a popular newscaster on television holds the same credibility as being a skilled athlete in the harebrained hacky-sack league. A highlight of a newscaster's career could be titled A Memoir of Deranged Remembrances. Here's one:

Tom Brokaw

Sounds like he's performing cunninglingus while talking.
like somebody inserted a microphone into a uterus and had him speak into it.

Sounds like he just gargled a mouthful of douche excretions that he's kept in a glass bottle corked on the shelf since the world premiere of *Network*.

Sounds like he sleeps with a tennis ball rammed in his mouth.

Talks like he has pubic hair growing on his tongue.

Sounds like his lips were sliced off by a speedboat propeller and the doctor transplanted Pamela Anderson's camel toe on Brokaw's face.

Speaks in queefs.

Brokaw's voice is really just reverse-rectal flatulence. A disease that strikes more Americans each year...where you talk out of your ass and defecate out of your mouth like the Brundlefly.

5.
Masculinity

The things I love most: Music, Sex, Food, Beer, Love -- are not impacted by getting rid of guns.

Some men clean their guns. I'd rather clean my manhood in other odd ways in misc orifices. Call it being a Real Man. I don't need substitutes...

My masculinity is not defined by firearms.
My masculinity is defined by being strong and vigorous in my love for other people.

Masculinity is the monster spurring Gun Violence. Men are ingrained with a brutal identity at an early age. Guns are toys, even shaped like peckers. Draw pistols before you can learn how to draw. Video games and action flicks like *Commando* inoculate the minds of youngsters to the joyous frenzy of killing. Blast your parents with a Nerf rifle then giggle about it. Adolescence occurs, so the weapons become bigger, and better. Being a crazy person is only relative to the society that raised you. Glocks are sucked on like pacifiers. M-60s shedding shells are the training tools for masturbation. Bazookas become punchlines. The flat line is our National Pulse when this sort of unrestrained violence is instilled into our Youth.

Men front like they're friends, ignoring the monster under the bed clutching hard steel that kills. And we become that killer. Why not? Get a blowjob while gripping a glock is the Ultimate. Pull it out. Masculinity is the best reason to kill. Somebody looked at you wrong. Walked in front of you. Said something dumb. Scuffed your Jordans. Didn't even acknowledge your presence. Fuck them! Pistol-whip the offender. Rakim knows what Masculinity is about: "Knockin' niggaz off, knockin' niggaz out." Fisticuffs give way for bullet-induced bloodshed once the masculine firearm fetish is allowed to flourish.

Masculinity can be a constant struggle between civility and caveman justice. It's a journey to become a man. At first, it was frustrating because I didn't fit in. I had too much masculinity for intellectuals, and not enough for the street crowd. And when a person has no niche, they get picked on…different people are to be ridiculed by the conformist mass that is called your high school class. Damaged goods take a while to heal. Abused and beat-up, I could become my tormentor, or remain a victim. So I faced my fears and became a person I would fear. Punching a person rarely made me feel better…mostly worst. So I soaked that truth with malt liquor and proceeded to the spiral: Got into fights, coveted weapons, and went to jail. That person was just a façade…it's taken me a long time to figure it out, but the masculine tough guy act is all bullshit. Not to say that I've cured it completely, but I recognize the true nature of being a Man. Purging yourself of negative aggression requires a minimum masturbatory schedule of one jerk per day. Religiously repeat this treatment for 36 months until you start to see progress, then up the jerk dosage to two a day. American Masculinity is a tough psychosis to shake.

The male elephant in the room with the 50-caliber cock is mostly ignored by our society. Mental Illness is the new cop-out/excuse for the pro-gun apologists, but Sigmund Freud couldn't change or rehabilitate an evil person who wants to kill women and children. You can't make someone less crazy by talking. Even the notion of normalcy is absurd. Everyone suffers from some sort of mental illness…whether it's a minor addiction or a major flaw; craziness is merely the cost of being human. Killing another person is a malignant tumor of the human condition that seems to be growing in America. Some of these killers are allowed to fester with malicious thoughts and evil intents. There's always going to be neglectful parents more concerned with drinking martinis and playing bridge rather than trying to figure out why their recluse outcast offspring sports swastika tattoos. And there is always going to be that crazy person who flips. Unless you have some pre-cog *Minority Report* fortune-telling device then there is no way to predict what evil person will commit an act of violence next. Gun violence varies from gang warfare to domestic violence to mass shootings…but the common item that binds them all is Guns.

The only sane rational solution to the epidemic is Gun Control…unless you're gonna geld every adult male in the country…and that would seriously impact my pursuit of happiness. I love a twirling tongue on my cock. Nobody cocked it. The only true happiness is head. Sounds crass, but pales in comparison to the bullet-crack echoes of people getting shot. Cries and screams of agony are buzz kills. I'd like to purchase a blowjob on the south side of Chicago without the ricochets. Capitalism chews up these victims like Pac-Man; fatalities are profits for the morticians. Even better, racism tastes better with hard statistics.

What does Racism taste like? Sweet? Sour? Or like Progress? And so many politicians love it. Sell out the lowest just to get elected to Congress. Minorities murdering themselves are mere opportunities to tout social movements based on bills.

Dollar Bills

Feel my balls; I still have those…no matter what. I didn't sell-out a gun bill, or talk up the NRA that decreases Everything. Men lesser than me have grander ambitions. Balls are better than bills – dollars or political endgames. There is a way to use Masculinity for positive purposes. Our Declaration of Independence is proof! Stand up for what is right when no one else will; no matter how much it ostracizes you from lesser peers. And it will make you an outcast from the norm. So what? Should your precious life be spent trying to be normal, or is life an opportunity to do something good?

I have no agenda. I have empathy. I only want the madness to stop. I want people to stop being shot. And I shudder to think how scared those Newtown children were when a gun was pointed at them. If a person is still pro-gun after that then they either lack an empathetic soul or a logical brain.

It is impossible to predict what crazy person will use a gun next.
BUT
It is POSSIBLE to control guns.
This logic should be easy to grasp.

Guns are so wack. If you have a problem with someone then knuckle up. Guns are for the weak. Get in the ring if you have a problem. I accumulated plenty of black eyes and I'm still here...and stronger for it. Fights used to be character-builders, and now they're life-enders. Put down the guns and put up your fists...That is my sane version of masculinity. I'm not sure there is a cure for Masculinity. Testosterone is a naturally occurring hormone…but maybe, just maybe, we can raise our kids better and not raise them with a gun.

JUMP SHOT

I shot the Nutter Center sign. That's right. And if you look close enough, what does that make me? An idiot.

Bullets. Holes. The smell of powder. Shells rattling around the back seat. Sounds like Iraq and only a dumb ass would try to simulate that in Paradise. Perverted Masculinity rears its ugly head in odd ways.

I was anti-gun before I knew it, but forgot. Guns were only something in the movies. I preferred playing basketball at JC Park and chasing girls, hoping that one day I could shoot a J and get some pussy. So I'd shoot jumper after another jumper. At least I can control that. One summer night I was out on the court alone, shooting. Taking a jump shot against the summer moon is a gift. And I'd miss more than I'd make, but it didn't matter. I clanged an easy eight-foot bank shot against the rim when a couple guys passed by on bikes. Derrick Dickey was one of them. He smiled...appreciated I was the only one on the court. Said I had to flick my wrists if I wanted to be a better shooter. Ever since, that's what I've been doing.

Sometime later, another kid flicked his finger and shot Dickey. It never seemed right that a nice guy willing to give advice of kindness could get shot down...and so it happened in my small town. Later on, I was rolling through Sunnyside with friends and saw his Killer drinking beer on the curb. Out on bail. And all I could think was what a Coward.

And I should know. I was picked on in High School. A lot. And I regret it...because I'm a tough guy yet shy. But I never once thought about shooting anyone. Instead, I lifted weights, and vowed to change my life. It didn't take a gun to do it.

Ass-kickings are learning experiences that I wouldn't trade for anything. Getting beat up is no fun. It is horrible, and it should be. Violence always is. You live with it forever...ingrained into your brain. It made me a better person who is not afraid of it, yet finds ways to avoid it.

The best thing that ever happened to me was when Steve Scales beat my ass in high school -- even though I didn't deserve it. Like Eastwood says in *Unforgiven*, "Deserve has nothin' to do with it." I realized one day you're friends with someone, the next day you have a black eye. Life is unforgiving and most tribulations are not earned or deserved, and that is when the survival instinct honed through confrontation kicks in. Getting bashed in the face forces a person to get strong & mean in the face of adversity. And all fights are eye-to-eye with one's self. Meaning, every fight is winnable so long as you're strong enough. Adversity is like sex...it's all mental. Think of it this way: In sex, your performance is primarily affected by your partner. Inversely, in a fight, your performance is really affected by yourself, and how you think.

Physical violence is no longer a learning lesson, but an end to life because of guns. A reasonable person can admit their mistakes and grow up. Gender specifically, only a real man recognizes his mistakes and grows up. Personally, I used to own a gun -- a 9 milli Llama -- but I got rid of it after the V Tech massacre because the thought of owning a gun repelled me.

The United States is over 200 years old...maybe it's time for It to grow up. Firearms and the cultural celebration of violence runs rampant. Gun laws didn't change after Newtown, and maybe they never will. And neither will the violence.

If you need a gun to get your point across then you're a pussy with a communication problem.

Author's note: *The American Masculine way of life is the Western. A self-righteous man with a handgun can solve all woes so long as he has enough bullets and whiskey. But what they don't show in the Westerns are innocent women and children getting shot. Nor has there been a movie made about the 32 students and staff gunned down at V Tech. "Sympathies go out to the victims" are shallow words printed on the walls of gun stores as the AR-15s and AK-47s fly off the shelves, all too easy to buy.*

We live in a sick country. A disease is consuming America. Is it fatal? I'm not sure...it feels like it...Americans kill other Americans every day, including women and children, and if nothing changes then maybe America should fail. Or just split it up. North and South. Let the heathens live with guns in the Confederate gutter, and if the Northern thugs don't like not having guns, then kick 'em out. Life is too short for this sort of senseless violence. The country is in a spiritual morass. And I'm not talking about religion. There is no sense of community. No love, or sense of caring and belonging. Even in my Summerlin neighborhood I'm constantly harassed by the HOA. The Melting Pot bubbleth over...consume and work, but stay in your place. Leave it to Beaver. And praise the pistol.

Cosmic Truth

God didn't help the victims of Newtown because God doesn't exist.
or
God is impotent.

Either way, God is an asshole idea to be despised.
The only entity that can help People is People.

But praying is supposed to make a person feel better, so go ahead and pray to a fictional superhero, or pray to an all-powerful force that doesn't care & wouldn't lift a cosmic finger to help a child. You pray to a malicious fuck of a myth and you suffer from massive brain tumor delusions.

As for me, I'll continue on the path of Knowledge & Wisdom, and do whatever I can to help Humanity progress...like working towards Gun Control.

The only thing that gives real meaning to life is helping others, or doing something to make the world a better place.

6.
God is a gorilla and we amuse Him

I was out sunbathing in the backyard and saw lil' baby Jesus wearing a golden fleece fly by riding a Pterodactyl. He winked at me and gave the thumbs up sign...I must be doing something right.

I never understood praying. If you believe God gave you life, then what more do you want? I have a prayer for you: say two Hail Marys while you go to Krogers and pick me up another twelve of Natty Light. Amen.

If I was God and all these needy sumbitches kept begging me for favors then I would send a comet the size of Idaho at the Earth.

Prayers are a fictitious form of panhandling. Welfare for the weak-minded. I'm a legally ordained minister and know what I'm talking about. I fart frankinsense & urinate holy water, and for a small fee, I also offer last rites for wayward gamblers, absolve sins with reason & empathy, perform baptisms in the Bellagio fountains, and promote the mind-freeing truth of Atheism. You cannot afford to go to Hell, so hire me. I guarantee a good afterlife or your money back.

The advantage of being an Atheist is that you can cherry-pick the best things from other religions and incorporate them into your life minus the voodoo.

For many Christians, Christmas is spent scrambling for Karats...shiny rocks called diamonds. Every Kunt begins with Kay. Buying these marked-up rocks sponsors civil wars in Africa, or gluttonous behavior in pig-drillers. Why buy something that only makes other people rich? It's just a rock for Chrissakes. Speaking of...the myth died on the cross so his children can celebrate his birthday giving gifts of diamonds to each other.

(Protestants have banned my book and added it to their "to burn" list. The word Cunt offends their delicate sensibilities; they prefer their profanities in private and expressed in a physical, more literal manner.)

I love Love. Both the noun (fam & friends) and verb (give and receive). Love is the most powerful force in the universe. It creates life. The best gift for the Holidays. I would like to see Earth Day become a full-fledged holiday like Christmas. We celebrate mythical figures of our imagination; why not celebrate something real, like the planet we live on?

For me, Christmas becomes a raucous celebration of family, friends, and life. Karma is a code to live by. And the yahrzeit candle is a beacon of love...though instead of lighting a candle, I prefer to perform an activity that the deceased enjoyed...which is usually some flagrant sexual act, and imbibing the sweet nectar of Manischewitz. Whether you're gentile or not, sippin' the Mani will turn you gentle. Or at least that's what my wife tells me. And she would know because she's got my handprints on her ass cheeks to prove it.

Every religion was created by man, so why not enjoy the best of what every man has to offer?

I'm not one for superstition, but that won't stop me from grubbing on Easter ham or eating burgers when Catholics pick at cod. If God didn't want you to eat, drink, or smoke something, then he wouldn't have made it! Only a heathen deprives himself of God's fruit and smokable green vegetation.

An Atheist is God's greatest fan because they espouse the joys of life while the pious religious fanatics rant & rave against their master's gifts. Sex, alcohol, and weed are to be shunned. These fools are the barbaric underlings of no fun. And without fun, what is the point? (GW Bush, a Christian, would answer, "War") We atheists have made a solemn pact with God to enjoy everything She gave us. EveryDay.

Most Christians are Pecksniffian pricks. They attend church on Sundays and spend the rest of their lives judging others; especially white Christians: morally depraved creatures with the social conventions of a flock of turkey vultures. Nothing boils the blood more of white Catholic Americans than having a pope from South America, even if he is a European. The great Christian mystery is how do they reconcile their Racism with their religious beliefs? Glad I have neither. Speaking of the pope, he's just another weirdo who likes to dress up in garish costumes and promote superstition...but at least he doesn't look like a ghoulish Sith emperor from *Star Wars* like the last Nazi pope.

"It's never too late to be saved." A constant refrain that hooligans promote. Saved from what exactly? I prefer to be saved from an ignorance-inducing mythology, but somehow I don't think church is the right place for that type of saving. Wars are started by the Saved. So are Savings and Loan scandals. Religious hope is a wooden nickel even though Religion is worth billions. Religious leaders have legs and know how to use them. Mysterious invisible legs that will save you from everything wrong so long as you believe they're real. And they are, though the only purpose of the legs is to kick the believer right square in the ass. I'd rather stand on my own two, thank ya very much.

The Bible is fantastical history written by barely-literate hacks. Karl Marx said religion is an opiate for the masses, but I disagree, opium is at least relaxing. Religion is a solemn waste of time that promotes patriarchy and war. God said to the woman, "Your desire will be for your husband and he will rule over you." In other words, get me another beer, bitch, or you gonna git it. God tested Abraham, and told him to sacrifice his son Isaac if he really loved God. And now God is the United States' military, and we are Abraham.

E.O. Wilson, the noted biologist, was quoted in *the Atlantic* describing the Book of Revelation as the ranting of "a paranoid schizophrenic who was allowed to write down everything that came to him." To counter that sort of crazy, my book is the ranting of a logical intelligent person who decided to write down everything that made sense. This sort of honest stream of consciousness is a palatable way to prove a point to the average reader. To make sense out of nonsense is not an easy task, and the gobbledygook Bible only makes matters worse. I don't need a book of gibberish as a moral beacon. The overall philosophy of an Atheist is to live an ethical life...not because you fear burning in a mythical pit of fire if you don't, but because you honestly care about your fellow man.

I accept other people even if they exhibit delusions of religious disease...so long as they don't try to sneeze on me and inhibit my liberty. Though I do have an allergy to Islam. I enjoy eating bacon with my eggs. Plus, I respect women enough not to cover them in bed sheets.

The reason behind the bed sheets is the Dark Age belief that if a woman shows an inch of skin then it would incite rape that the woman is responsible for. But I think it's also because Arab men have a secret obsession with stink and so they want Arab women to sweat profusely until their nether regions give off a musky otter scent...

Every month there is some Muslim riot. Know what these crazy dudes need besides education? Two things: Internet porn and weed. Seriously. A high dude who just busted a nut is unable to get angry. My new foreign Muslim policy: Set fires to dubees, not cinemas or embassies.

Women can't even drive in Saudi Arabia without death threats, and the inhumane animals on Muslim Zanzibar threw acid on two young British volunteers. Saladin would not approve. I wouldn't volunteer to help these crazy assholes. Let them rot. The oil will run out eventually, then what? Who will take them? Money can only buy so much when livable space is in short supply. If Allah is so great then how come his followers live in shit-bowl deserts?

Honor to a Muslim means killing gays or women who don't listen. Honor is another idea like Patriotism that incites bloodlust & rage. But Honor is not to blame, for honor is just a euphemism; the real reason for the killings is the moldy tumor growing in the Arab brain called Islam.

Liberal Hypocrisy decries any form of Muslim criticism...even though these same libs are quick to bash the Christian South for outdated right-wing policies. But -> if Muslims had their way and enforced Islam, their cultural policies would make the southern Christians look like Castro Street hippies. Maybe it's time for the libs to unglue their head from their a-nooses when it comes to Islam.

America has been lucky that the bulk of recent immigrants have come from Mexico, and not the Middle East. Allowing massive amounts of Muslims to live here doesn't seem to mesh with Democracy. We already have enough religion to stagnate our culture, we don't need anymore.

Religion is a disease to humanity. If Christianity is a cancer then Islam is the Ebola Virus.

I remember 9/11 and the Boston Marathon bombing vividly...and I can do without Muslims. They're free to practice their backwards-repressive religion in their home countries so they can just stay there. Just look at Europe, which is becoming swamped with Muslims. They move there and have no intentions of assimilating. Radical Islam is allowed to fester in Londonistan. Even after the London bombings, nothing was done about Anjem Choudary and his bearded followers, who insist on the "domination of the world by Islam." London has become a hotbed of radical Islam recruitment while Paris is a frequent site of immigrant unrest. They riot, complaining about lack of jobs. Well, hey, they moved to France...if they don't like the job opportunities then they should just move back to their old countries. 54 million Muslims (and counting) are in Europe, a disease to democracy.

I'm no fan of ethnic cleansing, so the Muslims already here in the States just need to be vaccinated with a rational dose of atheism. Barring that, they should at least assimilate and lose the bathrobes & head sweaters. They don't have to eat pork or celebrate Christmas, but they should socially & culturally acknowledge they live in a Westernized country and act accordingly.

The only kid who wore a turban in Sandusky, Ohio ironically attended a Catholic school. Maybe his parents thought he would be spared any bullying there. And maybe he was...but my experience with Catholics is that their favorite secular word is Nigger. They use this zinger to define a person who looks different...or someone who acts different. Or to even define a relative's spending habits. "He's nigger rich" is a way of saying that a spouse's spending habits are out of control. The said offender has a proclivity to purchase Schlitz and lotto tix with their paycheck. This is a biblical grievance, for a pious Catholic knows that a paycheck is not to be spent, but to be earned, then divvied up by someone more responsible. Hard work is best rewarded with a scolding. Catholic guilt runs deep. Maybe that kid with the turban escaped Saint Marys with his soul intact. Or maybe he just traded in one crazy religion for another.

   Despite my reservations for Muslims, I welcome other immigrants. Mexicans are hardworking people who moved here for the American Dream. Indians make fine doctors and skinny standup comedians. Asians are smart biological calculators with a knack for coding. An old *Dayton Daily News* article stated immigrant entrepreneurs account for a quarter of US tech startups. According to a Duke research study, immigrant entrepreneurs' companies employed 450,000 workers and generated billions of dollars in sales. Call me old-fashioned, but I believe that's what's great about America! Other white racist Americans who fancy themselves patriots would disagree. Xenophobia is quite common in the States. America has become the opposite of Hot Potato: As soon as you get it, no one else can have it.

   I always laugh when I hear white people complain that "illegal" immigrants are gonna take their jobs. My reply, "Well, you, or your ancestors shouldn't have crossed an ocean and moved to a country that borders their country."

   It seems a pre-requisite for ignorant patriotism is to be anti-immigration. We would have no country if the original immigrant white forefathers were patriotic. They would have just stayed in their own countries instead of coming here. Yet, they came here for the same reason Mexicans do: Opportunity. Patriotism is an image. It is propaganda used to get young men to die on foreign soil for rich people's purposes. It doesn't exist...just like God.

   The white God-fearing racists in America choose to ignore a sentence in their beloved bible: Do not mistreat an alien or oppress him. Jim-Bob and Billy-Joe thought that meant not to be mean to ET or Alf. So they stock up on Reeses Pieces only to see them disappear whenever their morbidly obese trailer trash wives are around. Ouch, stereotypes hurt. I welcome Hispanics with open arms. Especially the women...

The blacker the berry the sweeter the juice

   On that note I contacted an online genealogy company to trace my roots. So I sent in a DNA sample courtesy of Redtube and found out I'm a direct descendant of Jesus of Nazareth. He's my great, great, great, great, good, great, great, mediocre, great, great, great, great, not-so-great, great, great, great, aight, great, great, great grand-pappy. Yet some people say he wasn't all that great, of which I'm living proof.

    Don't worry; God has a sense of humor. Just look in the mirror...or turn on the news. Cultivating a sense of humor throughout one's life is a noble endeavor. For living life without humor is like eating food without taste buds.

    When I die I want to go to Heaven. A place where I can eat good food, drink beer, smoke weed, get a nobber, and be happy. Wait a minute; I'm already there.

Author's note: *Found this truth in a fortune cookie: Mudbutt in the morning will tame the most runaway of egos. (A self-fulfilling prophecy after eating fried Chinese food the night before) The only God I pray to is the porcelain kind for providing me with sanctuary during the dark days.*

7.
Homophobia

The one prejudice I cannot understand, much less tolerate, is homophobia. Why do straight men hate gay men?

Being a straight white man I embrace everybody. You show me respect, I show you respect. I have never been dissed or beat up by a gay man. Only straight men with crooked attitudes have dissed me. Or tried to.

Think about it. A gay man won't fuck your wife or girlfriend.

Go out to dinner with a gay man...and you will have good conversation and a nice time...without body odor. What's so wrong with that?

My mantra is this: More gay men the better. Less competition for women. And if you had a face like mine then you would agree!

At least "Don't Ask, Don't Tell" was repealed. Macedonia didn't have that rule with Alexander the Great. Or Rome with Julius Caesar. Yet, during Vietnam, straight arrows Billy Colby & McNamara were running the show. I'd rather have a general suck cock then suck at strategy and bomb innocent Asians.

So much vitriol over gay marriage wafting through the inner sanctums of right-wing suburbia even though the Real problem with the world is that too many dumb straight people are reproducing: a brainless mutant mass craving empty calories and immediate satisfaction. Spineless jellyfish that like to shop at Walmart. Stupid kids are the only real threat to American Values. At least if two dumb gay guys marry their stupidity is not replicated. No such luck for straights.

I'm all for equal rights, but marriage is an act of conformity that celebrates attrition. Best thing about having a wife: If you drool on your pillow in the middle of the night, just switch it with hers...or his. Why would Gay People want this? Would there have been an Elton John if gay marriage existed 30 years ago? If Gay People desire mundane domesticity then fine...It's their right. I just hope the arts don't suffer. Nothing is more dangerous to creativity than vanilla comfort.

The thing about gay people that straight people don't understand is that gays are just like straight people. Some gays believe in God, watch football, and even fondle rifles like cocks and go hunting. Maybe to prove to their backwards Repube-licken' family that they too can shoot straight. See, even some gays are ignorant. They're human. Last time I checked, humans are allowed to marry humans.

Why was Marriage Equality even debated in 2013? All the problems facing our country and the ancient fossils in the "Supreme Court" had to Debate an obvious moral issue: let everyone have the right to marriage; miserable domestication or not.

Global Warming, Debt, Overpopulation, Gun Violence, but they want to debate this. Gay marriage is fine...what I have a problem with is BP & Exxon committing ecological crimes and appealing their fines 'til the penalty is a hand slap.

"Supreme Court" -- what a stupid fucking name -- should be renamed the Appointed False Teeth Court...because someone else tells them when to bite.

Palin Tolerated Gay People

She may not like 'em, but she at least tolerates them. Hitler tolerated Jews right into the ovens and gas chambers. Palin is not that extreme, as she will only expel lazy-eye screwballs like her Juno daughter who keeps spitting out special grandsons.

The word Tolerate is morally bankrupt. Tolerate means you can barely stand someone different than yourself. I ACCEPT those who are different. I tolerate dirty assholes that don't wash their hands after they piss in casino bathrooms -- Newsflash: 70% of men urinate & don't wash their hands...filthy bastards indeed.

I cannot tolerate simple-minded politicians like Palin who try to impose their ignorant views on the people. Civil rights aren't taught in certain sections of Alaska. America was founded on the notion of liberty and freedom. Maybe they don't explain the constitution to beauty pageant contestants, posing and pandering to the right-wing radicals whose brains can fit in a teacup is what counts.

Tea-party scientists, all two of them, are busy at work trying to create a cure for homosexuality. Africans already beat them to it. Corrective rape is a known cure created by the South Africans. Any homosexual can be turned straight only if a straight man sodomizes the offending deviate. This remedy is known as tough love. Raping the gay out of someone is the selfless act of a patriot. It's only a matter of time before this method catches on like wildfire in the American South.

A dichotomy that has always puzzled me is that most conservatives who hate gays also possess a puritanical disdain of straight sexuality. They are petrified of the word Pussy. or Penis. I believe they just abhor pleasure, or do not understand sex. Myself, I have never understood trying to have a baby. It's like humping a putting green filled with warm custard. I'd rather pull out, shoot around, and we're all good friends again. Having kids just adds agitation & resentment to an already delicate situation.

That's why I'm a fan of nobbers. It's an understood act of pleasure. Nary a disease passed, and no unwanted pregnancies occur. I should run for president under the platform of Nobber Nation...the "cum out and see America" campaign. Get a nobber in every state. I still have 45 more to go. Through rain or shine: At least I possess Master Semen status. Dry ports or waterbeds, bodily fluids are best exchanged with a willing smile and a willingness to do better. My insistence on getting it just right rings true with the most naughtiness of females. Either that or I have a wild imagination that invents crusty sheets and curled feet. Hazy high-fives in hotel rooms filter up from recollections of reckless youth. Bad Dreams. Every man's favorite.

Why does the word Cocksucker have such a negative connotation? Probably the best feeling in the world is having your cock sucked, so why should the word be negative? It should be right up there with angel, saint, and prodigy. From now on, if I like a person, I'm calling them a cocksucker. It's such an unselfish act that only brings joy. The entire world can learn a lot from a cocksucker. Reminds me of a poignant song lyric: "Take what you give, then leave the rest."

The greatest sensation in the world is sex, so why do most of the movie trailers today highlight violence? Sex is the best experience of life, violence isn't fun. Even more popular than action movies are video games, especially violent ones. Whatever happened to *Pac-Man*, *Dig Dug*, *Donkey Kong*, and *Galaga*? And how come there are no sex games? With the Kinect and the superior Xbox One graphics there should be a pornographic video game. The porno industry rakes in billions worldwide, as does the video game industry. Combine the two and it would be a runaway success. Make it a Kinect game; your body is the controller. Call it Porno Hero. It would give the average dude the opportunity to bee-bop a porn star. And you could modify your avatar: black, white, hispanic, whatever. Modify the sex, and modify the schlong: pinky dick, 6 inches, John Holmes monster dong. I'll stick with the 6, I get intimidated easily.

I used to play video games until I found out my penis has a pulse and now I find myself checking it twice a day to keep the sluts away. Sex is always available...married or not. This is a first world problem for a first class mf'er. Baby-faced Heatt still gets carded with silver slivers in the sideburns. Wave the wedding band and it only exacerbates the inebriated situation. Unbeknownst to my slightly domesticated sensibilities, it seems that a man of my stature is a prime catch for the Summerlin penis hopping demographic due to my fabric softener quality of being non-clingy. An attribute of me a decade ago.

So I think of something. Anything. Sure, my many moles need kisses, but my conscience cannot allow such grievances. And I'm unable to get drunk enough to break my Bond. My word is stronger than Temptation. A wink & a whisper of "Thank you, but no thanks" is all I can manage. And it works...for now.

Irony: I was always a non-ass getting dude at OSU...so much so my dude nicknamed me No-Hoes. Now I feel like Mark Duper and Life is Dan Marino.

What to do?

Lucky for me, I'm a writer and the real pleasure is a well-written paragraph. Though I feel rotten, brains are a horrible thing to waste...
   Thinking about this quandary, jammin' Jodeci at a stoplight, and I swear that some floozy just flashed her silicone valleys at me. Whathafuck? Is my life on Candid Camera? Does the cosmos find my quandaries amusing? Toil & Testosterone is the epic storyline of my life. Every freakin' night and every freakin' day...
   I'm nothing special. There must be a serious dick deficit in Vegas these days. In a crisis like this the only smart move is to smoke a dube in the backyard.
   Puff, puffed, and figured it out. I have a baboonish sort of face. And believe it or not, women want a wild ape to fuck the shit out of them every now & then. The leftover desires of Evolution. And I'm surrounded by male sybarites with the sexual attractiveness of sludgeworms. So of course my cute chubby cheeks are gonna stand out. And most women want good dick. That's what they're primed for...their vaginas were created for interactions. Just make sure there's an understanding: Strings are allowed, but no feelings attached. Selah.
   Women like to laugh and have orgasms. Please the pussy and the mind, and a woman will never fault you. Keep it real and never lie. I've never had a *Fatal Attraction* stalker because I've never lied or strayed. And cool attracts cool. Maybe I'm a bit prejudiced because I've spent so much time with myself, but I have to say I'm a fun person to be around. And the twin Thai masseuses who just left the crib would agree...so long as you pay them like I didn't.
   Anyways. Ignore the tangent and let's get back to the topic. Homophobia is a disease of ignorance where the petrified person fears cum. One dick spewing sperm is enough to cause hysteria, but two rods jousting is reason to declare martial law.
   Get over it. In fact, embrace it. Sperm is a multi-purpose body fluid. I call mine Dr. Heatt's two-ball solution. It can be used as an adhesive or lubricant. You can shine your shoes with it, apply it as wallpaper glue, or even make babies. But my favorite use for sperm is Pranking. Just pop a load in someone's moisturizing lotion and let the fun begin. Nothing says "Got Ya!" like having your college roommate unknowingly smear spunk on their face. Gives a new & improved meaning to facial cream. They'll be sitting in their early morning Econ class wondering why their face feels like a French Cruller.

I'm not writing from personal experience...or am I? If you drop by my place for BBQ, just make sure to check your burger for organic mayonnaise. A condiment served fresh from the condom, straight from my penis to the dinner table. No artificial flavors, hormones, or antibiotics. Gluten-free. Actually, I don't know what a gluten is. Disease-free, does that count?

Just for the record, I have never *ever* put cum on somebody's burger. Freshly cut toenails - yes. Cum - no. And I was doing that person a favor. Toe fungus mold promotes digestive health and helps loosen stools. But that's another topic for another book. As you can see I have a psychic pipeline into the nether regions of bad taste. And that's exactly what my college roommate said after he ate his burger.

Author's note: *I noticed that grocery stores now carry Altoids minis. This product is designed for those with little dicks. So I told my wife to buy two packs.*

8.
Fishing for Anal Fissures

I don't watch much TV. A waste of time. Depressing. Dull. And the perfect example of what is wrong with this country. Littering the television landscape are putrid "reality" shows: competitions that crown the best singer, dancer, survivor, biggest Loser, and desperate bachelor/bachelorette. Mind-numbing material to be sure, these shows' popularity does not bode well for the future of this country. I don't know what was more harmful to society: The oil washing up on the Louisiana shore, or the *Jersey Shore* shit show.

"...the question deserves to be asked, who shaped the society this generation scorns?"
-Tom Wicker

    And the answer is television. TV dumb-downed the populace and it isn't this generation that scorns society, it will be the next generation that pays the price for our buffoonery...and they will ask the Wicker question then.
    Andy Warhol's 15 minutes of fame has been perverted into 30 minutes of TV infamy. Any lowlife lacking talent can be famous on a reality show. People tune into shows about repo men & pawnshop workers...dirtbags who make a living exploiting the downtrodden & desperate. Are the American People *that* mediocre they have to see their painful shortcomings reflected on TV?? David Mamet made a good observation: "Enron executives saw that the power to grow wealthy stemmed from the brave decision to stop making anything at all." It's only fitting that the American idea of celebrity should follow this business model as people with *no* talent at all become famous.
    These types of shows weaken the human race. Mediocre becomes good. Good becomes great. Reality shows reflect and reinforce fascist ideals of conformity and euthanasia. Vote someone out or off every week. Conspire and gang up against your fellow man instead of working together is the new American ethic. *Big Brother* was recently the #1 rated pogrom on Thursday nights. A house full of idiot racists entertains the country...which is kinda fitting if ya think about it. We've become the country full of idiot racists that entertain the world...when we're not too busy bombing it. *Big Brother* must be some sort of anti-American

propaganda designed to instill hatred in our enemies. The producer should be brought up on charges of treason. The swine is known to hide out in the Netherlands, and is a much bigger "threat" to national security than some guy named Snowden.

    We need to create a cultural climate that doesn't reward or idolize stupidity. In fact, it should be shunned and ostracized. Unlike fat people, there is no lap band for the mind. Put down the remote and pick up a book. The fact that an asshole can build a 2.2 billion dollar empire producing dreck like *Big Brother* is an intellectual indictment on Mankind. The idea of the show: Dumb People are cattle to be exploited...the show's participants & its passive audience.

    You can live life or watch it. Television is an impersonal medium that creates lazy voyeurs. Books are different. They're living, breathing things you hold in your hands. Reading is an intimate conversation, and the author has a direct connection to you. Nothing can take its place. Television dulls the mind, and causes the passive junkie not to care about anything that really matters.

    The average American cares more about D-grade "stars" dancing than they do about world news. Strife in China, Iran, Iraq, Afghanistan, Peru, Brazil, and a host of other countries goes unnoticed by the plebian, but Michael Jackson is on the tip of everybody's tongue. A Child Molester with a bad nose job overdosed; big deal. What about the Amazon Rainforest?

    HST wrote that after 9/11 the country suffered a nervous breakdown. Probably so, because we re-elected GW. And now, like any mentally ill patient, we are sedated///the most powerful drug being pop culture. The shift towards stupidity started with Britney Spears and other trailer trash icons. I can't think of anything more wasteful than paying money to see a no-talent slut lip-sync bubblegum pop songs, or other sluttish trash screech with tongue out.

    The American population is a herd of brainless buffalo whose overriding need for fast food and equally easily digested entertainment has deadened any vitality this country had after the Obama election. A foul mist of mundane mediocrity has descended upon US. Critical thinking has been replaced by a two-step. Kids are put on the television colostrum diet soon as they're born. And they stay on it 'til they die...though the brain usually encounters that fate several decades before the body does.

    Newsflash: A black woman was shot in the face while trying to seek help after an auto accident. This is shocking news?! Shouldn't be, this sort of thing happens every day around America. But what about the people who aren't on television? With no voice? Who airs their grievances? And would anybody care anyway? LeBron got dunked on. Did you hear? Know who else got slammed? Most of the

Children who attend public school in Cleveland. The same could be said for Los Angeles. Does Kobe or LeBron pony up the loot to bail these kids out? Nope. There are mansions to be built, and rape victims to be paid off...though the American Government bails out the rapists – AIG being one. Selfish sodomy never paid so well.

Gun Control is swept under the rug. Politicians are cowards, none more so than the Democraps. Unfortunately, it's the "best" we have right now. The Republican Party is composed of a bunch of charlatans and repressed sex fiends. Marijuana is illegal, and so is dog fighting...but it's okay if you kill somebody while driving drunk off Patron. A whirlwind of irrational chaos sweeps through our (in)justice system. Laws. I have no clue what that word means. Or the idea behind it. I guess the only sane thing to do is buy a large plot of land, get drunk, and keep the savages at bay...the politicians, police, and their stagnant laws.

The only thing more intellectually stultifying than American culture is British culture and its buffoonish pageantry and idiotic obsession with the Royal Family. The Brits' bad teeth and snooty accents are paradoxical elements of a depraved culture born from centuries of war mongering and imperialism: Two things that America is beginning to specialize in. The Revolutionary War merely separated the conjoined twins, and White Arrogance reattached them like an editor with splice tape.

The truth is, television is mind control...better yet, it's mind dosing. Or mind pausing. The mind sleeps while raking in hours of meaningless fluff. People used to read. Now we watch. When I tell people I don't have cable TV they stare at me like I'm some sort of creature from the Black Lagoon. Why pay for the mind-numbing madness when I can read a book for free? Am I really missing out? *Everybody Loves Raymond* set American culture back 50 years. *Boardwalk Empire* is an epic fictionalized history lesson sprinkled with incest, murder, corruption, and guns. *House of Lies* follows a group of sociopaths trying to make a living by lying. And the worst show of all is the most popular, *The Walking Dead*. No, it's not a documentary of American Society, it's entertainment for psychopaths, a daymare that celebrates the destruction of the human body.

I watched season two on DVD and found myself rooting for the zombies. The show is populated with a bunch of unlikable characters that spend most of their time whining and arguing and making bad decisions. The show grotesquely veered off into a brutal perverted wish fulfillment of guns & killing that appeal to the inner sadist of the audience. What's so wrong with the zombies? It's not like they wanted their condition. They didn't ask to be zombies. Rooting against zombies is like rooting against people with AIDs or cancer. Granted, zombies have a tendency to eat people, but they don't make nuclear weapons or poison the environment. In fact, zombies might be doing the planet a favor by curing the overpopulation dilemma. And who doesn't want some brains every now and then?

Watching season three was a chore that I only did for my book and may have suffered severe trepanation as a result. *The Walking Dead* (and *Game of Thrones*) is atavistic entertainment born from the apocalyptic New Testament defeatist mind state that all hope is lost so let's all act like animals and shoot guns. Watching this show turns the viewer into a zombie -- the new entertainment: Death-affirming. It has to be the most morally despicable television program in history where a boy walks around with a gun the entire show. A lil' cunt kid with a goofy hat shoots people in cold blood. Everyone dies and the true act of love is when the bastard shoots his own mom. Truly a sick show for sick people. This gratuitous gross show is a symptom of a diseased culture. The viewers are the metaphor: A brainless mass stumbling around seeking sustenance…on the comfort of their own couch.

Boom & gloom, death & despair, *the Walking Dead* is bleak dreary dreck. Nothing life-affirming about it. Characters sit around and reminisce about the good ol' days of killing relatives. I watched the entire season and wanted one of those overacting assholes to put a bullet in my head. An old lady walks around with an assault rifle, and the pissant boy carries his pistol with a solemn air Hitler would approve of. All in all, it's wholesome entertainment for the modern American family. In a perverse way, it celebrates the worst of humanity. Ain't nuthin' guns can't handle. Guns & bows, a hillbilly's wet dream. "Ya'll gonna be glad you had those guns & prisons when the zombie apocalypse happens!"

It already has. The season 4 premiere of *the Walking Dead* on AMC shattered a ratings record with 16.1 million viewers. The plague spreads quickly...

"How do you preserve yourself in a world where life doesn't mean much anymore?"

Paddy Cheyefsky's movie *Network* asked this question. And I still don't know the answer. Paddy's prescient ideas are still relevant. He said, "Violence brutalizes the audience." We are surrounded by the entertainment of Dehumanization. We are losing the human identification...meaning: we are losing the belief of togetherness. Cheyefsky believed, "Human life is a helluva lot more important than your lousy dollar." We are on the brink of becoming a lousy selfish brutish group of people known as the television generation. Rotten voyeurs.

"We learn life from Bugs Bunny." Television in a bloody nutshell.

"Reading is one means of emancipation for the working classes. That is why we recommend that they read widely."
-Luis Emilio Recabarren
(Worker's Movement maverick)

9.
The American Sleep

"In the time of the missionaries, in the time of the rubber, of the timber, and now the oil, they all lied to us. It is all the same person wearing a different mask."
-Wili Corisepe
Isn't it always? Maybe the devil is real, and he goes by the guise of capitalism.

The most important issue facing Humankind is Global Warming. This was the thesis of my final position paper a dozen years ago for a college English composition class. And yet, our society still does nothing but take baby steps when the problem requires a revolution of green political policies. This issue is ignored by the majority of American politicians because hard truths of reality can be a poison pill in our antiquated political system. Every week there are new scientific findings that support the Fact that the Earth's global temperature is rising due to human activities...yet all we do is slumber towards a glum future.

By now most people are familiar with the greenhouse effect. It is responsible for the absorption of infrared energy in the atmosphere, thus making Earth conducive to life. Carbon dioxide is one of the main atmospheric gases that absorb infrared radiation. The amount of CO_2 has increased over 28% in the past hundred years and could rise by more than 40% in the next hundred. This is a bleak prognosis to anyone with a sliver of intelligence...of which I'm quite certain our policy makers lack.

I extensively researched Global Warming for that English paper, and found that many scientists made dire predictions for the year 2150, and many of those predictions have already come true. Global Warming has accelerated. The New Orleans delta was not only endangered but flooded. Dengue fever has been reported in Florida. Sections of America that have had flood problems were hard hit...Colorado just one example. Massive droughts constantly occur. Stronger storms battered America: tornadoes in Oklahoma and Hurricane Sandy in NYC. Irregular weather patterns brought upon by global warming will continue to increase the likelihood of massive forest fires and floods. If I knew this a decade ago, you can bet the politicians did also, but they just didn't give any feces so as long as the feces are free and not lobbyist green.

The melting of the Antarctic ice shelf would only increase the global warming effect as the ice currently reflects insolation, while the rock below absorbs it. Another harrowing prospect is the frozen tundra thawing. This adverse event would release massive amounts of methane into the atmosphere, increasing the greenhouse effect even more. The byproduct of this would be a massive displacement of populations, leading to tumultuous overpopulation conflicts in many areas of the world. Natural resources are already being strained by population increases and pollution.

Desertification would increase as food supplies plummet. Temperature increases means an explosion in the insect population...which increases the probabilities of disease epidemics. Warmer weather also causes more erratic and deadlier storms...of which we are becoming tragically accustomed to. Global warming also causes extreme cold temperatures in some areas due to the complex effects it has on rainfall and ocean currents. Polar Vortex is a fancy media term for Climate Change.

The debate & discussion are over -- we are in the midst of Global Warming. Now is no time to be a selfish Yuppie. Irresponsible behavior is for children, not adults. The only industry not ignoring the problem is the Insurance industry, which will cease to exist decades from now unless things immediately change. The United States is the biggest polluter on the planet. We account for about a quarter of all greenhouse gas emissions yet we only comprise 4% of the world's population. Our burning of fossil fuels is the result of power & heating plants, and the use of cars. And our policies on environmental issues are controlled by these Big Businesses, whose economic fortunes lie in fossil fuel consumption. America's refusal to implement policies geared to the reduction of global warming is an arrogant attitude fostered by greed and apathy-induced ignorance. Bush & Cheney implemented anti-environmental policies geared to the whims of their Big Bizzy campaign contributors. Obama has finally realized this fact and announced a plan to reduce 30% of carbon emissions from American power plants. A great start.

Huge financial interests are at stake. The fossil fuel industry pockets over a trillion dollars a year. No wonder current restrictions on CO_2 emissions are non-existent. Bush's cabinet was composed of people with links to the oil & automotive industries. Unfortunately Obama dilly-dallies with the proposed Keystone oil pipeline. There will be no reform movement until people start getting pissed & protest. If people wait until massive population displacement occurs then it will be too late.

We are not the only problem. "Developing Countries" like China & India are embracing coal power even though these countries have had thousands of years to develop alternatives. The rest of the world shouldn't have to suffer the large CO_2

outputs by these countries due to their inability to modernize their infrastructure. And the world shouldn't have to put up with ours -- even though we act like the bully and completely abandon any sort of Treaty agreement. We have taken a passive role in a huge problem. Our reaction to Global Warming will define us as a people for generations to come.

We are all to blame. Political Leadership is an oxymoron. We need to institute change ourselves, not wait for wafflers. Energy conservation is important, and mass transit systems & car-pooling need to take on larger roles. We have to take control of the government...and stop subsidizing fossil fuels, and instead, devote that money to renewable energy & energy efficiency. According to Alden Meyer, an energy specialist with the Union of Concerned Scientists, study after study has shown that every dollar spent on conservation, energy efficiency, and renewable energies creates far more jobs than the equivalent amount spent on fossil fuels.

"Buy American, sell American, and keep a stiff upper lip when your sloth and stupidity catch up with you...why not?"
-HST

This quote applies to the Las Vegas high-speed railroad debacle that would connect Vegas to Southern Cali...and it was scrapped because it failed to meet "Buy America" rules. It was all a sham. Hypocrisy at its highest -- the railroads were partially built on the backs of Chinese immigrants, and yet, a high-speed railway that would create American jobs and cut back on CO_2 emissions is aborted because some materials are foreign. So, Toyotas, and Hondas, and Acuras, and Lexuses, and BMWs, and Mercedes, and a host of other foreign cars are okay to traverse the highways spewing fumes? But putting Americans to work building a railway is not "Buying American".

Do we just look stupid, or do the politicians just treat us that way because we are? Or because we let them because we're too busy chewing a Carl's burger on the freeway to care? Wouldn't that commute be a bit better if a modern transit system existed?

Smog clouds the Eyes

Scientists created the atomic bomb in 2 1/2 years; I would think that America could develop ways to harness the vast amounts of renewable resources at our disposal. Texas Instruments developed semi-conductors for the Cold War. Green Energy is just as important for the Warm War. Wind power and solar energy are invaluable sources of energy that need to be cultivated much more. The sun gives

Earth 30,000 quadrillion thermal units of energy per year. The total present global consumption of energy by humans is less than 400 quads per year. We have to develop ways to harness solar power that are efficient and inexpensive. We can do it.

Humans have always adapted and changed with the times. Now is the time for a rapid evolution. I don't want to see the Earth's future resemble the dark and dingy overpopulated cityscape of *Blade Runner* where the only hope of experiencing the serenity of nature is through virtual reality. Global Warming presents an opportunity to bring humanity together as a collective whole and to unite for a common cause other than war.

"Scientists have discovered a vaccine for apathy. However, nobody is showing the slight bit of interest in it."
-George Carlin

Even Carlin was guilty of apathy. In a 1992 NYC show Carlin railed against the environmental movement, sort of an apathetic exercise to give himself an excuse not to do anything. Instead, he'd rather criticize the people who actually give a shit.

Wake up!

We should be stewards of the planet, not the exploiters. A million years of evolution and we risk everything with mindless selfishness. Such a beautiful world, and people are so preoccupied with a car & home that they can rest in until death. Auto-Mobile coffins spewing fumes on the highways driven by unconscious consumers. *Wake up.*

Tesla is creating innovative electric cars. And GM has shed its junk credit rating and is creating the hybrid Volt. SUVs and Hummers are for cunts, hybrids are for forward-thinkers.

According to the Director of National Intelligence, everything "should" be relatively fine until 2030, but after that, who knows? Climate change will increase worldwide strife where wars are not fought for oil, but for necessities like water and land to live on & cultivate.

I like sports and grilling just as much as the next chubby guy, but everybody should devote some time to this important topic...whether it means driving less, consuming less, or HAVING LESS KIDS...the environment is being destroyed by the locust-like consumption of natural resources. It blows my mind that the proliferation of one species endangers every other one on the planet...and that the one species does so in such a greedy, callous, and ignorant fashion. When profits stop dictating morality then maybe some solutions can be found. Every individual has some power to help solve this problem. Either be a part of the solution, or remain a part of the problem! **Wake up**.

We know we are wrong, and we still do it.

Sign a useless petition against the Keystone pipeline if it makes you feel better, but it won't do a damn thang.
Thang.
Not thing...thang is an insult like a bloody nose. Why do I have to constantly sign petitions and donate money to non-profit organizations to get politicians to do the right thing? And even then the greedy rats still don't do anything! Waste a signature on a petition that nobody pays any attention to, or put your freedom on the line. Civil disobedience is the key. Let the bastards know the pipeline will not get built without widespread sabotage. Our government already acts like an au pere with a drinking problem and treats it citizens like unruly kids. They frack us, pollute us, flood us, and tell us it's for our own good. No more shucking shit and having to eat it too.
I signed a petition that was against Fracking (a process that pollutes our water) and then exporting the natural gas overseas. Nevada politicians Dean Heller, Joe Heck and Harry Reid emailed/sent letters in response stating pretty much the same opinion: They are FOR fracking. Skirting the obvious health concerns of fracking, they convolute the issue with paragraphs detailing bipartisanship support in Congress (whose true identity is corporate politics), and without conscience, tact, or grace, they both exploit the current events in Ukraine to justify the need for Fracking.
They say we need to frack & pollute our lands to help Ukraine reduce their dependence on Russia's natural gas supplies...even if that means increasing their dependence on ours. You can't make this shit up. And while we're at it, let's throw in a Billion dollars in loan guarantees for them. Because Ukraine needs that money much more than our schools do...
So let's all get used to Fracking and lighting water on fire as is drips out of the faucet so the Ukraine can diversify their energy supplies. It's all a scam.
Omaha dumps 6 million gallons of raw sewage a day into a river, while elsewhere 800,000 gallons of oil spilled into the Kalamazoo River, while elsewhere Louisiana floods Cajun country to prolong the inevitable inundation of New Orleans, and elsewhere, Cabot Oil & Gas shares rise as they frack our lands while polluting our watersheds. 300,000 West Virginia residents remember the good ol' days of being able to drink tap water without worries. Our country is

supposed to be the best in the world, yet this sort of shit happens everywhere every day? *Wake up*.

   The more I learn about America the more I realize America is not up for sale. Because it's already been sold. Guns, fracking, coal, oil, you name it. I read history books about the Civil War and WW II and I think: Did those marvelous men all sacrifice their lives so greedy pigs like Exxon can rape our country? Companies have bought the politicians and corrupted the legal system. It's time to take our country back state by state, county by county. Get involved. If it means risking arrest, then that pales in comparison to what our country's founders faced.

   An orange blanket of smoke covering the sky, the smell of a campfire wafts through an entire city: a reality for most people who live in the west from this time on. Two fires rage in Nevada, 22 fires burning 400,000 acres in the west as I write this. Firefighters battle the flames bravely, but they don't make the political decisions regarding Global Warming. Maybe they should. Forests are burning, and the future habitability of Earth is at stake. On the front page of the LVRJ, a despondent man stands surveying his burnt Mount Charleston property wearing a t-shirt proclaiming "American Speed Seeker" over a graphic of an American muscle car roaring past the finish line. *Wake up*.

   The government can fund a solar-energy company that manufactures solar panels, but if no one buys them, and the government allows cheaper Chinese-manufactured panels imported into the country then what chance does that company have? Everything has to change: Manufacturing, Distribution, and Protection of homegrown businesses.
   Everything did change when BP polluted the Gulf of Mexico. Millions of barrels of oil swirled in the Gulf because of BP's & Transnational Corporation's negligence. Media termed it "a disruption" and a "set back" while BP static-killed and bottom-killed to no avail. Pumping mud into a well was their best solution. BP should never be allowed to operate again in America. Gross incompetence that results in ecological devastation should be just as devastating to the company that caused it. *Wake up*.

   Dead dolphins washed up on the coast and the idiotic media proclaimed "oil's role unclear." Obama unfurled his panties and proclaimed a 7 year drilling ban...which reeked of common sense...which obviously had no place in the United States legal system. US district judge martin feldman overturned Obama's moratorium on new drilling. Feldman has extensive investments in the oil & gas industry and he would hate to see Transocean stocks suffer.

When the oil spill happened, I didn't feel bad for the drillers who lost their lives. They raped the Earth and suffered the consequences. They made the choice to have that bullshit occupation. I just wish Feldman were present on that offshore drilling rig when it exploded. Now I realize those poor drillers were just chasing the American Dream, just doing what they've been indoctrinated into doing since they were old enough to watch TV. I wasn't any better when I was younger, and I can't fault a man for trying to feed his family or put some coin in his pocket. But now we're all wiser. WE know better.

I wonder if the handful of American Olympic athletes who whored out to BP ever thought about the ecological devastation BP caused...prolly not...Capitalistic Cunts could care less. Oil-soaked turtles are nothing compared to crisp bills.

Cleanup costs are still being debated in court. No money will alleviate the irreparable harm done to the environment. If you buy BP gas then basically you're saying it's okay to destroy the planet. Same thing if you buy Exxon gas. BP may or may not pay back the cleanup costs...they and Halliburton and Transocean will try to litigate their way out of the fiasco and not assume responsibility. No wonder audiences rooted against the humans in *Avatar*. **Wake up.**

BP has a history of negligent pollution, only we didn't know about it. BP had to shut down their Alaska Prudhoe Bay factory back in 2006 because corrosion in their pipe spilt 200,000 gallons of crude. A year before in Texas, a BP refinery exploded, killing 15 and injuring 180 people. Why wasn't BP shut down and kicked out of the country then? Obviously these limey knuckleheads are not to be trusted. Why do we allow the Redcoats to pollute our country?

American't keeps giving these cunt companies access to pollute our lands. 4th of July 2011, an Exxon pipeline ruptured in the Yellowstone River. Tens of thousands of gallons of crude oil swirled in the waterway. Ranchers and fishermen had no answer for the grievance. The Forest Service likes to allow uranium mining at the Grand Canyon. And now our Prez still mulls over the Keystone pipeline that would send oil through our country to a dock where it would be shipped off to benefit another country. The oil would come from the Alberta tar sands -- a filthy mess -- destructive to the environment is an understatement. This scumbag operation produces 475 million gallons of toxic waste per day. An open pit tar sands mine is a complete raping of the land. These facilities really are nightmares -- an open pox that encourages deforestation. And they want to pipe this mess through America. Guess what? Pipelines rupture and leak.

If the American Governcorp does nothing to address Global Warming then it obviously doesn't care about its populace, and even less about other countries. Politicians see no profit in the sustainability of life on this planet. Bleed Everything. Our form of Government has been so far incapable of change. So now we must change the government and all its loquacious pandering ineffective forms.

    Obama's department of Interior gave Shell the OK to drill exploratory wells in the Arctic Ocean. Something happens there, forget about it. These companies are determined to make sure every fish caught in the ocean is polluted somehow. Japan already has the Pacific Ocean on radiated lock! Radiation plume petals love me not.

Wake up.

10.
Where's Mothra when you need it?

March 2011. Radioactive water spills into the Pacific Ocean…the Japs determined to make Godzilla a reality. How smart was it to build nuclear reactors on a coastline? Fukushima is tragic irony -- the only country to be bombed with an atomic bomb turns to nuclear energy to bomb itself. Years of isolated island inbreeding finally caught up to the country, and now it threatens the world once again.

Back in April of 2011 the LVRJ ran a story with the headline "*Radioactive water leaks into ocean.*" Then to insult the intelligence of the reader the subtitle was: *Seepage through crack not expected to cause health hazard*. The Onion would be proud. Radioactive water was *pumped* into the sea for almost a month! Afterward Tokyo Electric Power apologized. Then the PM reassured the victims, "We will support you so that you can resume fishing." ??!! Does the government wish death on its populace, giving it radioactive fish? Japan raised the stakes on the philosophy of shitting in their own backyard, contaminating a large percentage of their food & economy.

Do we need anymore proof that nuclear energy is not the answer? Ban Japanese food imports. The Chinese reported radioactivity in their spinach afterwards, but the news was poo-poo'ed in the US. What do you expect? Our government treats us like children…a reoccurring problem. Ironic, because they are the ones who act like children -- an irresponsible & immoral government that failed to warn citizens about Fukushima dangers. Believe in Santa Claus, make your bed, and if you ask any questions, shut the fuck up and suck on a bar of soap. Now we find out that babies born on the United States Pacific coast in March & April 2011 are 28% more likely to suffer from congenital hypothyroidism. Wonder why? Could it be from the Fukushima explosions that floated iodine 131 over the Pacific?

One country's incompetence affects every other country around them. Radioactive leak? No problem. Japs throw sawdust and shredded newspapers in the hole…thereby making North Korea look like an innocent girl scout. I still can't understand after WWII Why we would allow Japan to have nuclear power?????? This degenerate country is incapable of doing anything constructive except bellow

Karate routines and ogle at young schoolgirls wearing Scottish mini-skirts.

The Japs were a wicked race of people like the Nazis, and if you hear loud unbearable babbling in an airport, more than likely it's a Jap on his celly talking like Toshiro Mifune. You can tell a lot about a culture by the sound of its language. And there is no detestable noise more grating to the human ear than the Japanese language. It sounds like hogs rutting in the mud exhorting one another to sodomize the weakling of the litter. A debased syntax built around guttural exclamations that an animal utters in heat. The only thing worse is the Arab conjuring of loogies that passes for communication.

Eastwood attempted to sugarcoat shit with his movie *Letters from Iwo Jima*, but the truth is that the Japs are a psychologically screwed-up culture: a nation whose fathers were serial killers. The Banzai butchers had no respect for humanity. I never trust a culture that breeds butchers. The Japanese are a degenerate species that shows slow progress. Their culture esteems a filial obligation to ancestors...which is the Yamato Race. They preach harmony, peace, balance -- just linguist PR that really means the opposite. Their historic actions prove them to be cannibalistic cunts. Perfect companions for the Nazis.

The Germans were a restless pack of Huns who thought cat urine smelled like lavender, and so they followed Hitler. Phil Goodman once said that you can't argue with a thickheaded German. They're all alike and if you prove to them that they're wrong about something, they keep on believing their error more strongly. And they kept on believing until the bombs started falling in their own backyards. They were the masters of the death business, and that is why now all of the funeral homes in America are run by Germans. It takes a certain sinister genetic inclination to suffer a job like that.

Hirohito & Hitler were barbaric twins. Hirohito was one of the worst human beings to ever breathe air.

So much outrage these days over the NSA snooping, FBI flying drones, IRS probing, American generals outted in conduct unbecoming, and the Prez promising but not delivering. Big Deal. Hirohito reigned under the auspice of "abundant benevolence"...which has become known as chemical warfare, rampant rape, extravagant arrogance, and merciless murder.

Hirohito's Showa era can be defined as "Kill all, Burn all, Loot all." Those were his orders. Japanese escapades included The Bataan Death March (an 80 mile trek that killed thousands of Filipino & American POW's), Pearl Harbor, and the rape of Nanking -- the Asian massacre of 300k Chinese. The reason Japs are good at baseball is because swingin' samurai swords to decapitate people is good practice. A contest to behead a hundred people is like homerun derby.

Rape & looting was the Jap trademark in China, though the US didn't care until the pestilence washed ashore on December 1941. The Japs were almost as bad as the Nazis. The death rate for POWs was 30% and they murdered 6 million people, mostly Chinese, Indonesian, Filipino, Korean, and Vietnamese. The Jap culture was a determining factor...they prided themselves as ruthless conquerors. They would undoubtedly be fans of *Call of Duty* today...and probably are.

Hirohito was a modern day Muslim who offered afterlife promises. He was the Emperor, another cultish god-on-earth figure. And when things turned sour in 1944, Hirohito gave an imperial order to civilians: commit suicide rather than be taken prisoner. Yet he lived in a palace 'til his death of old age. His tomb in Tokyo should be treated like a nuclear fallout accident and sealed with steel-reinforced concrete to ensure his evil soul stays trapped there.

Hirohito lived like a king 'til 1989, free of war crimes...shielded by an Interest Group. Dead US GI's who served in the Pacific Theatre were sold down the River Styx by the OSS & Douglas MacArthur: the greatest act of military treachery committed since Benedict Arnold. Hirohito was fellated by MacArthur, an American general...proving that a general is not to be trusted. Never Ever.

Instead of building a pyramid to the sky, Hirohito was intent on forging an inverse dagger that would strike at the heart of humanity. In order to understand how deranged the Japanese were, all you have to do is drink warm sake. Picture lying on a beach with a big girl lathered in sunscreen. For hours. Then pour vodka on her stomach and drink it. That's what sake tastes like. Now you understand that those cretin samurais had cast-iron stomachs and a demented cultural disdain for pleasurable beverages.

A rotten apple returns to Earth

9/11 occurs. And people, including myself, ask, "How did this happen, and why?" Because the past is covered up, that's why. A corpse hidden like Hoffa diced up in a Hyundai. We don't learn from it because we don't know about it. There's nothing to be studied but an ongoing tragedy of malice.

"I can hear the future by putting my ears to the rails of history."
-Phil Goodman

The forerunners to modern American democracy began an enduring policy of turning a blind eye to evil so long as it suited their immediate interests. They rather lay their heads on the rails and wait for the quick solution. Right and wrong never mattered. Not even when the pigs were piglets. As long as they had something to suckle, all was right. And now that nipple is soulless power. Money has no flag. Nor a moral compass. The true north is what's best for the beast. And the beast is hungry. Always.

Too much of the old ways leads to ruin: The enemy of my enemy is my ally. That twisted way of thinking might win a battle, but it's not making the world a better place.

The Japanese were a destructive war-like culture. We are becoming our past enemy. To the victors go the spoils and the psychosis. A transfer of aggression. "No Retreat, No Surrender" is a Bone song blaring at a football game...our new anthem. Japs were a brutal bloodthirsty people...a product of centuries of warfare, a people that exulted war above all else. And they Apologized for everything only after they were beat. Official apologies are basically diplomatic erasers to wipe the slate clean. Governments want their misdeeds to be covered up, and won't acknowledge or apologize for them unless they're brought to light. An apology might be the most worthless man-made device ever. It just means you were caught and feel bad because your actions are frowned upon. That's why our history books are a candy land of half-truths. Japanese Nationalists deny that any war crimes took place, sort of like my ass denies hemorrhoids...bloody ones that demand itching. Jap PM's continue to pray at the Yaskunie Shrine -- they pretend their atrocities never happened just like we do.

The imperial family was pardoned...just like our imperial family decades later: Bush & Cheney were never charged with Iraqi war crimes. The UK even granted Hirohito 6 Knight honors...proving that awards have no special meaning, and are usually bestowed in relation to monies bequeathed to the giver. If you live a life seeking honours then I recommend the game *Pac-Man* to spare humanity from your arrogant horrors. This leads us to...

The CIA was formed with the philosophy of Bonner Fellows: exonerate war criminals to serve a purpose. There is absolutely no morality. Fellows was a John Birch radical whose ideology was more important than humanity. And there you have the CIA in a nutshell. Many of the Jap criminals who engaged in biological warfare & torture were not prosecuted...instead they were given cushy jobs in the Japanese pharmaceutical industry so long as they handed over the results of their heinous experiments. And this is the way the world has worked for the past 70 years. Once you understand that monsters run corporations & nations, the less you'll be afraid of the shadows under your bed. Unless those shadows are Monsanto...the company that created Agent Orange now produces our food.

Decades ago there was a Transition to the new order in Indonesia. Radical Islam grew popular through a horrible massacre of communists by Suharto and his death squads comprised of Muslims all too happy to kill others. Almost a million people were slaughtered, with the CIA's blessing of course, yet radical Islam was not a popular topic in the United States until 2001. We are taught about the Holocaust in school, but what about this horrific tragedy in Indonesia? I guess our state-sponsored massacres are swept under the rug. The criminal organization known as the CIA should have been disbanded after this debacle and its management indicted on crimes against humanity. The CIA is a seditious force: a bacterial virus incurred from too much warfarce. Time to get rid of it. A mad dog infected with rabies is not a healthy animal to have roaming the world while promoting peace...and that's just it. The CIA cannot survive in a peaceful world. War is necessary for its survival.

The CIA is a just a tool for American corporate power, and the Agency has no problem turning a blind eye to crimes against humanity (even if they aren't active participants). The often-ineffective International Criminal Court defines crimes against humanity as odious offenses that constitute a serious attack on human dignity, or grave humiliation, or a degradation of human beings. Sounds like high school. Here is a better and simpler definition: Killing another human being. Isn't the killing of an environmental activist in Nigeria by Shell a crime against humanity? A crime against one person is a crime against us all.

Every race and religion has dabbled in ethnic cleansing. The true guilt is that we as a global people keep allowing it. The Serbs massacred the Muslims in Srebrenica. Some of the demons that participated are still in power...but at least the Serbian parliament was kind enough to offer an official apology. The United States is no better. By now most people are familiar with the massacre of Native Americans...but more recently the United States engaged in a massive campaign of terrorism and bombed the Vietnamese people mercilessly a few decades ago. We even sent in platoons of soldiers to wipe out entire villages...acting more like WWII Japs than American soldiers. The My Lai Massacre is a famous example. At least 350 Vietnamese died yet not one American soldier served any time. William Calley, still alive & free today, killed 22 people and was sentenced to house arrest. General Westmoreland congratulated the gook killers on their outstanding job. Colin Powell tried to cover it up, the establishment's favorite house Negro. To be fair, the NVA carried out their fare share of massacres also, the Hue massacre being the most damaging. War makes a monster out of man. And so what sort of beast instigates wars? The CIA. The bulk of our foreign policy problems can be attributed to the CIA. Too bad JFK never got the chance to get rid of it...

Author's note: *It's worth noting that America helped defeat 2 of the worst psychopathic bully countries in the history of mankind during WWII: Germany &*

Japan. To honor our WWII veterans, it is up to all of us to make a positive difference in our country. Now.

It's time to fulfill the promise of a democratic society instead of wasting our potential on brainless consumption.

11.
Belch

America is the redneck rolling a pickup truck guzzling Budweisers then flipping the cans out the window littering the highway. After the Japanese nuclear disaster, a 2011 report came out detailing radioactive leaks in 48 US nuke sites. Tritium leaks in the groundwater causing cancer and genitalia to light up like glow sticks. These nuke sites need water to cool the reactors, and being insane, we place nuclear reactors next to the Great Lakes and other water sources.

The plant operators think safety margins can be eased without peril. However, if you do ingest tritium then you can make a healthy profit by selling your neon feces for $30k/gram. I think that's how Robert Rodriguez financed his first film, *El Mariachi*.

The NRC Cunts, aka Nuclear Regulatory Commission, looks the other way despite over 400 leaks. This is not a regional problem, but a worldwide one. Exelon stated that 100% of nuclear piping integrity is not practical. And this company is related to the proposed Keystone pipeline project. And they are the biggest US nuclear operator. Well, if they can't guarantee 100% integrity then shut the bastards down! (DMX voice) This isn't a fucking game! There is no room for error when it comes to Nuclear Energy. If Davis Besse or some other nuclear reactor melts down and contaminates the Great Lakes then kiss the United States goodbye.

Water is the lifeblood of the world. Without it, there is no existence. And procuring water is becoming an exploitation device that some experts estimate to be a $400 billion a year Bizzy. How can life be business? And why do we allow it? Whoever controls the water controls the world. And why should anyone control it? We all live on the same planet and everyone deserves clean water without having to pay for it. This sort of selfish insane profiteering makes modern day humanity a bane to the world.

The effects of our civilization threaten every other form of life on the planet.

BLM rounds up Mustangs to be slaughtered for dog food (but bow down against tea-bagging weirdos on the Bundy ranch). Bears are killed in Montana. Wolves hunted in Washington. If People do not like these animals then their bitch-ass shouldn't move to the states where these animals are. Simple. That's why I root for the shark in *Jaws*. The Vegas casinos serve shark fin soup to the limp dick Asians who need boners. I read an MSN headline: "Massive Killing Machine Caught." But the only killing machines I saw in the pic were the Caucasian cunts posing with a dead shark.

Sharks are killed at an alarming rate, mostly by foreign fishermen who murder the sharks for their fins. Check out the documentary *Sharkwater* for details. The media shouldn't glorify asswipes who kill sharks...but again, the media is responsible for the braindead populace in this country whose numbers continue to rise in direct proportion to the time spent exposed to media.

Prehistoric apex predators aren't the only things We exterminate. Overpopulation, pollution, and Global Warming kill off thousands of plants and animals. Our very exploding existence means doom for everything else on this planet. The Germans weren't satisfied with WWII and initiated "Elterngeld" which gives incentives for giving birth. Most other European countries have various newborn bonuses, and the United States allows tax benefits for couples having kids. Western Civilization has caught a major case of the Dumb Ass. Staring overpopulation & decreasing resources in the face, we reward people for *having* kids. There should be tax benefits for people NOT having children. **Do the world a fucking favor and pull out.**

America has had a hard time doing the world any favors lately. We export pollution by financially supporting transnational corporations. Shell polluted Nigeria for over 50 years and now is responsible for a one billion dollar cleanup. Hundreds of millions of gallons of oil were spilled into the Niger River Delta because Shell has no respect for black people...and life in general. Fining Shell one billion dollars for the pollution is like giving Jerry Sandusky community service for sodomizing lil' boys. Shell paid for the execution of the Nigerian activist Ken Saro-Wiwa. And now Nigerian pirates intercept Dutch Oil ships. They had their land raped for so long it's only right they share in some profits. Yet *Captain Phillips* is the movie Hollywood gives us.

Hunt Oil covets Peru's natural gas like a crackhead covets car stereos. Even worse: illegal gold mining has been devastating Peru's Amazon rainforest since 2008. Gotta love humans: Chop down the Amazon, pump mercury into the water table, and all for a shiny substance Lil Jon can wear in his teeth, or rich white hags can dangle from their ears. Capitalistic vanity is still used as a weapon of imperialism: funding mining, graft, and forcing underage girls into prostitution for the miners. Think of some weeping 14 year-old girl being forced to fellate a sweaty miner the next time you see an "Every kiss begins with Kay" commercial.

If South America doesn't resort to some form of socialism then their continent will be just one big polluted mining dump for the Nortenos. Chevron has its pederast eye on Brazil. And Transocean cannot wait to start drilling...even though we've seen their stellar work in the Gulf. Ecuador ransoms off their oil reserves in the Amazon for a hundred million dollars a pop. And our own President, at any given moment, is quick to strike a FTA with foreign countries for his corporate tops. I equate FTAs with exploitation and deforestation and job exportation. There should be a new clause inserted into all "Fair Trade" Agreements: If a country is going to take our jobs then they can also take our criminals. For every job a country takes from the United States, they also take two of our worst criminals. Fidel Castro gives two thumbs up!

   We're not the only country that pollutes. Hungary is known to turn rivers into toxic sludge that threatens the Danube. According to EU standards, this sludge, being a byproduct of manufacturing aluminum, is not considered hazardous waste. Tell that to the dead wildlife. Bangladesh also believes in polluting water with toxic waste. Dye from factory chemicals swirl in the waterways & canals. Fish & rice paddies come second so Americans can buy cheap clothes at Wal-Mart and JC Penney. The next time you throw on a shirt with a Made-in-Bangladesh tag, thank the little brown kids for having to drink polluted water so you can save a buck. China is becoming a polluted wasteland and their problems are well documented. They also like to rape international waters. Russia too. Fifty years from now China will be fighting water wars with India. This reality is a not a possibility, but a mathematical fact...unless a Global Evolution occurs.

   Pollution is a worldwide problem. Global Warming is the most important aspect, but other deadly side effects occur. The seas are facing mass extinctions. Overfishing will contribute to starvation. The global food chain will be stretched until it snaps in order to repair itself. Fertilizers create dead zones in bodies of water, and chemicals & plastics disrupt ecosystems. Air and water, the two necessary ingredients for life, are both becoming health hazards with a multitude of pollutants. The WHO classified air pollution as cancer causing...a higher risk than smoking. (this statistic includes Newports but excludes OG Kush)

   We need to change now. Everyone. And fast. In 2100 the sea levels are expected to rise three feet, and worldwide skirmishes will ignite as refugees pour over all borders.

"To understand a new idea, break an old habit."
-Jean Toomer
(Poet, Novelist)

   The number one priority for any government should be to develop green technology while the planet is still livable. Everything's about food, water, and shelter. Observe animals, insects, and humans long enough and this truth becomes clear. Knowing that, the governments of the world have to come together and ration out the resources in an appropriate manner. This idea will scare Americans...which is ironic. People immigrated to America because of the lack of resources in their home countries, and then, have no problem exploiting the resources of other downtrodden countries. What I find disturbing is that most people rather be opportunists instead of humanists.

If there's something you can do or say to help others then do or say it. Educate yourself and embrace green tech. And most importantly, pray to a God that actually exists & matters: Mother Earth. Lord forbid people worship something that's tangible. If people worshipped the planet half as much as some fictional God then there would be less pollution, less ecological destruction, and more environmental activism.

I understand that asking people to care about the planet is a tall order...because most people don't even care about their own bodies. Two things that qualify as biological "miracles" are the planet Earth and the human body, yet people have no problem destroying both. Just look at all the bad shit people eat, and the growing number of fat-asses in America. How can a person care about the planet when they don't even care about their life?

Two healthy people devoted to green causes are undermined by eight other people eating the world to death. And there you have America in a taco shell. Everything needs to change because it *has* to.

12.
Health Care Reform

A recent trend: the harder I work, the fatter I get. Food is being (mis)used as a stress reliever.
The result: bowel movements are longer, the sex is shorter, and my chins are many. Mediocrity is in the mirror.

Time to start working out again and find another stress reliever. Now I know how a crackhead feels. Just one more hit...but, for me, it's just three more chorizo burritos.

I'm giving up chorizo. It's not you, chorizo, it's me.

Eating a pound of succulent salivary glands processed from pork products is delicious but not healthy. It fills me up, then several hours later, empties me out. I'm getting off this culinary roller coaster once and for all. Go bother someone else's intestines you wicked meat you. (at least I think it's meat...still not sure)

That Barack is a villain!! Trying to give the American People affordable healthcare when the world is overpopulated as it is. Let the bastards die off already if they can't pay for a physical. Sink or Swim. Natural Selection. Survival of the Fittest.

I want freedom! I demand it. People should have to pay top dollar for a doctor. I hate sick people. Only the weak go to the ER.

My venomous criticism serves the sick right. Don't get a disease if you can't afford it.

And I will bemoan Obamacare 'til the day I die! Illness is a political issue so long as it doesn't happen to me.

How dare Obama try to make my life better!
Only I can do that! Even though I never have...

One of the most divisive topics constantly making waves upon the political wasteland is health care reform. "Universal" Health Care is a no-brainer, but I take being smart for granted, and those who argue against it usually have no cerebellum. Republicans are quick to proclaim that America is the greatest country in the world yet loathe to making it that way. They will shutdown the government just to prove how horrible they really are. Republicans are despicable human beings. I can't find any other way to put it. And anyone who supports them is Ignorant or/and despicable. But is Ignorance an excuse for being despicable? That is a Southern existential question for sure.

Universal Health Care should be provided for every American 17 years old & under, and 70 years old & up. In order to qualify for health care between the ages of 18-69 you must undergo an annual physical examination and fall within a federally mandated weight limit. And you must be a non-smoker of cigarettes. Weed smoking is not only excluded but encouraged.

Walk outside your house, or look around your place of work, and I bet that 50% of the people you see are fat. 60% if you live in Las Vegas: the fat fuck Mecca of the world. Three-toed sloths trampling over each at the buffet carving station a common scene. This diluted yet helium-inflated gene pool has started a new strain of Mankind: Flourish of the Fattest.

Do you want your taxes subsidizing health insurance for these gluttonous buffaloes whose main aim in life is to graze on fast food grease and cheese? Most preventable diseases like diabetes, heart problems, strokes, and a host of others are a result of being obese. These fat nitwits (I am sporadically fat so I'm allowed to call them nitwits) are a drain on American health care. Obesity is expensive and accounts for 17% of the nation's medical costs. According to a Cornell/Lehigh study, blubber-related illnesses cost the country roughly 168 Billion Dollars...and rising.

The best solution to this problem is to *make Americans responsible for their actions!*

If you don't want to die and want to receive health care then try eating like a normal human being. And try another thing: Exercise. But if you insist on eating like a two-ton rhino, fine, go for it, but guess what? You're gonna die. Don't cry when the bill comes due. Oh yeah, and you're gonna pay for two seats when you fly. No more sharing elbow space with a Klump.

If a person is too fat and doesn't meat (pun intended) a reasonable weight limit in proportion to height then their health care costs skyrocket. This sort of sensible solution would prevent young & healthy people's premium to rise. And lower health care costs would be a result as preventable diseases would plummet.

Now if a person has a medical problem like cancer or epilepsy through no fault of his or her own, or was born with a medical condition, then that person should be covered through UHC. There is no more heinous term than pre-existing condition. The greedy insurance companies would love to scan your DNA at birth and label any medical problem a pre-existing condition.

Everyone has a pre-existing condition: Mortality. And everyone should be afforded a modicum of decency and respect when dealing with it. Unless you're fat. Then go take a jog. If you want gastric bypass then go sell meth with Walter White. If you desire plastic surgery then go fight the Taliban. I hear mortar shells are effective in shaving off large swaths of skin...wanted or unwanted.

With the current threats of overpopulation and obesity "weighing" down our planet, mankind is evolving into a pudgy species of sedentary dinosaurs -- born for extinction. And it's not gonna take a comet to knock us all off, but merely a knife and fork.

True wealth is health. Having both legs to run, walk, and hike. Both arms and hands to be self-sufficient & play sports. Eyes to enjoy the beauty of the world and sexual acts. Ears to appreciate good music. Money is great, but no amount can compensate for the loss of health. And health shouldn't be dictated by money. Very briefly in our history there was a thriving middle-class born from unionized manufacturing jobs until those jobs were outsourced for profits. Pensions dissolved. Unions ridiculed & weakened. Historically, there has been an ebb & flow battle for workers' rights. In effect, a battle for Americans' right to work for a decent wage has been waged by the corporate tops and the people for 2 centuries. Health care is just another battle that the Republicans want to extinguish because a sick worker should be fired, not cared for.

House Rep's shut down the government in October 2013 because they disagreed with Obamacare and supported BonerHate. dr Joe Heck sent mass emails to his constituents that tried to explain his harebrained stance on the issue. He stated he is merely listening to the will of the American People by trying to delay the healthcare law. Call me crazy, but didn't the American People vote for Obama twice?

Heck acts like a scoundrel who raises a racist kid that popped out the womb wearing a KKK hood, but Universal Health Care would have taken that hood off and put a lollipop in the youngster's mouth instead of Heck's hateful penis.

Earn your way should be the American Way. But to Heck, Hate is a proper value to hand down to offspring, along with inherited wealth. That way they can have something without ever working for it: money & prejudice.

Give the Republicans credit for finding a new way to fix problems. A household chore had been troubling me for days. An MIT degree is required to operate my irrigation drip system. In order to properly program it you need to be an idiot savant skilled in the mystic arts of the Rubik's Cube. No owner's manual, no problem. I just unplugged it. I fixed it "tha Republican Way".

All Hope Is Not Lost

After lambasting fat people in this chapter it is only fair to share the secret to weight loss: Exercise & Eat Healthy. Sounds easy, rational, and sound...and it is. It doesn't take a PhD to lose weight. It's not astrophysics. All it takes is discipline...and a desire to live...not to mention an ounce or two of self-esteem.

My weight fluctuates -- I could be a disgusting 230lbs one month, and a healthy 190 a few months later. But I'm under 40 years old. Anyone above the middle-age line needs to be smart. No gastric bypass surgery is required. Lap bands are for suckers...just like Dr. Phil books. You're better off resorting to bulimia...a naturally occurring reaction every time I see his bald-headed ass on the tube.

B. Bonin Bough, the virtual reality adman of perverse corporate nightmares, dreams of a world made better through collaboration and technology...so long as you drink Pepsi Cola. I dream of a better world where healthy people drink Pepsi on special occasions and not on a daily basis. The only thing worse for your health is the constant bombardment of advertisements.

Avoid the media as much as possible. I was glancing through a *Reader's Digest* while organically indisposed and saw a ranch dressing ad where a man was pouring it on a "cone" of broccoli for some happy young girl. Here ya go, take MSG! This sort of ad makes me scrape my head against a brick wall then pick up the scalp peelings and deep-fry them. Sell them at the State Fair for a fare share of the proceeds. Ohio fried scalp is tasty. Anything is if you add trans fat and a heart attack. There are tons of statistics, but you didn't read my book for that shit. You bought my book to survive...so stop eating fried chicken...or at least only eat it once a year!

Eat Pussy, Beat Cancer

I munch on pussy and I look like I found the fountain of youth.

All I do to get healthy is eat satisfying meals and work out each day...so long as there is a sensible amount of pussy to eat. Cancer is a man-made disease...rare in Egyptian mummies. They always snacked on snatch. Building pyramids sure did build up an appetite.

If I can lose weight, anyone can...being that I'm an avid lover of pizza, wings, pussy, ice cream, and a prodigious imbiber of various spirits. HL Mencken once stated, "Most of the trouble from so-called overeating comes from under-drinking. Remember that, my boy, and you'll live to be at least forty."

Sometimes my kidneys & liver feel like the corns on Kirstie Alley's feet, but so long as I keep my weight in check then maybe I can reach 70. The quality of life is just as important as the length. So enjoy your beer, but please avoid fast food!

Just the other day I ate a wild boar burger at Fuddruckers and caught a bad case of the mud butt. The only thing worse than Fuddfuckers food is their Clive Barker nightmare bathroom. It looks like John Deere schedules tractor pulls in the stalls. The overall ambience is that of a New Orleans mausoleum during flood season.

Several sewer rats sat in the corner & sneered at me while bobbing their depraved heads to the Michael Jackson song "Wanna Be Startin' Something" that was piped in through a series of tobacco stained speakers.

Avoid Fuddruckers like the plague...unless you want to catch one...

I would describe the overall scene as Dada-Botulism or Ebola-Beyonce. To make matters worse it was "Kids Eat Free" night. The unbridled brats were running & screaming around like hillbilly banshees while the parents compared breast-feeding techniques and small-talked about their painfully mundane lives.

I'd rather shoot Roman Candles into my eye sockets or contract genital leprosy than end up like these domesticated wretches. I have enough existential angst, and adding mediocrity to it would just be too much. It seems a vast amount of people live to breed...I'd rather live to breathe and be free.

13.
Cure World Hunger

As engorged Americans search for ways to lose weight without cutting calories, millions of people scattered around the world go hungry everyday. Sometimes solutions to problems are so simple and obvious that most people look right past them. The cure for world hunger is one such solution. The answer is obvious: Eat dogs.

If all the dogs in the world were rounded up, cooked, and distributed to poor people then starvation would cease to exist. Not only would a worldwide problem be fixed, but also the quality of life in America would dramatically increase. No more mangy mutts at the local parks shitting and pissing everywhere on the walkways. Neighborhoods across America would be serene without the shrill or gruff barking of worthless animals. No more children getting mauled by pitbulls, dobermans, and rottweilers.

This program would boost employment rates as dog catchers are needed in addition to dog chefs. The possibilities are endless when it comes to cooking dog meat. First you baseball-bat the brute to the ground, shave and scalp the beast. Then carve 'em up like a Thanksgiving turkey. For the Asian demographic you can cut the dog into bite-size morsels and cook it up in a wok with a spicy Szechuan sauce. Poodles are best served on skewers with Thai peanut sauce. Pairs well with a Malbec. Another popular dish is the dog steak. Throw a flank of Lab on the grill, sprinkle on some garlic pepper, and watch how quick African countries become peaceful when they learn the simple joys of grilling. Dog recipes would flourish around the world. Hush puppies would take on a whole new meaning. Fido & eggs would become a staple of any complete breakfast. I have a hankering for beagle McNuggets. Bring on the sweet & sour.

You're probably wondering: what do we do all with all the leftover dog scalps? Again, another simple solution: Knit them together to make doggy bags. This endeavor could help subsidize the world hunger cure, as there is a flourishing market for fashionable handbags. Dior and Gucci would accessorize these bags with different furs, designs, and canine teeth.

This plan is perfect, but I know there will be critics. Blind people will be pissed. But just replace their seeing-eye dogs with guinea pigs. How will they know the difference? The bottom-line is that my cure will make the world a better and quieter place. No more starvation, and no more dog shit. What more could you ask for?

14.

Money Bloody Money

There's a foul stench in the air. Like someone left a bag of Wendys burgers in the backseat of a station wagon roasting all day in the desert heat.

I fart when I get nervous.

I have good reason to be, writing a book of such inflammatory material that no one will read, and the two crazed people who do will undoubtedly stalk & scalp me. And to make matters worse I ate fried chicken slathered with Sriracha sauce for dinner. Too hot outside to open the windows so the smell circulates through my house until it lingers to the point where I would barely notice it if not for my smoking nose hairs. My wife hides in the bedroom, but she can still hear the flaps of my ass reverberate as I release gas on consistent five-minute intervals. Sorta like a cash register that rings in a new American soul every second. Welcome to Hell, how may I direct your call?

"...I still feel rage at the cowardice of our time which has ground down all of us into the mediocre compromises of what had been once our light-filled passion to stand erect and be original."
-Norman Mailer

Mailer's frustration at cowardice still resonates today. That Cowardice has come full circle accompanied by an accomplice named Complacency. Spurred on by pop culture and consumer addiction, these two C words have combined and formed a bully called Capitalism: the new drug that threatens to destroy everything, yet there's a war on drugs, and It is never mentioned.

   Capitalism is like crack cocaine. Easy to get hooked. Hard to shake. A fiendish pursuit of luxury that Americans let dictate their lives. At its core, Capitalism is based on exploitation. Exploit the workers. Exploit the land. And this philistinal philosophy does not lead to stability. America in a nutshell. A capitalistic country that outsources its soul so long as there is a bidder.

There has to be a low working class to control. Capitalism cannot survive without it. Once Americans started to flourish and became a thriving middle class, the Corporate Powers decided to ship those jobs overseas in order to exploit lower wage workers and increase profits. Because that's all that matters: Money. It's better to increase profits than to increase humanity and better society. Corporate CEOs can't have middle class workers. How will the Fat Cats possibly afford three homes instead of two by paying decent living wages? And it *is* sort of absurd to think that people like Warren Buffett have billions of dollars and for what? To make more money. Pikers applaud his every move. The Buffett buffet is a living pledge of allegiance to only one thing: Profits.

Greed is a disease of the spirit, where the afflicted person only cares about how much money and property they can acquire, instead of how much they can help their fellow man. The 21st century version of the Hell's Angels is the Ivy League frat boys raping the country: Bush League spanky brothers walking Tall wielding Phantasm balls with drill bits & oil pipelines. Nothing is sacred except the delusion distilled to the people for purposes of hiding the fact that Everything is bought & sold everyday.

Democracy is now fueled by dollars instead of people. Republicans used to run for office under the auspice of pragmatism, now they are merely greedy opportunists and Confederate anchors. Democrats were the utopians: wishful thinkers trying to make a perfect world, but now they've become the pragmatists. And there's a serious problem when the Dems shift to the right because it leaves a void in Forward Thinking. Politics becomes a constant game of dodging dog crap instead of inventing non-stick dog shit retardant shoes. Policies are Band-Aids and business is Innovation for profits only. And the love of money over everything else is not just exclusive to Capitalism, for its wayward twin Communism uses ideology to cover up the financial exploitation of its people. China regularly sweeps mining deaths under the red rug, which sometimes total up to 5000 deaths per year. Greed knows no boundaries or political system...so long as small groups of people are in charge of powerful countries there will be corruption. Income inequality is common in both China & America...but America is supposed to be the beacon of democracy that shines throughout the world. Yet the only light it casts is shaded green with no morality, a beautiful sight to the Great Gatsby.

There's a difference between being fiscally conservative and intellectually conservative. Fiscally conservative is balancing your checkbook and living on a budget. Intellectually conservative is praying to lil' baby jesus and hating gays. If humanity stayed intellectually conservative then we would still believe the Earth is flat and the sun revolves around it every other week. And everyone knows the sun revolves around the corporations.

While the corps and their political pawns control the majority of wealth, the American People are mostly to blame for the Capitalistic disease because they possess the power and do nothing with it. Consumer spending is now the aim of life for the average American. Buy, buy, buy, and be happy. Don't worry 'bout nutt'ing else.

The only way to spend and purchase and consume is to have a job. Whether the job makes a person happy or serves a beneficial purpose to humankind is irrelevant. The only thing that matters is the pay. And what is a person worth? A silly question that no one thinks to ask. Questions cause people to think and are to be avoided. But...

What do you strive for? Is it fame? Wealth? Family?

The only goal that keeps me semi-sane is to fulfill my potential. Sounds like a cliché, but potential is that elusive shining symbol in the distance most people only dream about. It's not a lighthouse or the ark from *Indiana Jones*, but it's the thing you were born to do. Even more important is the ability to lay my head down at night and sleep without regret or guilt. If I can maintain that throughout my life then I consider myself to be a success...regardless of money. Once you free yourself from expectations and materialistic wants then you're able to live a free life. Full of discoveries. And I've discovered there are three keys to a fulfilling career choice:

1 - To better humankind/society.
2 - To earn a decent living.
3 - To be happy.

A great job is a combination of two attributes, and pure bliss is all three. Take BB King for example. He'll never retire because he genuinely loves to perform, and probably will do so until he dies. And there lies the secret to life: to find a worthy occupation you can do until you die. No retiring and playing bingo. No frittering away your last days on a golf course wearing silly looking pants. Your life's work should be just that: a job you do the rest of your life. To do a job well and to maintain a level of skill & professionalism is something to aspire to. And you don't have to be a guitar prodigy to accomplish this. It can be something simple as caring for animals. Or assisting people. Or tending to something beautiful and not materialistic.

This idea is not advocating working the middle-class to death like some people call for. It is a utopian ideal. I fully understand that blue-collar people (like my Mother) who work tough jobs Deserve a decent retirement. My Mom has worked over 35 years for the United States Postal Service lugging a fifty-pound bag for half of those years, which has contributed to her having two hip replacements. She deserves to retire. Now, not at age 70 like the dingbat Alicia Munnel of Boston College calls for. Maybe 70 years is acceptable for a talking head with manicured nails that sits on her ass all day long doing nothing...but not for real working Americans who keep this nation running. They deserve to retire at 60. MSNBC propagandizes the belief that older Americans are working longer because they can, and that there are big financial incentives. Bullshit. Older Americans work longer because they're broke and they have to. Eugene Steuerle of the *SF Chronicle* thinks Americans should work 'til 75. And if they die before that age, then put a call center phone in their casket...Nevada Water Authority does that now -- outsource their customer service to the deceased. It's cheap effective labor. And it's what we *deserve*.

Peter Baldwin of the *New York Times* thinks that working until we die is "a very small price to pay for the extra decades of healthy life granted to us by modern society." Sure, if you "toil" on your gluteus Maximus for a newspaper. And according to the loathsome political staffer John Feehery, society can't afford older people not working. His ancestors undoubtedly operated factories that employed children. Now that that practice is illegal it's time to run the old bones into dust.

These people who spout corrupt ideas are few...though they are given media exposure because those ideas benefit the Establishment...a system that should crumble. Capitalism is a living breathing tomb hovering over the horizon that sucks us all in unless we stand together. Now is not the time to be dormant. Not everyone is going to be a successful *Shark Tank* entrepreneur, so there should be decent manufacturing jobs for blue-collar people. Respectable jobs where the employees share in the profits, instead of the CEO raking in millions. Co-ops are the template to move America forward. Green Tech innovation is the industry.

Most people are good...they just don't know how to express it, but they want to. They just need leadership to the Promised Land. Not to death, war, Wall Street, and dishonor. Humankind is shuffling along the pipeline of Capitalism, but something's missing and the people can sense it. A feeling that gnaws at the soul. We are meant for more than buying. And selling.

"Man truly achieves his full human condition when he produces without being compelled by the physical necessity of selling himself as a commodity."
-Che Guevara

So many people are selling nowadays. Everywhere and everything. Selling yourself becomes more important than what you're selling. And at the end of the day you're left with nothing but a green piece of paper you can put into someone's pocket for a pretty piece of Purpose. A warped reason for contemporary existence is consumption. Dangle the carrot and watch the hamsters run in place, and trample each other, and when they can't catch up to it, they cannibalize one another because there is nothing left to do. Like a young man on the Strip once said, "A muthafucka gotta eat." Even if it means robbing someone who looks like a relative.

"Cash rules everything around me. Cream, get the money. Dollar, dollar bill, ya'll."

Wu-Tang created the anthem. Go for self and exploit your brother, or we can all starve together. A helluva decision for a person to make. Especially being surrounded by Capitalistic fervor. Imagine being at a Baptist church and you're the only person sitting down while everyone else praises Jesus. Now be that young man in the hood while everyone else chants C.R.E.A.M.

In 1979 Jimmy Carter delivered a prescient speech known as the Crisis of Confidence. He bemoaned the fact that our human identity was not derived from "what we do, but by what we own." He warned that this sort of thinking would result in constant conflict ending in chaos. We must face the truth that the late 70's were a turning point and we went down the wrong road. Chris Hedges would say we currently exist in "the throes of a giddy intoxication with illusion." This is what the Establishment wants: Profits and an easily manipulated populace of zombies playing *Angry Birds* on smart phones. You're not a sports fan unless you have the Dish. You're not a respectable American unless you have a shiny F-150. And so, instead of living a fulfilling life, you waste it in a passive state of purchasing things you don't really need. The hacks of DC thank you for your cooperation. The Congress whores get a bonus for every braindead constituent that votes for them. Democracy is expensive, and only the rats can afford to play these days.

"...the whole country was doomed unless somebody, somewhere, could mount a new kind of power to challenge the rotten, high-powered machinery of men like Daley & Johnson."
-HST

That high-powered machinery that the Doctor loathed is still humming, but the good news is that I'm someone who can mount a challenge. And so are you. Social Capital is the key. And we all have it, and we now have the means to use it. Social networks can elect politicians, and those networks can replace lobbyists. A political candidate is vetted by the Internet, and that candidate's verified deeds become more important than how much money they raised. People decide candidates instead of corporations and special interests.

I have a dream, and the dream is the website I will create...but the reality is that our mindstates have to change also. Stop chasing the carrot. Be content without being rich. Work less. Consume less. And be *more* happy. Happier. We all can live just fine without excessive wealth...besides, that sort of wealth is usually earned by nefarious means.

"I've not only pursued the American dream, I've achieved it."
-Kenneth Lay on the witness stand

A sociopath's dream is our country's nightmare. How can the American Dream be something only one person can aspire to? The entire country should realize it. Tony Montana loved the American Dream with a vengeance. Our country isn't the criminal Serengeti where a few lions devour the other animals in a coke-fueled rage. The reality of a man pulling himself up by the bootstraps is fine, but not at the expense of everyone around him. Destroying people's pensions and 401k plans for sleazy profits has become our new Horatio Alger story.

A WSJ headline: Lay Uses Optimism as Defense

Well, I'll use Pessimism as Offense

The rich sit on their rumps and reap tax windfalls in the form of capital gains and dividends. Money makes money without doing anything. Yet some CEOs still can't stop being crooked. Tyco, WorldCom, HealthSouth, Qwest, Enron, and other corporate CEOs were indicted on a variety of charges. Everyday there is corruption by business leaders, but the only thing you see on the nightly news is blacks and his-panics. Robbing a bank for a grand gets the publicity while larceny by a bank manager for a million isn't a story.

Jeffrey Skilling gets his prison sentence cut from 24 years to 14 and it only cost $40 million. One of the seediest human beings on the planet who thinks fraud is funny; Skilling is the poster cunt of corruption. The Enron ethics manual is to eat the canary, laugh about it, hire crooked lawyers, burp, and floss your teeth with the feathers.

The economy and GDP increases, yet wages stagnate. Economists call wages compensation costs...meaning bust your ass for a wage and get compensated with pennies. Get a second job selling weed and go to jail, but Mark Belnick steals $150 million from Tyco and gets a five-year ban from serving as a corporate officer. Damn, that settlement stings...sign me up. And Belnick went back to practicing law...proving that practicing something the wrong way will never make you great, but rich.

Bribery is an inherent talent of the jet set regardless of political affiliation. Richard Scrushy gets caught with his talons in the cookie jar and screams racism...though he's whiter than porcelain. Scrunch up your face when indicted for fraud and holler scapegoat. Works for Dems and Republicans.

CEO pay is shaking salt on the country's open wound. Company stock can decrease while the "Chief" executive pay increases. Astronomically. Verizon wished the shareholders couldn't hear them now when they wanted to raise Seidenberg's compensation 50 percent back in 2005.

Even worse was the recent bailout of banks, investment firms, and other unsavory institutions, yet many execs received mad bonuses. Brokers gulp down 300k and bankers inhabit penthouses...compensation for jobs far from well done.

Citibank has a long history of being a cunt. Investigated in 1933 for a role in the stock market crash, Citi later introduces a MasterCard -- making its users slaves, then pays billions in settlements regarding Enron and WorldCom, still hungry, it Swept customer accounts for millions over a decade, and does Bizzy with Saudis. This worthless company historically accumulates massive debts and constantly gets bailed out by us! Subprime loans were another specialty. A Free-market society allows institutions to fail and let others take their place, but not ours, because we are not free...we are chained to the dead-weight anvil anchor of Capitalism that is sinking slowly, and will continue to do so until we find a way to sever the chain and right our ship.

A stock option is legal larceny. Throw ten pounds of feed in a trough and tell the pig he'll get it for the price of a pound when he wants to in the future. Maybe even cheaper if their accountant backdates it. So the pig snorts and signs up. Gets 10 lbs of swine cereal for the price of a couple ounces. Yet the government has a war on drugs and overlooks the real weight. Financial terrorism is a domestic specialty and the official word is the crisis is not to be disturbed. Give the press a case here and there. And so for every one publicized case, another two dozen pass by, with the regulators waving the graft through the system like blind traffic cops.

I can hear the noise now, "If you're against Capitalism, then you're a Communist!" Bullshit. I don't like Communism either. But I really loathe Capitalism because I love America and I see the damage the financial disease is doing to my beloved country. And guess what? Most corporations don't give a flying fuck about America. Caterpillar makes a killing in the global market when the dollar is weak because expensive currencies abroad means more bucks in our country. The *Wall Street Journal* agrees. The lower our dollar goes, the better news for corporate earnings. And so I ask, Why the fuck do we care what the Dow Jones average is? Back when our dollar slumped in late April of 2007 the Dow was up to 13120. Call me crazy, but don't call me capitalistic, because I care about my country over corporations and some bullshit DJIA. There is no loyalty or patriotism on Wall Street. Everything is about profit and the dollar going to the toilet is a good thing for them...one way or another. And if it's not, then they'll contrive a way to make a profit instead of trying to fix the problem. These scumbags are opportunists on steroids, and it's time to stop letting them hold the country hostage with their elaborate financial schemes.

According to *Forbes*, the Waltons who own Walmart are some of the richest people in America. They are worth about $136 billion, but are unwilling to pay their employees decent wages. And they get away with it because they are plugged into the political system. We the people also support the seedy Waltons. The cattle of grazing American'ts stampede through their doors everyday to buy cheap goods, and are a perfect example of what is wrong with our country. If you want to experience the ugly underbelly of the American condition, spend an hour in a Walmart. It's hard to do without wanting to cuntpunt a cow wearing spandex, or pile drive a wayward ratfink fuck of a kid who displays the obvious grace of truckstop hooker progeny.

Our public consciousness is starting to erode and corrode like a rusty bumper on an old Chevy truck stalled stone-dead in Janesville, USA. Why would the fat cats care about us when we don't even care about us? The heartland is an afterthought. Flyover country. Empty the septic tank and recline with a Tanqueray martini. Spit the olive seed down the drain. Maybe it will drop in a dry farmer's field and sprout something that Monsanto won't sue over.

Opportunity is outsourced to India. IBM, GE, Infosys, PriceWaterhouse Cooper, and other corporations built skyscrapers in Calcutta to handle various business matters...and to take advantage of Cheap Labor. Bharat Desai has made a 2.2 billion dollar fortune outsourcing jobs and is lauded by *Forbes* for it. Microsoft expands to China and spends millions of dollars to help the Chinese government. Intel builds a chip plant in China and will employ 1000 workers. And why should We show loyalty to these cunt companies? Is Capitalism now ingrained into our own DNA so much that we start to hate anyone who loves Democracy? I won't apologize for my love of America, and my book is in response to our country being shit on by Corporations while their commercials proclaim it organic fertilizer to grow the country.

We are on track to a corporate aristocracy that is similar to the China Princelings. Unfettered Capitalism is Communism, where the privileged few control everything and designate resources: Power consolidated at the top while the rest of the population scrambles at the bottom of the ladder...fighting each other until one is lucky enough to climb it...and that lucky one usually has bribery money. Why not just kick the ladder and walk away to a better system? Corporations do business here and in China. Let's kick them out and force them to move HQ to Shanghai.

And once the locusts are gone, it will be time to start something new. It's do or die. Bare your teeth and bite. Because the middle class are targets. Record corporate profits are not possible with a strong middle class. Blue collar is beneath a few dollars. We are now buying our own nooses.

"We survive on adversity and perish in ease and comfort."
-Livy (a Roman historian)

I'm the problem with America. Passive People like myself would rather watch March Madness and drink Pabst Blue Ribbon beer instead of getting out of the house to see what's really happening around the corner. We'd rather root for sports teams than assist normal people who could really use our help. Those normal people look like me. Those normal people struggle like me. Maybe the mirror is just too painful.

Unions are the last bastions of economic hope for the middle class. The last trench. A Maginot Line being surpassed by Conservatism and their corporate Tops. (What's a Top you might ask? Go to prison and run out of Newports and you'll find out.) Wisconsin and Ohio were political scenes where the middle-class was attacked. Class warfare waged against Unions and Education by the Koch-backed Republicans. Granted, there should be some changes to Unions -- it's a privilege not an abusable right to belong to a Union. There should be standards for employees, but overall, Unions level the playing field and are a necessary protection against exploitation.

The Struggle

A Peacock puffing of tail feathers was being waged on a warm spring afternoon at Red Rock Casino. It was exciting. I felt invigorated. And realized action is the American Way. So I went home to drink, eat, and sedate myself with the false & mundane comforts of the Middle Class.

This unexpected gathering of Commoners was the ideal lightening rod to call attention to the foul economic cloud that hovers over our beautiful Las Vegas blue skies. And I chose not to participate because I had plans. There was a game to watch. Athletes to root for. And a cause to ignore. I might or might not agree with the cause, but I should at least aspire to learn about it. And participate one way or the other. Station Casinos are anti-union. The Culinary Union believes in better wages and benefits. Pros and cons get muddled by greedy ideology...however, the bottom line is that the Union was out there on that beautiful day standing up for their cause...while I admired their plight on the car ride home to get wasted, watch sports, and play video games.

I'm no better than anyone else, and that's disappointing. Because I know I can do more. And so can everyone else.

Back in Feb 2011 the Culinary Union protested outside Palace Station...not for OJ's release from prison, but for the right to unionize. 22 people were arrested and a photo of the event stuck with me: The secretary-treasurer for Culinary Local 226 being led away, handcuffed by two Metro Cops who looked like confused, saddened pawns. Police are supposed to protect the people, not corporate interests. The police officers of our nation should all unite and refuse to arrest any peaceful protesters. Failing to clear a street is not an arrestable offense because it is our street. This country is ours! Not the corps or the incs. If the police join the evolution then crime would certainly go down. Crime decreases as exploitation decreases. The more self-esteem a person has, the less likely they are to commit a crime.

Decades ago people busted their asses and got their skulls busted to get unions formed. Real courage is not only standing up for what is right, but also standing up for what is right even though you know you're going to get beaten. And the Big Money-controlled government employed an effective ruse: get the police to beat the same people they're supposed to protect. Sound familiar? Still happens today. Woody Guthrie wrote anthems for the struggle. The anti-Jay-Z. Build your peers up and form a strong community. A Wobbly state of mind. And the key is education.

College Education is the big equalizer of social classes. Knowing that, the Establishment has hiked the rates of college education so high that the middle class can't afford it, and if they have the temerity to attend then they acquire extensive student loans. Loan-sharking 201: Consolidate power and exploit your community by turning the ambitious into indentured servants to be bled for decades. And this will keep them feisty upstarts anchored in the same social class. Upward mobility is a hindered movement reserved for a chosen few. But make sure to advertise the university with the standard white girl, indian boy, black girl, and asian guy. Mix it up to keep it interesting -- propagate the illusion of diversity.

To gain a better insight, here is George W Bush's freshmen essay on college education:

It's something I do cuz daddy told me to. I like it. Keg stands. Jello shots on the tummys of girls. I like the ones shaped like turtles. That way I can bang on their shells with a ballpeen hammer while I bam away on their rear. They love it. And so do me. Most times I wake up in pissy sheets and suck my thumb. I yell for mammy and my conscience ignores me so I snort a rail to wake up.

Cockadoodle don't -- I skip class so I can help the Mexicans trim the frat's hedges. I shape the bush under the front porch as a pair of hooters. We all got a kick out of that.[snort] So much so I slept underneath them with an empty tequila bottle. Found the worm wiggling on my chin in the morning. Or was it Cheney's pecker? I don't like that interloper from Wyoming. He eyes me with lust and chuckles when I run away. He can't follow...bad heart or something. Heard a rumor he doesn't even have one, so they implanted a hog's heart in his chest and have to charge it every 12 hours with a couple clamps and a car battery. So I keep my Chrysler's hood locked. Screw him.

Anywho, Grandad visited and keeps telling me one day I'll give the family a bad name. Says he should of let the crows peck my eyes out when I was born...regrets shooing them away. Dad just chuckles and says Aw Shucks. Well, I'll show both of 'em. I'll do something great one day. You'll see. Aww Hell, Gotta run, my buddy Osama is here and he has a beer bong. Those A-rabs are craysay!

Yale is a meal ticket to be bought, not a real education.

"Sitting on the park bench, eyeing lil' girls with bad intents."

Aqualung is not us. We watch these politicians fuck us over and over and over again. Aqualung is the perverted system peering back at us. The arduous ordeal of coveting head creates headaches.

Bill Clinton got some brains and didn't even proclaim blowjobs the ultimate American pleasure. Catherine Hill of Vassar College started a new transsexual program where she had a goat's penis implanted on her sternum so new freshmen can suck it when they enroll. And that's the last freebie they'll ever see. And so Vassar breeds blind troglodytes who abhor society...their only aim is to keep suckling the collegiate nipple of conformity. The first semester is a class sequestered inside a cave to blind the bastards. Second semester they dye the students' pupils red. Pretty soon they're all begging for cheese.

And so it goes...

Ali Velshi, an immigrated merc assimilated to the mastah's bowsack, writes in *Money* magazine that students should enroll in college to become Petro engineers, Big Pharma stepinfetchitcunts, and pursue other worthless financially worthwhile endeavors. Smile. Congrats. You're an American't. For Velshi, this is the land of the haves and have nots, and there is *always* opportunity for the haves.

While you go to college to study Cuntery 303, you can stay at Campus Apartments -- owned by Singapore. So learn how to fuck the country you were born in and financially benefit a foreign government. Call me naive, but that is seditious behavior promoted by our own government, which is a government for the people, by the people. The only question is which people? The small percentage of people with money willing to foreclose their country for a few bucks?

We're all tenants on the sphere of unpredictability. Some communities are nobler than others. Like it or not, we are related. America is an idea of freedom whose carpet is being sold out from underneath our feet while we dicker and dally over formalities. The transnational corporations have no qualms about making us a country of indentured serfs. Who owns the property? The houses? The businesses?

We need to devise a new Boxer Rebellion. Nobody should own property or businesses here unless they're an American citizen. No more ownership by proxy. The country is being sold on tiptoes, and Congress allows it.

And so do we.

I went to the 4th of July of fireworks show outside Red Rock Casino and the lady next to me asked her family how old America was. I gave a disgusted glance at the clan and realized they are the clichéd troupe that constantly dilutes our gene pool. Maybe our government should give out life jackets in the shallow end.

Maybe dumb fucks shouldn't have so many kids also. Wanton reproduction feeds into the Establishment's eugenics. We can adapt, educate, and overthrow the system. Or we can keep reproducing and overthrow the system by mere numbers and stupidity. By then it will be too late and Mad Max will be driving dune buggies.

Dystopian predictions are created by cynical people who give up after the first yank of a lawn mower. Screw that. We are strong. We can do it. It just takes Will and Courage. (those are my muscular gay neighbors with the mortars and RPG's...but if they're not down, screw it, we'll do it the old fashioned way of protest)

This is my fuckin' country and I'm not leaving. The rich fascist Establishment pricks can follow their money to the Caymans, but I was born here and I'm gonna die here. I'm Helen Keller reincarnated; only I can see & hear, and I'm more abrasive.

"The few own the many because they possess the means of livelihood of all. The country is governed for the richest, for the corporations, the bankers, the land speculators, and for the exploiters of labor. The majority of mankind is working people. So long as their fair demands -- the ownership and control of their livelihoods -- are set at naught, we can have neither men's rights nor women's rights. The majority of mankind is ground down by industrial oppression in order that the small remnant may live in ease."

-not written today, but...
1911
by Helen Keller, an IWW member

Pie in the Sky

Long-haired preachers come out every night
Try to tell you what's wrong and what's right
But when asked how 'bout something to eat
They will answer in voices so sweet

You will eat, bye and bye
In that glorious land above the sky
Work and pray, live on hay
You'll get pie in the sky when you die

And the Starvation Army, they play
And they sing and they clap and they pray
Till they get all your coin on the drum
Then they tell you when you're on the bum

Holy Rollers and Jumpers come out
And they holler, they jump and they shout
Give your money to Jesus, they say
He will cure all diseases today

If you fight hard for children and wife
Try to get something good in this life

You're a sinner and bad man, they tell
When you die you will sure go to hell.

Workingmen of all countries, unite
Side by side we for freedom will fight
When the world and its wealth we have gained
To the grafters we'll sing this refrain:

You will eat, bye and bye
When you've learned how to cook and how to fry
Chop some wood, 'twill do you good
Then you'll eat in the sweet bye and bye.

"Pie in the Sky" is an American song that helps offset the group psychosis promoted by the soul-snuffing magazines like *Money*, *SmartMoney*, and *Kiplinger's*. Fictitious Pie in the Sky is what these mags like to sell to saps. The May 2007 cover of *Money* had the **bold** headline: HOW TO WIN IN REAL ESTATE NOW. They ran this imbecilic story during one of the worst housing crisis in history with no sense of irony or conscience. The schmucks who followed that advice now own Frigidaire cardboard homes and shopping carts to transport their valuables to recycling centers.

Later, in October of 2007 *Money* proclaimed: WE ARE SO MUCH BETTER OFF. And backed this proclamation with faulty stats by comparing median family net worth from 1983 to 2004, which has doubled. Sure the median may have increased, but that rise rises with the rich, not with normal people. Misleading propaganda is *Money's* specialty. They did mention that life is riskier, and key costs are steeper...none more so than being a *Money* subscriber. Yet a person can be c-squared following *Money's* investing advice. In order to qualify as a Capitalistic Cunt, one must invest in Exxon Mobil, Wal-Mart, and IBM. These are the THE PICKS according to *Money*.

Not to be out-cunted, *SmartMoney* touted the Return of **Fossil Fuels**. Just what the Global Warming doctor ordered. *SmartMoney* is a magazine for dumb people.

Kiplinger's agrees...they proclaim these blue chips to hold forever: Philip Morris, Nestle, McDonalds, Monsanto, Exxon Mobil, Teva Pharmaceutical Industries, and IBM. Lung cancer, water exploitation, obesity & diabetes, GMO, oil spills, and pills are the best ways to make money. Who is *Kiplinger's* financial adviser? Satan?

On the cover of that issue, April 2009, was the All-American couple: White, conservative dress & hair, with the shallow woman making it a point to show off her Rolex and wedding bling...and ingrained crows-feet ten years too soon, proving that soul rot ages the body prematurely. The cover models for plasticized existence: Finely coifed rats leading the race.

Vermin is loved and promoted in the pages of *Kiplinger's*. Lenny Dykstra had a full page spread touting his business acumen and benevolent financial advice. The readers would be better off taking mental health advice from Amanda Bynes. Dykstra is a renowned maniac, prone to bigoted homophobic rants, sexual harassment, bouncing checks, vandalism, and that's all on his day off. In 2011 he was bankrupt and faced fraud indictments, then sentenced to three years in prison on March 2012. Not to mention, Dykstra is a renowned embezzler prone to grand theft auto minus the Xbox. The title of *Kiplinger's* article was "Saving Pro Athletes From Themselves." Well, I'm here to save *Kiplinger's* subscribers from themselves. Cancel the subscription immediately. Save your wallet and soul in the process.

Everything is a game to be played, and the people who lose Smile in the *Wall Street Journal* on the way to court. During the Enron trial the WSJ ran a story on Lay's & Skilling's wardrobe...like they were 2 actors attending the Oscars. And in a way, they were. They lied for a living and got justly rewarded.

If this economic sleaze turns you off then you can always devise security products for the prison complex industry. Or follow the *Reader's Digest* advice and become a pearl diver, hacker, oil-rig technician, or maybe repo airplanes. Anymore these days the majority of hack the media generates is an occupation all its own: dumpster diving.

I don't have all the answers, but I know one thing -- the only jobs worth having don't hurt others or the environment. Start a business...something that helps people or brings joy. I want to open a topless barbershop. "Get a trim while you're getting some trim."

One day when I retire from giving a shit, I'm gonna open up my own bar called Beer & Nobbers. (my 2 favorite things in the world)

I could build it in Pahrump, a saloon along Homestead Road. Cold beer, good food, and affordable nobbers. Put a quarter in the jukebox or tip your waitress fiddy bucks for migraine relief. It's your choice.

And the bar would be a sane choice...Write scripts behind the bar while serving drinks to the regulars...everyone enjoying life. Maybe I could succeed or not...but I could do something that is fun.

Sometimes I read cowardly statements by "business hacks" saying that your personal life is separate from your job, which is probably the most horrid idea to bring down American society. A large part of a person's identity is derived from their job. And they should be proud of their job. What makes a person an individual is what makes them valuable to their employers. To conceal and/or destroy Identity is what creates soul-less automatons capable of exploitation. Or worse. No person is perfect, and anyone who claims to be is not to be trusted. I don't trust a man who doesn't cuss…that same man contends he doesn't wipe his ass or play with his pecker. That sort of sociopath is prone to backstabbery and other devious machinations. People that have faced tribulations & disasters and came out of it are the type of people I want to hire. Scars are the beauty marks of life, and the strong people bearing them may not be unscathed, but they're not beaten down. Couple instincts with intelligence and you have a person not subject to boundaries or bullshit. Any difficulty in the business world pales in comparison and I want those fighters who can persevere under pressure. That is the sort of perspective I will use when I create my company…thereby creating my reality.

Joseph Conrad wrote in his book *The Secret Agent*, "Money symbolizes the insignificant results which reward the ambitious courage and toil of a mankind whose day is short on this Earth of evil."

If all a person wants to achieve in life is to make money then their results will undoubtedly be insignificant.

Where hastening creatures pass intent on their way,
Threading like ants that can never relent and have nothing to say.
-DH Lawrence: Flat Suburbs in the Morning

15.
Politicks

Ducking a rare Vegas thunderstorm I met a homeless bum that grew up with Obama in the dark dank alleyways of Bangladesh. They used to chant "Allah Akbar!" while sucking cock for cash. God is great so long as he came quick and paid with paper money.

Barry always had a plan: Pay his way through school then have to apologize for it. The bum swore the tale was true. He pleaded with me to take his word, and to give him some change. Then I noticed he was wearing a weathered Bush/Quayle campaign pin. Aha! A crackhead will make up any sort of story for a buck. I gave the bum a dollar, but then he wanted two. A typical encounter with a Republican...they deftly exploit fictional storylines for profits. Though I did concede that Barry sucked BP's dick after the oil spill: "BP is a strong and viable company, and it is in all of our interests that it remain so." Whose interests, Barry? You and your corporate johns?

Conservative pundits constantly proclaim that liberals are awful. But who got America through the Great Depression & WWII? FDR. Conservatives at the time labeled him a socialist.

Who got America through the Cuban Missile Crisis? JFK
Who got Bin Laden? Obama
Who wants to give America universal health care? Same person

Our country's Founders were influenced by the Enlightenment thinkers Rousseau & Locke, liberals of their time.

Obama has only done a fraction of what he promised during his first campaign, but he's done all he can in an antiquated system. His only fault: he believes in a broken system. He's content posing with past presidents instead of orchestrating an Evolution. At least he's finally showing leadership by having the EPA cut coal power plant emissions. A start. If only a bit late.

I was an innocent kid: Trusted family, trusted friends. And when a violent act popped off I didn't know how to react. I was under the assumption that we were supposed to love one another. It took awhile...a long while...for the reality of the world to sink in. I am Public America. A naive ignorant eight-year-old in the schoolyard waiting for the morning bell to ring. The sun is coming up, sprinklers wetting the fresh grass. Four kids come over and inform me that they're goin' to kick my ass. Why? Why?! It doesn't matter. Because you're there.

And you can grow to embrace This, or fight back. Become the animal your enemy is. Do you relish violence, or does the **Smak** your fist makes against another person's cheekbone invoke revulsion?

Too many people crave violence, and therefore, have no problem with the bullshit our government does. We were all raised on violence through movies, video games, and music...so what's so wrong with it?

The only thing more violent is the intellectual dishonesty passing for domestic policy. Conformity is a nefarious act of stripping away whole populations of their potential. Capitalism has more in common with Communism than it wants to admit. Point the peons towards the salt mines. Both C words are fascist forms of government that prevent the full expression of humanity. Both ideologies pervert minds without thinking about what makes a person Feel.

A person needs a purpose. A person isn't born to serve. A person is born to live. To be something special. To serve a master isn't it. Having a unique contributing part to a community or culture is the most primal urge a person ever feels. To be part of something special. That is *culture*.

This culture should be one of caring. Too many people hate others because they hate themselves. Love yourself, flaws & all, and you can love everyone else. Disregard the sadomasochistic self-flogging man-made creation of religion. The only creed that really matters is leaving this planet a better place than when you found it. Doing something positive soars the heart.

Our current culture eschews Utopian ideals for the easy way out...which becomes hard for everyone. We suffer from a void of leadership. The Elected are good at one thing: raising money & playing the same game that is holding us back.

A fitting metaphor for the American political system: America is the prison. The people are the inmates.

The wardens are many: Big Oil, Big Bizzy (corporations), MIC (Military Industrial Complex), Wall Street, and Big Pharma.

The President and Congress are the trustees...if they step out of line then they get their privileges revoked. If they try to change anything Important then they get shot by the tower guard (JFK & RFK are prime examples).

Once you understand this metaphor, you understand American politicks. Now it is possible to escape from this prison by becoming self-aware and educating yourself, and check out of this prison and commit yourself to a new political process.

If enough people do this and demand a new system then the prison crumbles and a new co-op can be built. But most people don't escape because inside the prison, ignorance is bliss. Each cell has reality TV, fast food, and pills that make you feel better and your dick hard. Women clean the cells with feathered dust-busters and smile serving coffee. The prison is sexually repressed, so sex becomes a rare victual, vital to the men, and a chain to the women. The best things a woman can do are bare healthy boys and pray really hard when her husband is hard.

The American Problem is a smart person who bitches and moans about issues, but does nothing to solve them. We are the problem and We are the answer. The obstacle is not insurmountable.

HST wrote an Elko screed in 1974 that is relevant now. Three vital questions to ask:

1 - Decide if the patient is worth saving.
2 - What's basically wrong with the patient?
3 - If the saving is worth the effort. How to define and begin dealing with the basic problems.

1 - Yes, we are worth saving. And so is the planet.
2 - We are experiencing a fever called militaristic Capitalism. It is not fatal...yet. *almost*
3 - Make every effort to benefit Humankind...in every discipline. We face a global crisis of diminishing resources & Climate Change. Everyone has to do his or her part.

Evolution is the only answer. On every level. On all levels. Discard the old prejudices and the ancient superstitions. GW vetoed federal funding for research of human embryonic stem cells so Snowflake Babies could flourish; Eugenics disguised as social policy. Now the war criminal paints nude self-portraits. Good riddance to bad rubbish.

The last presidential election was particularly brutal. A tame Democrat incumbent running against a money-hungry power-mad bigamist. Romney gives me the creeps -- he seems like the type of guy who would pickpocket a corpse. He's nothing more than a used-car salesman...content with selling broken goods, and can't help but to smile because he knows that once some poor schmuck drives the lemon off the lot there's no warranty. Romney's private equity career equates to destroying businesses for bucks through leveraged buyouts. He's just another gangster skimming off the top, hanging with the other Bain capital buzzards eating pond scum because it tastes yummy.

Liking Mitt Romney is like liking a dog that's been dead for 3 days. It stinks, and its glassy eyes and lifeless smile will re-affirm whatever philosophy you cling to. Watching Romney debate is proof that he's a reanimated Mormon shephard needing brains.

Though his campaign jingle was kinda catchy:
"I got my binder full of bitches, smackin up these snitches, pockets full of riches, and I'm blingin' like it's Christmas."

Romney's been watching too much *Hustle & Flow*. The only thing worse than Romney's condescending attitude towards women was the GOP convention. The Delegation of the Damned: Romney & Ryan, plain white guys with Stepford Wives, waving to a crowd full of idiots applauding for aggressive action with Iran even though not a single person there would actually be the ones going to war. Romney looked nervous, out of place, but public speaking is really not Romney's shtick. He's much more comfortable lurking in the shadows of the finance world...chasing the cheese through a labyrinth of tax loopholes.

The Eastwood empty chair debacle captured the most attention, but what really disturbed me was the blatant air of superiority wafting through the convention. An air of Entitlement. Old white men think they own this country...just 'cause. Demographics are a changin' and it's not Bob Dylan's fault.

What I find repulsive is that right-wing Hollywood types like Eastwood & Duvall love them some Hispanic women, but only vote for white dudes. It seems these fossils find it okay to screw another race so long as the transfer consists entirely of bodily fluids and no power. This philosophy dates all the way back to Thomas Jefferson.

"Just because a person can subject himself to the degradations of a lifetime in politics and finally end up in the White House is certainly no reason to respect him."
-HST

I didn't plan on voting in the election, but Mitt forced my hand by backing the Keystone oil pipeline. I swore I would never vote again...I guess my actions define me as an optimist. Many people died for the freedom to vote, so I might as well exercise that right. It would have been nice to see both presidential candidates suspend all their political ad spending and use that money for Hurricane Sandy relief, but that would have been too responsible of an action for a politician. And politicians & responsible spending is like Michael Jackson & responsible babysitting. Hee Hee.

Romney really never had a chance in the election despite the media trying to pump it up like a lopsided Mayweather fight. Republicans increased the deficit with runaway war spending, gave tax breaks to the rich, and allowed unregulated greed on Wall Street. The GOP's current stance of Deregulation as an economic accelerator is a myth. Deregulation leads to Trough Economics: Good for you if you can elbow some room at the money trough...if not, have fun in the manure fields. The next step for the Republican decline is to stonewall Obama for the next four years, effectively vilifying themselves outta business.

Unfortunately, Obama tried to avoid real gun control policy and established a faith-based office that promised Pie in the Sky policies to offshoot the varied problems facing the ghetto. This religious action went into effect in 2009, and so far God has not stopped one bullet in Chicago. Obama vowed to assign a theological council to research this omnipotent grievance. "There is no religion whose central tenet is hate." So says Obama while reality proves him President of that tenet -- Capitalism.

Initially, Obama tried to please everyone, but ended up pleasing no one...especially the people who voted for him. Like 90% of politicians, he resembled a corporate lackey. To paraphrase George Carlin: our government was bought & paid for long ago.

Obama has been ineffective. He promised Change and all the people got was a couple pennies from his pocket. Stagnation cripples DC. His environmental policies were inconsistent. He didn't address gun violence until his 2nd term. His lip service to the issue did nothing to change the laws. And he neglected Global Warming until his 6th year in office, refusing to pay attention to the issue with the expediency that it demands. Yet his arrogant ass has time to hang with celebrities at press functions & shoot hoops with Clark Kellogg. But give Obama credit when it comes to campaigning -- he really knows how to exploit people's hope, treating it like a disposable commodity to gain votes. He's not the only one...

Republicans, Democrats, they're all lawyers fighting a slight ideological battle of profits. The Repubes want no big guvment, dagnabbit. Conservatives embrace the "value" Progressives dismissed yesterday. Republicans: the slime behind the snails of modern-day Democracy. The Democrats are meek profiteers with guilt complexes, and rarely impose their will even after they win two elections in a row. And the Teabaggers are a bunch of reactionary racists who still can't come to grips with having a black president. Their fiery rhetoric spawns assassinations and outright racism.

Global Warming, Peak Oil, Overpopulation, and Water Pollution are all pressing issues that Obama does his best to ignore. At least he finally took a stand for Health Care.

Republicans despise Obamacare because they despise Big Government...even though America is a great country because of Big Government: Public Education system, Police & Fire Departments, Highway creation, Mail Delivery, Armed Forces, Libraries, etc. Don't waste your breath and explain this to them because *trying to reason with a Republican is like teaching a snapping turtle how to chew bubblegum.* Republicans like Rick Perry publicly decry government spending, but plead like paupers for federal assistance when natural disasters smack their states. Conservatives cannot understand that their unbridled bloodlust of war could not be subsidized without Big Government.

Don't Believe the Hype

Capital Hill is full of pork belly warhawks on both sides...which is really one side. D- & R- means that the shyster found a way to be elected. And they have arrangements. Even more important, they have responsibilities and are held accountable to the special interests that got them elected. The country is for sale and the House of Representatives are the go-betweens. Fuck the people. CWA. (Congressflackies With Attitude)

American interests are not the interests of the Republicans. Their anti-union privatization plans hurt workers. The Bush-era Postal Accountability Enhancement Act required the US Postal Service to fully fund retiree health benefits for the next 75 years. This was a brutal blow designed to bankrupt the postal service so the conservatives could privatize it for a buck. Payday Loans couldn't have thought up a better scheme.

The Republicans are a party of rotten mercenaries, embezzlers, and money launders open to the biggest bidder. An escort service for lobbyists. Fred Thompson made a grip by fighting people dying from asbestos. Mitt Romney collected bank from China and Iranian stocks. Rudy Giuliani was "tough" on crime even though he owned a stake in Oxycontin. Get paid off the solution and the cause. Rudy isn't dumb...just greedy. Your average conservative cunt. And that my friend is your free civic lesson of the day.

Politicians cannot identify with the American People because the Political Swine live in mansions, estates, lavish condos, ranches, and other extravagant houses fit for aristocracy. And the top hogs have multiple houses. How can these connected yuppies connect with the Average American? Our ordinary income is taxed around the 35% mark while these fat cats sit back with their capital gains taxed at a scant 15%. So they live like Kings & Queens sucking the lifeblood from America while encouraging us to Vote. Because they are different from the other rich guy or gal.

Blue State Red State Schizophrenia

True leaders are supposed to bring people together...not divide them. Though maybe our country can still not be completely unified due to historical differences. Georgia & Alabama & Ole Miss and many other southern states always vote Republican no matter what. Sometimes I think the country should've split after the Civil War. Lincoln was a great Prez, but I would've cut ties after the victory. Let the south have their backwards Pakistani-like country, and we'll have America. Keep your friends close, and your enemies closer is a surefire way to always have constant strife, one way or another.

I came across the following sentence in Stephen King's book, *Insomnia*, and thought Mr. King could have included American Politics: "...the similarities between loneliness and insomnia -- how they were both insidious, cumulative, and divisive, the friends of despair and the enemies of love..."

Politicians latch onto divisive topics for their own selfish purposes...they're more than willing to pull the country apart for their own gains. They recognize the rift and are adept at ripping it further./././even though Americans have more in common with each other than they do differences. Everyone loves his or her country. Everyone loves his or her family. Everyone wants to make a decent living and be happy. Which begs the question: why don't politicians seek out the ways in which Americans are similar instead of concentrating on the few ways we're different? Because we are easier to control when splintered.

Politics have become a time-consuming crossword puzzle for the populace. They keep the spaces blank and feed off our blank stares. Time on the board of Life has been reduced to scraping for leftover scraps. Our era is the Power Suck. Power is the only thing that counts. Money is Power. And it sucks. It buys elections. It buys complacency. It buys souls. It buys us.

"Our two party system is a bowl of shit looking in the mirror at itself."
-Lewis Black

Obama and Boehner refuse to sit down & share a dube and come together and do what's best for the country. And then you realize Politics is just a game of And. Vote and __ will do __.

And it never happens. And history repeats itself because our politics are set up to do so. At least Bush and Cheney are gone.

There has never been a more vile person than **Dick** Cheney. His veins pump vinegar and his anal gland secretes sulphuric acid, leaving a slimy trail of sizzling pus everywhere he shuffles. He is the puppetmaster war criminal who only laughs out the sidecrack of his rigid mouth at collateral damage. Or what they say in Wyoming, "pop goes the weasel cuz the weasel goes pop." There is no layer specially reserved for Cheney in Hell because he is a wandering demon that jumps broken body to broken body on this earthly plane using weak constitutions as entry points. Cupid he is not though he uses the same methods: Up the loose asscrack with an evil soul arrow of malicious intents. Make sure the mark wears baggy jeans because malignant intents have a tendency to expand.

Studying politics and analyzing the photographs of politicians will surely drive a person crazy. John Murtha's face is designed to drive the observer to a state of helplessness. Louis and Clark couldn't navigate every crease on his sanctimonious forehead. He scowls at the fact that our defense budget is so large that Galactus pales in comparison. To the non-nerds, that comic book reference means that we are making the Roman Empire look like rookies in squandering away the economy on the Military. Even ancient Spartans would be a bit hesitant to designate so many resources to War, slaves or no slaves. Ask a Confederate senator and he would posit the problem was freeing them.

Defense spending creates jobs...so they say. Send a young man off to war and when he returns he searches for work. Creating an existential quandary in the soldier: Why protect a country that doesn't give a fuck about me?

GW never had the problem. The country was just some slot machine to play and continually lose until he won two terms at the helm. Don Quixote wants his windmills back.

There is a skewed sense of morality here in Ameritown. The Republicans piled onto Bill Clinton for getting a nobber while Bush/Cheney got away with crimes against humanity, bombing innocent Iraqis. Sex is rated R. Violence is a palatable PG.

After our 9/11 response in Iraq there should have been a military coup against the Presidunce Bush. Go fight for your Master while they extend investment-tax breaks. Invest your life in their Cause, because a life is a horrible thing to waste for no profits. Uncle Sam wants to Sodomize You!

You got a Purty Mouth

Chevron kickbacks Saddam for oil rights. And when he doesn't want to play fair then Condoleeza Rich...I mean, Rice, the Chevron director, sets nefarious actions in motion with her white Masters to take those oil rights. Exxon is thankful. Extremely thankful. Bombs, bullets, deaths, injuries are nothing to these swine. Fight for your country and be exploited.

We no longer live in a world of nations. We reside in regions controlled by corporations. Hu Jintao came to America to meet with Cisco, GM, Goldman Sachs, and Home Depot...our government was an afterthought. Sort of like a Pimp taking a holiday to Miami and not wanting to be bothered with the hoes who owe him money. The bitch-slap will come later...and it always does in one form or another.

The United States Chamber of Commerce members have resorted to taping their eyelids diagonally when they sleep. Shay Shay. They've been bowing so often lately that their backs run at 90-degree angles when they crawl. Just last week the mayor of Main Street got caught rubbing his body with banana peels, hoping to transform the pigment of his skin. And to think, just a couple decades ago this same person was bombing thatch-hut villages in Vietnam. Terrorism. Napalm. My Lai. Genocide. Economic Opportunity.

The buck stops here, Bubba. The leaders reflect the society and vice-versa. We allow this shit to happen so long as our happy meals are warm. We act like children then get mad when the government treats us like it. Pulling out the passive-conformist pacifier is rough at first...especially when teething with knowledge, but you can't be a baby forever. If the Establishment tries to stick it back in, then bite their hand...or, in political matters, their sexual organs.

When you have a government ran by political hacks & lawyers instead of brilliant humanitarians then you have a society prone to decay and stagnation. HST wrote that politics was a way of controlling your environment. That heavy task shouldn't be in the hands of people who have no real care for community...locally or on a national level. These cicadas have no problem spending hundreds of million dollars on presidential campaigns yet the public schools are always facing cutbacks.

Obama had good intentions, but the antiquated system is set up to stall progress. Corporations have seen to it. This is a problem that has frustrated many a writer. HL Mencken was a deplorable misanthropic racist, yet 15% of what he said was true. He termed Democracy "the darling of demagogues, who exploit the people, who are made to believe that the demagogues are their best friend." This prophecy came true in the sixties & seventies...the era of Dr. Gonzo. Hunter Thompson was the insightful jester of the 20th century who realized the tools available in his time weren't sufficient to enact change. *Now they are.*

The solution is simple. Most things in life are simple. People who try to complicate issues usually have hidden agendas. The solution is a New political system: Ran by the People without the interference of corporate influence. A third Party is necessary, and can be mobilized through the Internet and social media. I will devise websites that will aid this transformation. Dems & Reps will resist and join forces against the Idea, but that's to be expected. Sheisty local tactics of re-zoning districts will be common. Snapping crack (pop) and other Rice Crispy routines are practical politics of the Tammany Hall jetset. The specter of George Plunkitt has possessed American politics for the past 150 years. His ideological offspring continue getting rich off "honest" graft, kickbacks, and controlling the system though various political high jinx. But these whores can't re-district the entire country. It's time to hammer the spike into the Bram Stokerish hearts of special interest groups. Their soulless nights spent feasting off the lifeblood of the middle class are over.

Voting needs to change also. Vote for the candidate based on their verified actions and qualifications instead of what the candidate promises. And please, vote blindly without regard to the candidate's appearance, religion, gender, race, and wardrobe. Voting with prejudice does nothing but change the names...the game remains the same. If you can't vote without prejudice then do the country a favor and never vote again.

A social movement can be successful if objectives are achieved through a chain reaction of strategic momentum. Grassroots participation is vital. A Bolivarian state of mind is necessary. One sows the seed. Another fertilizes it. Another raises it. So another may harvest it. And that is how an Evolution grows.

And this movement can be called Americanism. I'm no fan of labels. Labels are for medicine so the old man doesn't take boner pills instead of Lipitor. I'm no fan of Capitalism or Communism either. If you must label this movement then label it Humanistic Democracy. Or just being an American for short. A state of Being. Doing. Standing for something. Being something. Not buying something. Being something. Being something greater than you. Being a human being. **Being**. Label me that.

The Evolution won't happen overnight, but it can start tomorrow. And it won't take long. Our minds work faster than congress. Follow my lead. The Internet will be the spark, and we can all come together as a whole. First it will be healing communities one at a time, large and small. Then growing. A long overdue Renaissance. Where everyone has something to contribute. And share. And Give. If you want to stay passive then this isn't your country. America is action.

"Character gives us qualities, but it is in actions -- what we do -- that we are happy or the reverse. All human happiness and misery take the form of action."
-Aristotle

Some people have already started. Michael Tubbs was elected councilman in Stockton, Cali at the age of 22. Tubbs helped extend Project Ceasefire, an effective violence reduction program. He is also a teacher and promotes literacy. Nike should be making shoes for him...he's a thousand times more admirable than any basketball player. Michael Tubbs is the Truth. Imagine if there were a Tubbs in every city in America. Multiply that idea and change can happen.

Malala is another inspiring human being. She is the future of Islam and has the potential to lead the Muslim world out of the Stone Age. Malala is a brave young woman who doesn't let violence deter her from seeking equal education rights for girls worldwide. Her courage in the face of adversity gives me hope that one day peace will prevail.

Courage can be contagious. An entire community who exemplifies this trait is Greensburg, Kansas. In 2007 a tornado destroyed the town, but they pulled together and partially rebuilt the town using green technology. Now Greensburg is a role model for perseverance and coping with tragedy. They turned destruction into an opportunity to rebuild in the spirit of sustainable living. Greentown is a grassroots community organization that spurred the idea to use wind energy, solar panels, and geothermal energy...proving that every town could be a green town.
  Tubbs, Malala, and the people of Greensburg are all beacons of hope, proving that humanity has the potential to achieve great things. Everyone can pull together to further the cause. Devote time, knowledge, even write a book or run for office. Do something.

I get bizarre ideas when I'm sick. Once I had the flu back in Fairborn, Ohio and decided to record a rap album. So I spent $500 in a studio and recorded 20+ songs in one night. It was epic, but overwhelmingly Amateurish. Recently I had the flu and thought it would be a good idea to run for office as the Radical candidate who would unite the Occupy movement with a concise vision of reform. But now I realize to never trust a mind gripped in the demented throes of fever. Because any egotistic hunger to run for public office is a sickness akin to bashing one's skull against a brick wall because it "feels good."
  An Aspiration of power is not the reason to run for office. Aspiring for power is what makes politics rotten. Instead: Aspire to help people. Wanting to better

society is the way to go. And if that means running for office then do it. A public office is a public service, not a pork belly job to inflate your bank account. Aspire to contribute in a meaningful way to the evolution of Society. And there are many ways to do that. Create a dialogue: A new system. A new way of thinking. A better way of living. Everyone is capable.

A person doesn't want to enter Politics, they Need to. And we all need to help institute change. Attend council meetings and public budget hearings. Form organizations and clubs. Start a youth commission or a labor union. Get active, be stalwarts of change; from community colleges to the state capital, the time is now.

Author's note: *Optimism is the real American state of mind. Never get discouraged by ignorance -- we live in historic times and it will only get better. Only if you help make it better.*

16.

President Heatt aka Mr. Mojo Risin'

Everyone has that "If I were president" fantasy, and I'm no different. President Heatt has a nice ring to it, but I wouldn't last a year in office before being assassinated. Rational thinking negates this because I would never even be elected in the first place. I have too many faults: I drink like a guppy in the Gobi, I love pussy more than JFK & MLK combined, and worst of all, I tell the truth. Even though I'll never be President I can still offer Evolution Solutions.

    We live in unprecedented times. Climate change, depleted resources, and overpopulation are obstacles to our species' survival. Anything less than radical improvements are merely pat-on-the-back platitudes to the plebes. My book is a means to inspire the next generation to solve the problems of our society.

    What if it's too late? Or what if nobody reads this book? Sometimes I feel nervous like a fat naked guy living in a village composed of cannibals. As long as the ravenous beasts feast on wild game then everything's okay, but what happens when there's no more boars to devour?

    The problems I identify throughout this book are not insurmountable...yet. The solutions I posit are not easy-fix schemes, but Evolutionary steps to take in order to ensure a stable society. The only interests I have are for Humanity & the Environment to exist in a sustainable tandem, which will conflict with big-money corporate interests. This conflict will be significant and will be waged in the sphere of pop culture & popular opinion. And my opinions in this book will be decidedly unpopular. That is okay. Maybe I'm naive to think a human life is more important than a profit, but I have to believe that this universal truth will win out in the end and spur change.

    People need to regain that Evolutionary spirit. It has been lost due to corporate conformity. A diseased spirit of self-preservation is a symptom of Capitalism. Bow down to the forces that be and inhibit your sense of self-identity, or lose that cheddar. Basically, save your own ass in order to save your pocket book. This sort of fractured mind state is what weighs down our society. Materialism has driven a wedge into our communities. People find petty luxuries more important than the revolutionary spirit this country was founded on.

I'm not asking people to give up their homes and live in mud huts, but something even tougher: change their way of thinking. No more thinking "it can't be done." It can be done, and *has* to be done. Change is a necessary ingredient for any progressive society, and here are a few changes that would revitalize America as being the stellar democracy of the world.

Green New Deal

FDR was one of the best presidents in American history. He guided our country through the Great Depression and WWII. His New Deal policies shaped our country. We are in need of an upgraded New Deal for the 21st century while still abiding by his humanistic vision.

Green tech is the future of our country and we can all take part and prosper from it. A revolution of industry is a good thing. It's not like the casino industry, which is based on an exploitation that creates a society of servitude. Green Tech is an opportunity for everyone. New construction projects. Planning. Upkeep. Creating a new power grid. It won't all happen overnight, but there will be plenty of new jobs created by the evolution. And that benefits our society *and* the environment. The only people it doesn't benefit are the Greedheads in the oil, coal, war, and fracking industries.

If our tax dollars can fuel solar panels on schoolhouses in Afghanistan then why not here? Millions of American dollars are plugged into the development of solar & wind power in Afghanistan. This sort of thing should infuriate us when our schools are not only under-funded, but lack solar energy. But what can you expect when Congress is full of ass clowns and the Prez is held hostage by polls? Self-preservation is a political disease that wears this country down. Green projects can benefit every community and turn this country into the vibrant trendsetter it once was. It is up to Us to impose our political will and make sure it happens.

NV Energy has a goal of renewable energy of 25% by 2025. That goal should be 100%. Nevada's new transmission line, ON Line, is a good start. A grid of solar plants dotting the desert could power all of Nevada and a portion of California as well. Nevada will eventually be a desert sprawl of solar panels that feeds the west a pollution-free source of electricity.

The Green New Deal would fuel Relief & Recovery of the American job market. Relief in the form of government jobs for the unemployed would speed economic Recovery. We would start a Civilian Conservation Corps and hire men & women to work on green projects. There was an unemployment rate of 2% during WWII; we can replicate that with the war against climate change. Our green public works projects would build the renewable resource energy grid, solar fields, wind turbines, geothermal facilities, desalination plants, water pipelines, transit systems, and rebuild our infrastructure of bridges, dams, and roads. These projects would also include reforestation, and other conservation efforts. Start a program of co-ops and bring green energy to rural communities *everywhere*. The prize of all the projects would be constructing a high-speed rail system connecting all of the major cities of America.

A major question is how would we fund these projects? Several ways. America is slacking and spends about 1 percent of its GDP on infrastructure buildup. I would immediately cut half of the current defense spending and use that money towards the Green New Deal. The Iraq War cost $800 *billion* dollars. Bombing a country that had no connection to 9/11 sure was expensive. The United States military scrapped 170 million pounds of vehicles & other military equipment during the Afghanistan withdrawal, which totaled seven billion dollars. This is money better spent in our country.

Also, I would repeal the prohibition of marijuana and regulate & tax the green plant, then use those proceeds for these projects. I would also use the marijuana proceeds to create jobs for writers, musicians, and artists. What good is a society without art?

"Morality is temporary, wisdom is permanent."
-HST

Alcohol was once illegal, now it's consumed everywhere. Recent medical studies have confirmed that alcohol is more addictive than pot, yet marijuana is still illegal. The only "dangerous" aspect of pot is the munchies. I went to bed last night looking like Jon Favreau in that Rocky Marciano movie then woke up this morning looking like Jon Favreau in *Iron Man 3*. So yes, pot is dangerous...to your physique.

The feds & police cracking down on weed dispensaries and conducting "major" operations like Operation Green Venom are a farce. It just gives these lawmen errands to run instead of doing real work like cracking down on the Mexican drug cartels. Legalize pot, beef up gun laws, and enforce the borders, and the Cartels lose at least 50% effectiveness. They'd be chopped off at the knees. It doesn't take a genius to solve these problems, but our corrupt system values the money made busting weed dealers and incarcerating them in privatized prisons. This is unacceptable. Unless the feds are going to raid fast food companies, liquor stores, and tobacco farms, three industries that cause significant health problems, then weed should be legalized. The tax revenue would be beneficial to our Green New Deal. Weed is not the bogeyman, prescription drugs are. Pharmaceutical drugs create addictions. Big Pharma has created a culture that needs to get up to get down. In our skewed society that values a perpetual war on drugs, the manufactured ones are fine, but a plant is not. The insanity stops now. Weed promotes creative thought & happiness, and its popularity would raise much-needed revenue.

    The best and most controversial way to raise the money needed for the Green New Deal would be the Redistribution of Wealth. I would institute a tax rate of 80% for all incomes exceeding $15 million. That's more than enough money for a person to earn in one year. I would also raise capital gains taxes to 50%. Conservatives would oppose this vehemently due to their allegiance to Big Business, but our country is in desperate need of a visionary like FDR. The low and middle classes would not have their taxes raised, and the added tax revenue from the filthy rich would be used to complete the funding for the Green New Deal, help erase the deficit, and institute other beneficial social programs.

    In order to ensure all my programs are financed, and the budget is balanced, I would immediately abolish all inherited wealth over one million dollars. This would end the genetically defective dynasties like the Bushes and Romneys. "...some of whom have been bred up distinctly to inherit a large share of the property, and have been, from their cradles, specially disqualified from devoting themselves to any useful pursuit," Charles Dickens stated with much insight in his book, *American Notes*.

    A well-raised kid will earn his or her own way. Hard work and earning what you have is an old school way of thinking that still rings true. Kids that inherit wealth don't really do that, do they?

2nd Bill of Rights

    FDR had the idea for a second Bill of Rights that would cover employment, housing, medical care, and education. Obama has already instituted the Affordable Healthcare act, so I would use the added tax revenue to fully fund Obamacare and social security. I would also create legislation requiring a living wage for workers. Wal-Mart & McDonalds, and every other company would pay their employees aged 21 years & up at least 13 dollars per hour. Ed Hudgins and the Cato Institute and the Republicans believe that subsidizing low-wage earners through food stamps is the American Dream, but I do not. I believe in paying People an honest wage. I would also limit the workweek to forty hours for these jobs so people can spend more time with their family and working in their communities.

Another major jobs creation program would be to refurbish and/or build better inner city housing with green tech upgrades. A goal would be to have no city in America with slums. If people are forced to live like animals then they act like animals. Get the people involved. Instill pride in their communities.

Education would be another priority. No more launching hundreds of millions of dollars of missiles per day at some middle-eastern country. Those funds are going to schools. I would also significantly raise the tax rates on casinos & lotteries with the designation of all funds going to the schools. Inner city schools would be upgraded and technology would play a vital role. Inter-connectivity & creativity would boost learning. I would undo the sanitized version of education that allows the populace to be exploited. History and current events would be a priority to learn. Schools should encourage students to be free thinkers, not treat them like cattle to be scolded and indoctrinated into capitalistic conformity. Students need to be *involved* in the learning process, and the education system needs to incorporate more ways for students to be active participants instead of passive patrons of the state. Jean Jacques Rousseau thought that education should incite children's natural instincts without restricting them. Schools are not tyrannical havens for bullies; they are sanctuaries of self-discovery & opportunity. John Locke believed in the importance of education as a means for improving equality among the people. According to Locke, everyone is a product of his or her environment. Due to inadequate education, many people do not fulfill their potential and succumb to the seduction of crime. Building more schools are always better investments than building more prisons.

There are already some great innovations happening, and I would get the individuals creating those innovations involved. Dick K.P. Yue, a professor at MIT, is working on a project named OpenCourseWare that offers 2100 free college courses online. This is a good start, and should evolve into a system where credits can be earned and verified online then integrated into a website like LinkedIn, where an online resume is constantly being updated. College Education courses should widely be available for free online and I would offer Mr. Yue the position of College Education Dean. I would also implement a local tuition initiative to combat brain drain and empower communities. Local business owners (and local taxes) sponsor a full-ride tuition for a local student to the state university with the stipulation that the student comes back home to make it better. Imagine if every community did this. The genius behind this program is that it is a self-propelling evolution that regenerates.

I would cut military spending, and create a smaller yet more effective armed force. Morale would improve with the creation of a new GI Bill, which would give any soldier who serves at least four years free health care for life, and free college education or guaranteed employment upon discharge. If a soldier died while serving then their spouse and children would be exempt from federal taxes. And a veteran would never be homeless. Any country that can afford football stadiums and golf courses can afford reasonable housing for veterans. I would also institute a new military policy of the Family Draft. This basically ensures that any Congress & President that declares war will have to send all capable relatives between the ages of 18-40 to war first, before any other soldier goes; a morally-fair policy to prevent any more criminal Vietnam or Iraq wars. To put things in perspective: our country spends over 50 BILLION dollars on the nuclear weapons complex…cut that in half and there's more than enough to spend.

A few other things I would do: create a Farming task force and kick Monsanto out of the country, and outlaw GMOs. Organic farms would get significant tax benefits, and purveyors of high fructose corn syrup would not receive any tax subsidies. I would re-install & improve the Glass-Steagell legislation to prevent any more Wall Street meltdowns. Greed is not good, and three-strike laws would pertain to stock market thieves.

If I had the opportunity to be President then these laws/acts would be implemented immediately. Why else elect someone if they can't get shit done? So I would have to abolish the Supreme Court. These old white anchors hold the country back. I would also have to decrease the amount of power the House of Representatives have. Many of the goons serving there get elected pandering to the base emotions of fear & ignorance of their uneducated constituents. Getting rid of the Electoral College is another necessary step to having a true Democracy, where *every* vote counts. Dems would campaign in the south and Republicans in the north. This would also help alleviate the bitter divisions of the country.

In order to make sure a Big Business dictator is not hired as President and repeals all of these beneficial changes, I would enact a law that severely limits campaign expenses. That way a blowhard can't ad spend his way to the white house. Air travel would be kept to a minimum, and the major candidates would conduct transcontinental train tours using the extensive high-speed railway system that the Green New Deal builds. How can a person govern a country if they have never really seen it?

We are already becoming what Harold Ickes warned "a big business Fascist America." An enslaved America beholden to the whims of the few. Without instituting the changes I propose, America will suffer in the long run, and become another ruined empire. Every one of the ideas I offer are positive Evolutionary ideas that will benefit America, and in turn, the world. We will again become a beacon of hope and a role model of progress.

17.
Smoking Guns and Stray Bullets

Artists are affected by what happens around them. That's why they're artists. Hacks continue on like nothing happened: Business as usual. Movies are big business and Hollywood is hack city. Tragedies are mere inconveniences to the Moguls instead of life-altering events that require change.

The famous line from the first Spider Man movie: "With great power comes great responsibility." It's time for Hollywood to heed its own advice. The bulk of Hollywood's product has the cultural significance of a tube of Pringles...and just as disposable.

Hollywood has become Corporate America...an industry rotten to its core. They promote projects coated with candied violence that neither explores the human condition nor comment on it. The time is right for another 1970's independent upheaval.

I've written unproduced scripts saturated with guns and violence, and the only solace I can take away is that they were never made. It's frustrating to spend years of my life developing projects that contribute no cultural value to the society I live in. I'm against guns and violence, but how can I criticize someone who owns a gun when I make movies that celebrate guns? So I won't. I can't in good conscience contribute to the violent psychosis that currently grips this country. It's time to grow up and make mature movies that don't exploit the public.

Nobody is perfect, but everybody has the potential to change. An artist is affected. A hack is oblivious, blinded by bucks. Too busy climbing a stairway to heaven while the rest of us are trapped in the cellar of Reality. Arny SchwarzenNazi & Sly Stallone cling to past glories, shooting anything that moves on celluloid. Old steroidal fucks pointing guns at the audience while their personal lives are in shambles. Five foot five Psychotic Killers on the big screen contributing more carnage than a Michael Myers wet dream.

"And it makes me wonder..."

Led Zeppelin swells in my office, contributing truth to my book. Yes, there are two paths. There's still time to change the road you're on. The piper will lead us to reason and the forest will echo with laughter. Well, I haven't seen any fucking piper anywhere, only guns on the big screen spraying 3-D bullets. And now there are 3-D guns you can download & print when you get home. To protect you from the fictional threat that has become fact. Yourself.

And she's buying a stairway to heaven. She is the Statue of Liberty. Peace and justice for no one.

The Last of Us, *the Purge*, Zombies, Guns, and apocalyptic violence...another half-hour watching Fox TV. And I'm transported to another dimension. It's Nazi Germany in the year 2014, the victorious nation of WW II and III and IV. Ride or Die. The 6th Reich is strong so long as their pop culture on steroids keeps the masses docile. Goebbels' grandson is the television czar of Fox. He feeds the masses bite-size nuggets of blood every half hour. Dispatch a few negroes here, another dozen wetbacks there. You know, the bad guys. The men who clean your streets, cut your grass, fold your towels when you're out of town, and replace the Kleenex you wipe your nose with.

We beat the Germans & Japanese only to become a warmongering culture that idolizes war & violence. Hitler roams the halls of Fox, still alive due to a cutting-edge medical technique known to the layman as Red Bull blood infusion. He's a bit uneven, staggering here and there, demanding that his favorite movie, *The Dark Knight Rises,* be played on a continual 24-hour loop. He absolutely loves Catwoman -- dressed in tight black leather, brandishing guns like a lunatic. Wait a minute...that's Obama...he loves Hathaway in that movie. America's sweetheart: young, white, and eager to please. AKA America's Fuckpot.

"I was sittin' in a crummy movie with my hands on my chin. All the violence that occurs, seem like we never win."

A week after the Aurora massacre I went to see Batman 3 in a Vegas theater. There was an armed officer there to make sure everything went Right. And the movie began. A million bullets were shot onscreen. And the only echoes I heard were the giggles of the audience at the mayhem. And it makes me wonder...

What kind of people are we?

Superstitious people who cross their fingers for a field goal and make the sign of the cross when someone dies. Praying to God even though the reality of their Satanic lives is an afterthought. God, Devil. Both entities live in US. Apathy is the subtle devil that allows greater evils to take place. Say you wanted to launder money...do it like the guys of *Office Space*...take 2 cents for every person per day. 300 million people times 2 cents adds up. Multiply that on a global scale. And you see that people are becoming their own worst enemy. Their own devil. Apathy is that 2 cents. Their own two cents is a "Like" button on a computer screen.

Religion is a man-made metaphor. Unfortunately, most people look back 2000 years instead of looking forward. I'm a legally ordained minister of the Universal Life Church and never lie about matters like this. I don't need superstition. Everything I need I was born with. My heart is pure and my spirit is even stronger.

I love my fellow man, and no book taught me that.

A book can teach many things...mathematics, spelling, but love is not one. You're born with it. Most people are anyway. Some ain't.

Hungry eels swirl around the Hollywood Hills, searching for another fix as they develop another project. The Rest in Peace Department never sleeps. By day Tom Cruise and Hugh Jackman tout Wal-Mart as role models then at night they suck each other off repeatedly while counting the shares they gained. Empty Vessels shilling for corporations. Beards with hundred dollar bills for smiles. Ironic.

They bust nuts of blood money. Fuck too many people too many times and that's what happens. Thumbs up. We are all customers to be bled by the "Artist". You know, the tough guy with a gun, the guy who pulls a trigger a dozen times onscreen, and then retreats back to his trailer to drink a goji berry smoothie to relax. Tough work actin' tough.

Lift a couple weights, hop onscreen as a hitman with edgy sideburns, and bellow at the unfairness of it all. An Actor Prepares.

Food stamps are a good thing...that way the poor bastards can afford to go to the movies. Wal-Mart is a role model because their employees are either on welfare or stamps. The fact that Wal-Mart is the largest private employer on the planet is a sad comment on our progress as a people. Fuck reality, pop in a Blu-ray and take the pain away. Hugh Jackman is so handsome, I'm sure he has no problem at the dmv, or the bathhouse.

If stars like Cruise and his Wolverine bud hate themselves to the point where they hide their individual truths in order to make money then what do you think they think about you?

Suckers to be bled and sold...just like their souls...

Murder Incorporated

It's a bit disheartening & frustrating to find out the industry you hoped to be a part of is full of scumbags. So don't aspire to "industry". Instead, aspire to creation...because industry is an assembly line of conformity...or worse.

After Newtown I thought our culture would stop glorifying guns and violence. Boy was I naive. Pop culture has a gun fetish and it's to the point now where guns are phallic symbols considered to be cool accessories. The reality is that guns are instruments of death that are not regulated enough.

Hollyweird liberals are intellectual despots that rigidly resemble NRA nuts who love guns. They are all for crazy people giving up their guns, but proclaim violent movies to be harmless. A self-serving analysis. They create the culture of violence that contributes to craziness. "Everyone has to change, but me." A common opinion of filmmakers/rappers. To these elitists, art is created and consumed in a vacuum. At the very least, isn't it sick to entertain a populace besieged by gun violence with fictional gun violence?

Producers give all sorts of lame excuses for their violent dreck. The producer of *Kick-Ass 2* compared his fluff to Sam Peckinpah's movies. Peckinpah hated violence so much he filmed it in slow motion to show the brutality of it. He made violence dirty. And he made you feel bad for seeing it. *Kick-Ass* glorifies violence with kids partaking in it...a sort of detestable activity akin to serving soiled baby diapers for dinner. A little girl in *Kick-Ass* runs around shooting guns. Sweet child.

"What passed for society was a loud, giddy whirl of thieves and pretentious hustlers, dull sideshow of quacks and clowns and philistines with gimp mentalities."
-HST

I made the mistake of "friending" Don Murphy on Facebook. He's the prominent producer of such violent fare as *Shoot 'Em Up*. After another American mass shooting I tried to engage him in an intellectual discussion about violent movies, which led to him insulting me, talking trash about the shirt I wore in my Facebook pic, and deleting me. An ugly, obese, morally-depraved Neanderthal with a fat bank account and prominent IMDB page got bent so out of shape by my logical comments that he felt it right to bash me for no reason. The essence of a scumbag -- it is rumored that Don Murphy makes love to holograms of himself while jamming "Space age Pimpin'" by Eightball & MJG. Whereupon he strips naked, shimmies down the railings of his house overlooking the hills, and strangles the stray animals that wander upon his property. After draining the animals of bodily fluids, he lurches home & rests his bloodstained cheeks on his silk pillow and sleeps like the baby he really is.

Anything for a Buck

Hansel and Gretel is now a fairytale advertised with douchebags pointing 2 guns at the audience. *2 Guns* is even the title of a hack movie with 2 well-known actors shooting each other only to live another day while real people get gunned down in the streets. "Make it rain" bullshit. Pacman Jones made it rain bullets outside of a Vegas strip club a while back, and it just so happens the comic book writer of *2 Guns* lives in Vegas, using a slang term 7 years past its prime. And like many purveyors of culturally-degrading violence, the writer of *2 guns*, Steven Grant, is an old crusty white dude who fantasies about violence...thinks it's a cool literary device to get paid with...no matter the reality of violence...or the consequences. *2 Guns* was a comic book published by Boom! (I didn't add the exclamation mark; the company's name is Boom!). *3 Guns* is the sequel and Mr. Grant looks very proud posing for his contribution to American Culture in an August version of Las Vegas Weekly. A bad man with psoriasis who hasn't experienced violence outside of a cinema, he walks his pup, shops at the local grocery story, and writes clichéd stories. So he deems guns & tragedy worthy aspects of American Life to exploit.

An even worse movie is *Olympus Has Fallen*. Probably the most morally reprehensible movie I've seen in a long time. After 9/11 the destruction of American landmarks shouldn't be considered entertainment. This mean-spirited cruel movie with an execution fetish touts a blatant disregard for Life. Torture is a plot point, and socking women and stabbing slanty-eyed terrorists is brainless set dressing for this horror show.

Foie Gras is the new hot genre that Hollywood favors: shoveling shite down your throat with a funnel that enlarges your liver & shrinks your brains. And the new hobby is sucking China dong.

Bad Taste makes big bucks. *Iron Man 3* was released after the Boston Marathon Bombing, and a major plot point was bombings. I would consider this poor taste, though I doubt if the creators have any taste at all. This cookie-cutter boring movie was all too eager to sacrifice national pride for the Chinese Yuan. The Chinese cookie line was cute at the expense of America, but there was nothing offensive to the delicate Chinese sensibility in the movie or else the movie would be banned or edited for the commie audience. Maybe that explains the red herring, the Mandarin. In the comic books the Mandarin was a Chinese super villain, but Marvel changed it. Despite the greedy implications of catering to the Chinese government, the movie was just flat-out bad. Does Iron Man really need another mentor in the third movie? Especially a hillbilly lil' boy? And the Mandarin character doesn't make sense. The real villain wants to remain anonymous yet creates a terroristic character designed to draw attention to the bombings. This might have sounded logical when the writer was on LSD, but it makes no logical sense. *Iron Man 3* also had tons of guns and shooting in it...which is not creative. Lazy writing. Tony Snarks was merely a drone pilot in the movie wearing janky-ass weak suits who had to be saved at the end by Pepper Potts. The laziest writing of all is having your main character saved by someone else (*Dark Knight Rises* falls victim to this cunty flaw as well). Overall, the movie was wack, had a score that ripped off *T2*'s score, and made a shit-load of moolah. I resent it because my bucks contributed to their cause. And I will never spend BO bucks again for a Disney superhero flick.

A part of the problem is that the Europeans come from a war-like culture. "The Song of Roland" extolled the gruesome excitement of dying on the battlefield. Violence reigned supreme in feudal times...and the contemporary cinematic offsprings are the *Chronicles of Narnia* and the *Lord of the Rings*. British writers love war, and so do Americans who write *the Avengers*, *Iron Man 3*, and other movies that glorify men killing other men.

How do you abstain from war when it's ingrained into your culture?

Culture defines society, so war becomes glorified. In Narnia the children fight upon the bloody battleground...the same type of fervor that fueled the Crusades. We have become the 21st century Samurais. The current definition of Cinema: Conflict is necessary for the soul in order to ward off evil. And evil is the enemy. And to thwart that enemy, a populace must arm itself even though that populace uses those arms on each other. Friendly Fire. All the while, the movies promote war. Yes, there's strife in the world, but do we have to constantly entertain ourselves with cartoonish versions of it?

The masses may react to bloodthirsty swill, but that is not a good reason to feed them it.

Corporations spend a quarter billion dollars with the mission to water down the human genome. Derivative douche action-packaged for the hermaphroditic drooler. Walt is freeze-dried with a smile as awful Oz movies are rolled out. Fortunately, Disney had to pull the plug on his cryogenic unit after *the Lone Ranger* debacle. The racist anti-Semitic HUAC squealer has finally been laid to rest.

Disney isn't the only company wasting money on bombs. I'm still trying to figure out why New Line would make a Jack & the Beanstalk movie for $200 mill. I could make at least twenty movies for that price.

2 reasons not to make $200 million movies (excluding *Avatar*):

1 - A sane rational business decision. It's better to make several good movies instead of one gigantic piece of beanstalk shit.

2 - Ethics. 200 years from now people will look back on our society and be flabbergasted that a debt-ridden society facing Global Warming and depleted natural resources would regularly make $200 million movies for their entertainment. Insane and irrational.

    Steven Spielberg predicts an implosion of the film industry after a few $250 million movies flop. I predict a cinematic revolution akin to the 1970s: lower budgeted movies that have something to say and/or explore the human condition. First, we have to turn our backs at the crappy corporate shit being shoveled onscreen. Second, recognize what is going on. Superman, the soldier of steel, is a National Guard recruitment campaign riddled with product placement. Most of these movies are mere two-hour commercials. Expensive ones that sacrifice story for spectacle. A narrative that is becoming a mirage to mask our nation's shortcomings.
    Special effects are the new star according to the WSJ. Scott Ross of Digital Domain believes that they improve upon something like the Venus de Milo, without really thinking if it should be improved upon. The Strause Bros are self-proclaimed nerds rolling Bentleys and are obviously happy about the inflated cgi costs. The studios too often rely on computer wizards to create big screen alchemy...without the same regard for Story. The plot is several points to a crossword puzzle and each studio has their own answer key. Marvel's is starting to run dry while their profits are flush with stupidity-infused cash.
    Hollywood is not the only Industry with an obsession with violence. The Video Game biz is infatuated with blood, guts, warfare, and guns. Designing video games is a lucrative social experiment breeding a sociopathic class of patriotic killers. This depraved industry feasts off the bloodlust of warped people...whose numbers continue to increase.
    Carjacking and shooting people is the goal of *Grand Theft Auto*. *GTA 5* cost $250 million to produce and made $1 Billion worldwide in three days. Wow, that is quite depressing. There are a lot of sick people out there with expendable cash and time to waste. If I was a woman and carried some bastard around in my belly for nine months and expelled that sucker out through my vag only to see said bastard sit on the couch carjacking people then I would abort the bastard on the spot.

The only thing more entertaining than *GTA* is War. War is fun. It's a game! Death & machine guns are all an adventure to be played. And our militarized culture eats up the fecal matter titled *Call of Duty*. *Battlefield* and *Killzone* are other games that trivialize war in an unhealthy way.

If these gamers want to get the full immersive experience of a real battlefield then they should play *Call of Duty* with metal hooks. Grip the controller with hooks for hands and see how fun it is to lob grenades at pixilated enemies. Or even better, zip yourself into a body bag with eyeholes cut out, and play your war porn until you ass-phyxiate yourself with noxious Mountain Dew farts. At least the bromaylated vegetable oil is flame retardant in case one of your nerdy buddies tries to light it. Strange Days indeed...

The new *Call of Duty* game advertises cunt propaganda with the tagline: "A man who truly loves his country doesn't just give his life, he gives his sons." The best military recruiting device ever made was this video game. Don't fall for it, and don't buy it. Unless you like to be used. And many do -- *Call of Duty: Ghosts* made a billion dollars the first day it was released. Yay. Sacrifice your frontal lobe for your corporation; your ass belongs to the army. Express your patriotism with two thumbs and an unhealthy amount of bloodlust. When you beat the game, enlist.

or drop the controller

Fuck dying in some foreign desert while the people back home don't give a shit about you except for about twice a year when some bs Holiday tells them they have to care.

We have become a perverse people. PlayStation 4 advertises a game with Dresden-like destruction. Instead of building civilization we are becoming trained to destroy it. What difference does it make if all a "civilized society" does is play violent video games and watch shoot 'em up movies?

The Message

Movies have messages. Writers and directors put these messages into their movies, whether it is subconscious or not. M Night's movie *the Village* has a message: In order to escape crime you have to move away from urban areas into an all-white backwards village. Crime may happen there too, but guess who commits it? The retard. So according to M Night's worldview, ethnic people and retards are the ones responsible for crime. Another Night movie, *Lady in the Water* had mostly caricatures & stereotypes as characters. But what do you expect from a spoiled kid who grew up in affluent settings and surrounded by white people?

A writer must not only amuse the mind, but inspire and elevate it as well. Unfortunately, too many Hollywood hacks fill their scripts full of Murder & Mayhem for entertainment sake. Violence is glorified, not artistically presented to try & understand the state of Man. A hack believes that a dollar in the pocket is worth more than a thought in their head.

"Writing is like prostitution. First, you do it for the love of it, then you do it for a few friends, and finally you do it for the money."
-Moliere

Violence presented as spectacle has been ingrained into our culture for thousands of years. The war-mongering European sense of drama is esteemed. That history seeps into our culture like radiation leaking into an aquifer. Ratings prove it. *Game of Thrones* is one of the most successful shows on cable television. 15 minutes into the pilot episode the main character executes another character by beheading them. A child watches, and so do we. When a Muslim performs this execution in real life it is horrible and something to be despised. But when a white man does it on a TV show it's entertainment. This cruel & vicious show is a nightmare of some sick man's fevered imagination, spewing skewed and warped knowledge & philosophy of diplomacy that was undoubtedly regurgitated by a child's interpretation of Machiavelli's *Prince*. Sort of the perfect entertainment for a psychopath...America. The key art for Season 4 of *Game of Thrones* touts the tag line: All Men Must Die. Charming.

People get all wrapped up in the fantasy world of *Game of Thrones*, but lord forbid they have to face the reality of their own history: Crimes against humanity that happened not too long ago. Slavery, civil rights abuses, Native American genocide, and ongoing gun violence. So instead of trying to facilitate progress they numb themselves with brutal fiction. Give the psychopathic baby a sword and a bottle of blood to suck on for an hour every week. It almost seems these shows are designed with the explicit purpose to divorce the audience from any type of benevolent reality.

These shows that are so popular posit the fact that mankind is brutal and the only way to survive is to show no mercy towards your fellow man. Kindness is a weakness and butchering your fellow man is a virtue. The exact opposite of what mankind desperately needs now. There is something good in man, a kindness that is currently being suppressed by many factors. Pop Culture is the glue that holds the rickety suppression together. The *Game of Thrones* fantasy celebrates a mythical middle ages...a sort of Dark Age devoid of art and meaningful culture. And modern day audiences love it. The episodes are rife with nudity and violence, everything to appeal to every man's base instincts...equating sex with violence where true love is an arrow in the back. Throw in torture, cold-blooded killings, and some T&A for good measure. It's *Lord of the Rings* for the large demographic of Old White Men working shitty jobs and trapped in even shittier marriages. How many men have boned their wives then drifted off into sleep dreaming of dragons?

Roman Polanski does both. The possum-faced director, who possesses a slimy countenance only a blind mother could love, prefers fornicating with passed out victims so much he invested half his wealth in the organic mannequin industry. He recently lamented the fact that offering flowers to a lady has become indecent. Slippin' mickeys make much better presents when given as surprises. Polanski understandably longs for the good ol' days of raping on the first date. Sodomizing a thirteen year old isn't real rape according to his Hollyweird friends.

Even worse than anti-rape laws is Ethnicity...

Black People Scare Peter Jackson

They haunt his dreams and keep him trembling underneath the NZ sheets at night. Don't believe me? Then watch all 3 *Lord of the Rings*. All of the heroic characters are white -- very white, some even with white hair, while the nasty, brutish, evil onslaught is filled with very dark ethnic heathens. Granted, these movies were based on books, but it is Peter Jackson who visually interpreted the evil characters and brought to them to the big screen.

The *Lord of the Rings* franchise was very successful for a myriad of reasons...an overlooked aspect is White Fear. A subconscious (or very conscious for some) xenophobic fear of different ethnic groups encroaching upon white terrain. Whether it's a Black family moving into a suburban neighborhood, or Hispanics becoming the majority in some American cities, White people are scared of changes to their status quo. Thus, the popularity of Lord of the Rings. And the director is all too happy to depict ethnic people as the bogeyman.

Still not convinced? Then please watch *King Kong*...another Peter Jackson directed movie...an ethnic-fear as parable. The white women being snatched by the Big Gorilla.

The natives on a long lost island are the scariest blak people ever brought to the big screen. Now I know Jackson has a team of costume designers, makeup people, and prosthetics experts, but it is ultimately Jackson's vision to portray savages in such shocking fashion. He even admits to getting the idea from reading *National Geographic*. In the book, *The Making of King Kong* by Jenny Wake, Peter Jackson admitted he saw a portrait of a man with "ultradark skin" and bright red eyes and was unsettled by it.

Maoris, Hispanics, Samoans, Indians, and mid-Easterners are all groups that frightener Jackson, but he is absolutely, positively terrified by Black People. Like it or not, filmmakers' obsessions, fears, and loves are depicted in the movies they create. In the horror scripts I write, the villains may consist of a ghost, killer with a knife, werewolves, or a giant spider; but in Peter Jackson's films, the antagonists to be feared usually have black skin.

Ramblins of a Red-Blooded American Man

I was chewing sunflower seeds, kicking rocks alongside a set of train tracks just north of Las Vegas. Trying to clear my mind. The wind was at my back and I almost didn't hear the train behind me.

A whistle rang out right before I stepped out the way. The rushing train blew oven air against my cheek. Thirsty, I took a drink from the brown bag I was holding and watched the graffiti-laced beetle race by. An open door caught my eye. Some Mars-colored man wearing a straw hat gave me a grimace and tossed out a paper airplane.

I ducked on account of instincts. It nearly punctured my right eye, but flew on by. I tracked it to a ditch. It had writing all over it. So I sat down, unfolded the projectile, and read it:

-Tarantino might not be a monkey, but he made a movie that glorifies 'em!
As a Red-Blooded American Man I'm appalled by so much violence directed towards the white man. We built this country by making other people build it for us!
I demand my freedom! My freedom to own guns! My freedom to watch violence! And my freedom to own slaves!
If I wanted to work for a living then I woulda been born black!
Tell that Tarantino feller to come down to Alabama and I'll give him a history lesson he'll never forget.
I'm tuning up my banjo now...Tarantino better start practicing his pig squeal.

-That *Gangster Squad* was a crowd-pleaser at the local Tuscaloosa Cinemark. Me and my local brethren cheered every time someone got gunned down.
Yee-hah!! Those Yankees shore do make some good movies.
I love to watch violent trailers while I swill Busch Lite and watch football. Speaking of violent trailers, it's time I got out the belt and teach the young'uns some manners and not to eat all the Pringles in the doublewide.

-My old great grandpappy would call last year's Golden Globes a Self-Congratulatory Circle Jerk. At least Braveheart was in the front row makin' crazy eyes at all the yellow-belly libs! I taped it for him on our VHS player.

-Woo-hoo, now *Won't Back Down* is an educational movie that I can root for! There's nothing that satisfies a redneck more than bad taste, and this movie has it in spades...though I'd prefer it if Hollywood would stop castin' 'em.
I couldn't wait for another unflattering movie about teachers. Thanks Hollywood for caring about Sandy Hook.
Maybe ya'll can cast that Maggie Gyllensomething in everything! She is the Hollywood authority on the public education system...having spent so much time in it herself.
K'up the good work...maybe you libs aren't so bad afterall...

-*The Last Stand* is my nomination for best movie of 2013!
That Kraut shore knows how to pull the trigger. Who needs Viagra when there's so much bloodshed onscreen?
I just left the Tuscaloosa AMC with lumberjack wood...now it's time to break out the moonspit and call up my cousin for a nite of rip-rompin' billyhopper boogaloo. My only criticism of *the Last Stand* is that not enough Mexicans were gunned down by SchwarzenNazi!
Maybe they can increase the body count for the sequel.

-Melissa McCarthy stole Miss Piggy's identity! Put a lipstick on a hog and it's still a hog...though a good-lookin' one that I wouldn't mind sharin' a bottle of moonspittle with.
Ya'll yellow-belly libs just settle down. I thought this was America -- freedom of speech and all. You PC porkbellys wanta fire a man for pointin' out the elephant in the room?
Guns are bad -- but obesity and diabetes is funny! Something to be snickered at? I American't understand ya'll...

At this point the paper plane had a yellow liquid stain on it that smeared the rest of the writing. And it smelled. Bad. Like he'd been hiding this foul thing in his groin region for the past 600 miles. So I took it home with me...and set it on top of the TV set. It couldn't be any worse than what plays below it.

Love/Hate Relationship

I honestly love movies and try not to criticize a good movie for several reasons. First, there is no such thing as a perfect movie. And second, I do not like being criticized for writing a good script. When writing, or especially acting, you are baring your soul somewhat, and criticism can sting. Movie critics do not contribute any value whatsoever to the arts or to society in general. It's probably the most worthless occupation in the history of mankind (with the exception of a food critic who engages in douchebag pomposity & writes pretentious snobby reviews of foie gras and other horse manure that normal people don't eat). Movie critics just sit on their pretentious asses and sniff at other people's hard work. At the end of the day his or her opinion is no more valid than anyone else's. If you wanted to, you could nitpick any movie to death until it's not enjoyable to watch movies anymore -- which is what most professional critics do.

It is so hard to make a movie. It takes months to write a script. Then preproduction to cast the movie, location scout, etc. Then the actual production commences, which can be a logistical nightmare fraught with unforeseen problems, all the while trying to beat an impossible deadline. Then comes postproduction...a time-consuming haze of editing, scoring, sound design, etc. When factoring in all these variables it's amazing that any good movies are made! So I try to be lenient on any good movie because they entertained me in some way, and when you get down to it, that is what movies are meant to do...though the Great Movie does even more: Inspire and/or investigate the human condition.

But at the same time, if the movie is bad, dumb, glorifies violence, or sends a morally bankrupt message then by all means I criticize it. Unfortunately, the majority of movies that Hollywood produces exhibit some or all of these negative criteria. It is very rare to find a good movie these days. For every dozen bad movies, you may stumble upon a good one. That dismal ratio hurts American culture, and economically speaking, is not a sustainable business model. Common decency is an amoral act in the movie biz. After the Colorado movie theater shooting the movie *Dark Knight Rises* ran in thousands of theaters in all its uncut gory glory. Catwoman's idea of fun is guns and killing. And the other bad girl in the film orders her minions to "kill them all" as they gun down police officers. Two nights after the Martin/Zimmerman verdict, HBO aired the harebrained comedy, *The Watch*. Jonah Hill's character agrees, "I can get behind that."

Hollywood doesn't **care**. There is no sense of responsibility. Only thing that matters to the mice and Rat (Disney) is dollars. Their only "moral" obligation is to make money. No matter the cost. These entities are corporations with claws. And Disney has fangs. *Iron Man 3* grosses $1.2 billion worldwide yet ESPN layoffs

400 employees. And the Rat owns 80% of ESPN. In April 2013 the Rat Studios fired 150 employees even though net profits were up 18% to $5.7 billion.

The Rat is running shit like GM. On 8/25/13 the Vermin made 2 billion dollars at the international box office for the 4th consecutive year, but this year was in record time. By November, Disney broke its 2010 record and banked a profit over $3.8 billion. And we all buy this shit! Disney, Marvel, and Star Wars are all one large rodent. Where's Galactus when you need him to shove a gerbil up the Gere's orifice? Disney Studios have come a long way since Walt's snitching years to the FBI from 1936-1966. Apparently Jews weren't the only loathsome things according to Walt...anything the opposite of fascism was bad.

Studios are corporations. Get that. and get out! Don't pay for stupid movies anymore. And don't let your stupid kids do it either.

Agents are just as bad as the studio moguls, if not worse...My advice: fire 50% of the morons & hacks in Hollywood and integrate new talent immediately. In addition, make having an imagination a prerequisite for holding a job. Most moguls love money more than movies and that's why there is so much shit splattering the screen. The agents sit in their glass towers and have no interest in real stories that matter. Bricks are something their Mexican helpers pile in the backyard, not evolutionary movies of change.

Serious American filmmakers need to bypass the studio system and make their movies independently...be the Underdog versus Money. Everyone loves an underdog.

The Garden is a documentary that motivates me. Gordon Gekko said, "Greed is good." But in real life, greed is a disease. A disease of the human spirit...and it can infect anyone regardless of race, religion, and gender. The afflicted person only cares about how much money & property they can acquire, instead of how much they can help their fellow man. Any aspiring filmmaker should watch *The Garden*. Matta fact, everyone should watch it no matter what they aspire to...so long as those aspirations are not compulsions for cash.

Aspiration Jungle

BLOW is a classic movie that hinted at the filmmaking potential of Ted Demme, who would die soon after directing it. I like everything about this movie, especially its timeless tragic journey of George Jung. It's hard to create empathy for a character that lived so recklessly, but this movie pulled it off by showcasing the damaging effects a criminal lifestyle has on Family...and the damaging effects Family has on an impressionable individual. Family reminds me of a Vietnam song: no one gets out of here alive.

A few years back I met a friend of George Jung...he came over to my house with some racist handyman from Arkansas who was supposed to repair a variety of maladies. Instead, the Razorback brought an 18 pack of MGD that never made it past noon. Soon there was more beer to be drunk, then things got ugly. But before...

The friend of Jung was also named George, a ragged Greek who sniffed every ninety seconds...rubbing his septum, missing the powder monster. He made the mistake of feeding it back in the day, not worrying about its future appetite. Despite the sniffling, he was a nice guy. His stories of Jung, and Anthony Spilotro, and Lefty were all entertaining. And true.

Jung was an ordinary guy who liked to hang out and have a beer...only difference being that Jung's garage was bigger than most people's house. He probably would have never been busted if he didn't let his excessive coke habit spiral out of control. The events depicted in *Blow* were based on fact; Jung was pretty cozy with Pablo Escobar. This is the reason I heard this story. The Greek accompanied Jung to Columbia and met with Escobar, who wanted the Greek to sell coke throughout the country in Greek Delis. The storyteller was content with selling a kilo or two a year to survive and refused the offer. Imagine the fear of saying no to Pablo. He thought he would be killed, but he was Jung's friend and Pablo respected that.

It's true that it takes a certain kind of person to be Boston George, but after conversing with someone who knew Jung, I found it scary that Jung's journey into the drug underworld could be easily duplicated by anyone with a similar temperament. Not saying that I would ever want to be a criminal, but after beating my forehead against the brick wall of filmmaking, making money taking risks that many aspiring filmmakers take for free does hold some appeal. Risking years of your life without a payoff is an artistic sacrifice. Maybe if I wasn't scared of prison, or if I didn't believe that I had the talent to succeed, then I'd consider Jung's path.

Blow is a cautionary tale to people like me who think they are smarter than the system. George Jung is not much different than the average American. The only thing that differentiates him is his life experience growing up, and his lack of fear in pursuing his particular career. Before you criticize a criminal like Jung, dig deep inside yourself and see if there are any of his traits lurking in the inner recesses of your psyche. Maybe the only thing that separates you is fear - or - timidity that passes for good sense.

Speaking of which, I didn't drown the Razorback redneck in my pool...even though I spent a good five minutes in my kitchen contemplating it. The drama started a few minutes before. We were all outside laughing, drinking, and enjoying the Greek's story until the redneck turned ugly. The former drug provider to the Hell's Angels started to make fun of the Greek...and the Greek's downtrodden situation in a mean way...the sort of way scorpions eat each other. Paw around with pinchers, latch on, then sting. Death comes. All at once.

Then the hick would look my way, searching for a smile and finding none. I wanted to end the party but there were buffalo wings on the grill and another 30 cans of the redneck's beer in my fridge.

Then the Razorback disparages the Jew landlord who employs him and houses me, then curses the "Niggers" down the street. After I expressed my disapproval, he spit on the ground and told me to tend my nigger wings on the grill. Which I did. I flipped them. Then walked inside my house. Grabbed my trusty brass knuckles then stepped to the back door. Bout to open it and the Razorback's skull with one nice jab.

But I stopped.

Why? Damn it! I circled the hardwood floor in my kitchen enough times in five minutes to burn a hole. Then I realized that I don't want to be Jung's cellmate.

So I pocketed the brass and grabbed the crate of beers out of the fridge...slammed them outside, next to the poor excuse for a man. Told him it was time to go. We locked eyes and he silently agreed. A slight recognition of being lucky flashed for a second in his pupils...then he grabbed the beers, and walked away, muttering curse words, the Greek nipping at his heals.

Heresy

I confess to having an intense contempt for going to the movies. Sounds crazy, idiotic even, for a screenwriter/filmmaker to hate going to the movies.

Three reasons:
1 - People
2 - Prices
3 - Inferior Product

The main reason to loathe the movie going experience is People: asshole rude idiotic people. If they're not yapping, they're chewing popcorn like a herd of rabid bison. Or tapping they're feet, bumping my chair, or Coughing & Sneezing. Sick bastards infected with the swine flu shouldn't go to the movies in droves. Instead, they should wander into some barren field and fall on pitchforks.

So many ignorant people these days. Not like when I was young and went to the State Theater in Sandusky, Ohio to catch a matinee. There I could sit in the back row and pee on the floor and watch it drizzle down the theater in silence. Now I pay 8 bucks to hear mongoloid commentaries throughout the movie...punctuated by squeals, hocked loogies and hacking.

Most movies released are not worth the money or the trouble. Even the occasional decent one is ruined by the Experience. With the sophisticated home theater technology on the market there is no reason to suffer fools at the cineplex anymore. Grab an affordable fifty-inch 1080p HD widescreen LCD TV, Blu-ray player, and surround system. Throw in the new Xbox system then wait a decade until it's time upgrade.

If you must go to the movie theater then at least time it right in order to sneak into another movie for free. But I recommend signing up for a library card and getting DVDs for free. Let the zombies take over the cineplex...I'd rather reign supreme at home. Grub on some pizza and pound a couple Fat Tires. It's only a matter of time before the studios start concurrently releasing DVDs along with that movie's theatrical release...which is becoming the only smart way to battle piracy.

The last time I went to the movies I felt besieged by heavy-set hyenas with kids. The hillbilly family to my left had their shoes off and rested their bare feet on the seats ahead of them, and the rats to my right devoured popcorn & candy like a bunch of refugees who were never taught how to chew with their mouths closed. And the demographic I despise the most was out in full force -- Women in their late 20's-early 30's who pop out kids with the frequency of an Alien queen. They waltz around with an absurd air of superiority, sporting tight shirts that showcase the potbelly prego look. Why do these hogs with heathens think they're the shit? Wow, they had kids, big deal! How hard is that? Lie on their fat backs, spread their chunky legs wide, wait nine months, and voila, another obnoxious brat.

Spend enough time in a movie theater and you'll be rooting for the Armageddon asteroid.

18.
The Only Honest Movie

is a horror movie.

Making horror movies is the ultimate form of having a sense of humor. Being defiant in the face of Death. Thumbing your nose at the inevitable. Yeah -- everyone dies -- making a horror film is joking about it -- plus you can integrate social satire in the film. Horror movies are an enhanced intense sensation of facing an end that binds everyone in the audience together. Nobody wants to die, and the death metaphor is stalking the characters onscreen, creating instant empathy in us, the audience.

Cling to life Characters that want to live are the first necessary attribute. Faced with death and mortal danger is the only real way to see the true colors of a person. Everything else is talk, and action defines character. We all wonder what we would do in a tense situation, and horror movies are the visceral thrill that helps us appreciate life. It's better to never know evil stalking us...a realization by the end of the movie. Horror makes us all honest.

Horror flicks are reminders that real evil exists in the world -- and it's not always Freddy Krueger or Michael Myers, but sometimes your neighbor! Or yourself. Or something Different... And there is no age limit on evil. And the absolute necessity is to scare.

The art lies in the music. A surreal or moving score matched with visual trepidation is Cinematic. John Carpenter's score for *Halloween* is the prime example. And who can forget the scores for *Phantasm*, *Exorcist*, or *Psycho*? Argento knew that. And...Every time I want to comment on Dario Argento movies, or Vittorio Storaro's cinematography, there is something happening in the world that makes my comments seem trite.

Every day some type of Horror occurs in this country...making the genre closest to Documentary. Gun violence and Newtown are real terrors that I can't forget. Horror movies pale in comparison. Poppin' popcorn in my mouth watching werewolves now seems quite quaint. Man is much more dangerous than vampires and lycanthropes. Real evil has evolved while our mindstate stays the same. We live in a vacuum of selfishness. Clutching pillows to soak up drooling mouths. Apathy is the new Blob. Americans are oblivious to Outside protests throughout the world clamoring for something resembling freedom. Brazilians made their point about the corrupt World Cup spending. They stared down the plastic shields and tear gas with a Purpose. Nobody spoke a word in America -- a nation of nerds -- more concerned with some fictional superhero like Superman on the big screen or Jesus on their cross -- complacent in the fact they are entertained while others partake in a social evolution.

Maybe the zombie movies that we've become familiar with, the walking, talking, texting Dead, soften our hearts to real protests. Fascists behind a shield pointing a gun at a young man are necessary after a decade of zombie propaganda. Anyone with a brain acting abnormal is a target.

And who's the zombie? The man with the shield? Or the one dismissing it so they can eat breakfat with a clear conscience? The hired muscle behind the shield love complacent people. It won't be but a minute 'til they're doing it here again over the Keystone pipeline.

World War Z was termed an "original movie" by the Hollywood press. What was so original about it? Just another zombie movie that made a quarter of a billion dollars for Paramount & Viacom. And the shitty movies spread like the plague to Australia, Korea, and Argentina, among others. Zombies are lucrative. The subgenre used to be subversive like the original *Night of the Living Dead* where the black male character survives the zombies only to be shot by the white posse. Now that posse mentality is in full effect in our era's zombie movies. These flicks woulda played to full houses in Ole Miss during the Freedom Riders hoopla. Any crowd walking down the street that doesn't look like me and wants my brain must be dealt with in an extreme manner. What's ironic is that the zombie movies on the television are really eating the viewer's brain. It's no longer about conformity, but about guns, bullets, more guns, headshots, with a touch of right-wing survivalist paranoia.

The Zombie subgenre is a popular fixture of the post-apocalyptic movie craze. New Testament fantasies realized on-screen. It's almost as if subconsciously our culture has accepted that the world is going to Hell, and instead of trying to fix it, we'd rather fantasize about how it's going to be *after*.

Another apocalyptic subgenre that skews towards doom is the alien movie. Alien Invasion movies are an expression of guilt -- a cinematic metaphor for the plundering the Europeans did to the Americas. A sadomasochistic fantasy about what it would feel like...all in the name of Entertainment.

Actually, I'm a big fan of alien invader movies. That sort of invasion is just what this planet needs -- to thin the herd and help solve the problem of overpopulation. The Human Race has mutated into a viral strain of de-evolving parasites...where the least intelligent have the most kids, thereby diluting the gene pool to the point of creating a race of mongoloid slob-creatures that exploit every available resource on this planet like a pack of rabid cannibals. Survival of the Fittest is now Flourish of the Fattest. An alien invasion may be the only thing that saves the Human Race and the planet.

I watch a lot of horror movies and most of the new ones are lame. I usually mutter while bored, "I've seen the true face of man, and this is supposed to scare me?" The only movies that have scared me in the past decade are *The Strangers*, *The Conjuring*, *The Descent*, *Hostel*, and *High Tension*.

Reality constantly raises the bar. We live in a semi-continuous state of horrors. Movies have become mundane. And what does that say about movies, or, more importantly, us?

Maus

Balance. I keep preaching that the entertainment inhustletry needs balance...in particular the movie biz. And not just a balance of genres, but subject material...

Escapist fare can be fun to watch, but dramatic movies that have the potential to make a positive contribution to mankind should also be produced & distributed on an equal scale. There's plenty of room in the marketplace for both popcorn movies and movies that matter. One such movie that should be made is *Maus*, the Pulitzer prize-winning graphic novel written and illustrated by Art Spiegelman.

Violence runs rampant in our society. Moral values are in decay and communities are crumbling. And Movies are not helping matters. Too often violence is used in movies without regard to how it is digested by the audience. Realistic repercussions and the ramifications of violence are not depicted. Violence is treated as a special effect, a device to elicit an adrenalized response from its salivating audience. This sort of inane violence deadens the audience's empathy for victims of violence. They may not watch *Saw* or *Hostel* and want to cut people up, but they may be less likely to help a victim of crime. Why Care? why? Because movies teach us that violence doesn't really matter.

Most American children get used to violence at a young age by watching cartoons. Whether it's Bugs Bunny outwitting Elmer Fudd with devilish pranks, or the Road Runner making life hell for the Coyote, children are entertained and amused by violence. Animated violence is fun! Violence makes the kids giggle. The *Madagascar* Christmas special even has violent content -- Santa gets shot down, and the head rat chucks acorns at the heads of other rats in order to get on the naughty list. Tis the season...

Now I'm not saying these buffoonish cartoons or animated movies should be outlawed, all I'm asking for is Balance. And that is where *Maus* comes in.

Maus is a story of the author learning about the Holocaust by interviewing his father, who was a survivor. The father's memories are heartbreaking and brutal. Maus should be faithfully adapted into an animated movie...leaving nothing out, especially the violence. The characters in Maus do not get back up after being shot. They are dead...the ultimate consequence of violence. Apathy allowed the Nazis to slaughter innocent people. Nazis were manifested Hate: a tangible form of evil that kills people in Maus...not some theological absurdity residing in a soup-spewing girl. The emotional anvils dropped in this "cartoon" cannot be brushed off...or leave little bumps on the heads of its victims...rather, they tear families apart and kill men, women, and children. Violence is portrayed in a realistic manner in Maus. The victims of the Holocaust can never shake the effects of it. Violence is permanent Injustice.

The reason the movie should be animated is obvious: the Jews in the graphic novel are depicted as mice and the Nazis as cats. This use of simple metaphor would make it palatable to young audiences without being too gruesome.

A child's mind is malleable, free of prejudice & bigotry, violence & hate. These sordid facets of life are taught to children by family members and/or community members. But if children watch Maus at a young age then they would be more likely to empathize with people different from themselves. And that is the key: turn apathy into empathy.

If violence has no repercussions in movies then why should someone care if it happens to people around them? Watching a movie like *Pirates of the Caribbean* is such a mind-numbing asinine experience because there are countless sword fights with nary a consequence...half of the combatants are already dead! Sort of like the brain cells that enjoy this type of entertainment.

Maus is a story based on truth...a factual document of evil that really happened. It pulls no punches, and neither should the movie...thus instilling a more humanistic worldview in its intended audience: Children. (Though I think adults would be equally affected by this tale. I know I was)

We as a people need to treat each other with civility and respect. Shrug off ignorance, complacency, and apathy. Care about our communities and environment. Movies like Maus could help spur this positive change. The horrible dark chapter in history known as the Holocaust happened less than eighty years ago. Yet most children in America are ignorant of this event. Maus would help rectify this ignorance by presenting a creative historical document in an entertainment venue. The Holocaust was an Evil event perpetrated by men. Evil is not a fictional character running around with a chainsaw and hockey mask. Evil is what happens when humanity no longer has the ability to empathize.

19.
Exploitative Documents

I love documentaries, especially the ones that explore important issues and exotic locales. Unlike many of the fictional movies released theatrically today, documentaries have the power to entertain and provoke discussion & debate. Some of my favorite movies are documentaries: Michael Moore's *Bowling for Columbine* and *Fahrenheit 9/11* are a couple.

But -- there is a subgenre of the documentary industry that is based on exploitation. This greasy undercurrent of slime is ran by hacks who exploit other people's pain for selfish gain... these filmmakers are disguised as "blanket" liberals. It's easy to be liberal when a person lives under a blanket of ideology. A Blanket liberal lives in a bubble where nothing affects them, ensuring they are able to document/exploit their subjects through a camera lens. Problems are plots without hopes of a cure. Sick Entertainment made under the auspices of art.

This type of filmmaker Exploits other people's pain as a device to make a movie. Sundance, PBS, it doesn't matter, so long as the maudlin masterpiece is distributed. They are the documentary paparazzi. Pain is used as a narrative device to elicit sympathy. Poverty, AIDS, and Cancer are all fair game. Especially cancer. And if pain depicted onscreen isn't entertaining enough then these filmmakers will resort to snorting asbestos and drinking formaldehyde in order to get cancer themselves. It will make a good story at Sundance: a documentary about cancer by a filmmaker with cancer. But the only malignant tumor that the filmmaker possesses is extremely bad taste.

These career filmmakers don't even consider it exploitation because they haven't had a real job in decades; expert game players who soak up state grants and abuse migrant workers for the sheer fun of it. The people who do the real work on a movie -- the gaffer, grips, PA's -- are the ones who get the least amount of credit. The glory hounds are usually college professors who encourage their students to work for free, especially if they want to curry favor and be selected to direct their own student films: a process in full bloom at Wright State University, which is strategically located next to Dayton, the armpit of Ohio.

The small film department is hidden away on campus in a basement corridor like a mongoloid stepchild and is overseen by a race of humanoid possums who fancy themselves liberals yet conduct business in Nixonian fashion. This cabal has been surreptitiously engaged in a brutal white slavery ring for decades while simultaneously squeezing the tuition tit of strung-out college students. I made the mistake of attending their film school, leapt through hoops, petitioned my case, and all for the dishonor of directing a documentary as a class assignment. I had empathy for my subject, but was the process patronizing? I don't think so because I was a person who could relate to my subject. But what if my patronizing documentary was intrusive only for ratings? What if my false empathy was for Sundance?

Some would call that behavior disgusting... like jerking off in your college roommate's facial cream for kicks then watching him unknowingly apply it the next day, and laugh when it hardened on his face like a crusty Michael Myers mask. Only difference is that a nice hot shower will wash away bodily fluids, but nothing will wipe away the soul-sucking sting of exploitation.

I could sense impending exploitation. It's like a fuzzy feeling tingling on the edges of your fingers after shuffling across the carpeted floor and you're just about to flick on the light switch. I got that feeling back when I was in film school and it was the all-mighty junior film selection process. I proposed several viable film projects to my instructor and the only one the dragon-breathed bastard responded to was a documentary idea. My aspiration was to direct a fictional film as I was burnt out with documentaries as I had just done a couple the previous quarter. My professor insisted on the proposed documentary -- my Aunt's factory was closing down and I would document how that event affected people.

Then I felt the tingling. Why should I showcase those damaged people just so I can get a good grade and appease my prick of a professor? That's when I decided to do a fictional narrative based on my personal experiences...but my professor told me that I would fail. According to him, it's okay to exploit other people's lives, but don't try to make a movie based on my own life.

I disagree with that philosophy. Instead of living life and making movies, these Wright State fucks sit like snails and exploit the tragedies of others. They can't create so they extricate misfortune.

Slime trails are measures of accomplishments.

So I dropped out. School started to be suffocating and I dreaded having to attend class in such a venomous snakepit. Hollywood might be no different, but at least I don't have to pay tuition to be flogged. And I don't have to exploit documents.

WSU FILM PROGRAM:

1. An institution that breeds subservient weasels that are taught to conform and strive for mediocrity.
2. A waste of time and/or money.
3. An ass-kissing contest blind to talent or merit.

20.
You're Only Friend

The meek shall inherit the Earth.
Maybe so
But that's only because the Bold inhabit the stars!

You might hear King Crimson blaring out of my house all hours of the night. If so, don't pay it any mind; I'm just chipping away at a script, sipping a Pabst.

You might even see me in the front yard, chilling in my skivvies. Or doing naked wind sprints up and down the street. If so, don't worry...I'm just working on my physical fitness. The desert heat in the summertime forces me to exercise at night in my birthday suit. Silently performing nude jumping jacks in the front yard with the sprinklers running is a seemingly innocuous activity, but add in the intense King Crimson guitar riffs rising & falling with an ever-changing tempo gives the whole scene a sinister vibe. Just to add atmosphere I like to have a strobe light flashing through the front windows.

Music is the accompaniment to life that gives the whole charade meaning.
Music is the lifeblood of existence. Without it, what's the point?

At the very least, Music might just be the most enjoyable aspect of life (besides nobbers...and the best music to get a nobber to is, you guessed it, King Crimson. So kick back, crack open a quart of Pabst Blue Ribbon, and enjoy yourself).

David Lee Roth believed in keeping the flaws/inaccuracies of a recording intact when making an album. He believed that process is when Rock is at its best. It shouldn't be perfect. Life isn't either...but add the two together and that's about as perfect a feeling a person will experience.

I'm a fan of phallic symbols and playing the guitar just might be the best job in the world. John Lee Hooker must've had indestructible game back in the day with pickup lines like, "you got dimples in your jowls." If I say that to my wife, I'm not gettin' any ass for a week. Only a guitar player can get away with that phrase.

I try to listen to a new album every day. Just yesterday I listened to Jimi Hendrix, Warren Zevon, Incubus, Jethro Tull, The Doors, Bob Dylan, Snoop Lion, and

Nirvana. I must've played "Where did you Sleep last night?" a dozen times. I never want to be the guy singing that song...I'd rather be the muse to the muse.

Even better than new albums are old albums, trusted friends that provide solace no matter what. Music doesn't ask questions. Doesn't pry. Doesn't ask why? A really good album just makes you feel better. The songs may not provide a lesson to life, but they at least provide comfort. Underlined by a great singer that has style. For example, Bob Seger's voice is like an old dusty book full of amusement a person wanders upon in a forgotten attic. Lucky to hear it.

Music is meant to be shared. The soul of an artist touches other people, letting them know they are not alone. Primal needs, feelings, emotions, aspirations, and fears are all real. Important yet esoteric, these Human Realities are grappled with and explored through art. The immediate art is Music. A Heightened Rush pumped straight to the brain. Psychic energy manifested in a real form for the enjoyment of others. A sense of community shared through ear canals. As a favor to my neighbors I installed a pair of 15-inch Cerwin Vega subwoofers in my car, and roll up & down the block blaring Led Zeppelin's "The Ocean" at 3 am in the morning at least twice a week. It's my civic duty.

"How wonderful life is, while you're in the world."

I had free tickets to an Elton John/Billy Joel tribute concert at Suncoast Casino so I drank a twelver of Heinekens and went with the intent to cause mayhem in the midst of an elderly demographic. But two older ladies sitting next to me gave me pause. They had kind smiles and laughed at a corny joke I cracked about owning a honky cat. And they were both in love with each other and seemed completely happy with life. They had found peace & happiness. And it was catching. I sat content and watched the concert; realizing brief moments of bliss are enough to make it through.

Music is a high that can be tapped into every day. The art has a power to cement memories forever. Hear a favorite childhood song and certain sensations are instantly remembered. Smells, colors, and situations. A couple of kids dancing on the front porch to Weird Al Yankovic's "Who's Fat" while passing cars honk their horns in approval. Driving into Windsor for the first time with a pocket full of money to gamble, listening to Phil Collins "In the Air Tonight." Waking up to a Sunday breakfast of eggs & bacon my Mom cooked while Journey drifted out of the stereo.

Music can instigate the truth about life: Everyday is a Poem

...recognized or not. The Rolling Stones song "Blinded by Rainbows" came on the radio as I was driving on the east side of Las Vegas...somewhere around Maryland Pkwy & Desert Inn, and it was the perfect song for the moment -- watching the tumbleweeds and dust swirl around...old men sitting by the side of the road, their faces etched by the harsh sunshine of winter. A sense of desperation pervaded the area. Then I turned west and drove home -- admiring the clouds rolling over the mountains. The sun peeked out for a second -- glowing against the maroon mountainside, and then was gone. A fitting metaphor for life.

True art is the distillation of the artist's soul into their work. Music is a teacup that captures it. Let it spill out, and share it every day.

I really think Jimi Hendrix hated to end a song because his entire soul was invested into each song, every time: The epitome of living in the moment, and expressing it.

And who wants to see that end?

Watching Jimi Hendrix perform "Voodoo Child" is a treat. A gift to be given to children so they can grow older with taste. Any parent who buys their child a Justin Bieber cd is guilty of abuse and boosting the popularity of eugenics. Instead of Barney, give youngsters *The Song Remains the Same* blu-rays. Get the Led out!

In the 60's & 70's, Music was just as important as the writers and protesters. Now it's the great Pacifier. The tinny induction to a rat race that no one wins but the hogs that own the country.

Music is a craft that requires dedication. Not an act used to exploit ignorance. If it were then I would start a rock band and name it Drunken Toddlers. I already have a few songs written:

  -Rattlesnakes, Scorpions, and Venomous Spiders
-HonkeyBreath
-Shakin' like a Dog shittin' Peach Pits
-She's Got a Shovel-Tooth Smile
-Bi-Polar Bears

Instead, I'll stick to being a true fan of the art form. A man may not have limitations per say, but being a master craftsman requires more than mere predilection.

I contend that the Rolling Stones album *Sticky Fingers* is one of the best rock albums of all-time. There are at least three songs that are classics, "Dead Flowers" probably the best. Another great rock album is Van Halen's self-titled debut album. Listening to it will soothe a writer's mind all hours of the day. Or at least provide the necessary inspiration to seek the truth.

Truth. A rare commodity dressed up and forgotten like ET in a kid's closet. Something we think is cute and try to hide. The truth is, most acts gracing the billboard charts these days lack anything resembling truth, artistry, or courage.

It's rare when an artist has all three. John Lennon had the world in his palm and realized he had a conscience. So he moved to America during the Mess...and made a difference. And was shot later. He met a most common American end.

I identify with Lennon not because I share his talent, but because I share his humanity. Listen to his song "Watching the Wheels" and think:

Maybe America is a rabid beast that incites it ticks to destroy the few brilliant fleas residing in the fur of its reality.
or
(if that's too hippy for ya)

Maybe America is a psychopathic country prone to brutal outbursts of violence,
punctuated by cries of patriotism & protest,
then murmurs of sorrow and whispers of conformity
or

Maybe America is still a work in progress...
where the citizens will one day wake up and care about each other as much as they care about reality shows and fast food
or

Maybe America was the Robin Hood
that mutated into the neighborhood bully...
quick to spew Agent Orange and drones to get what it wants
or

Maybe America is stunted from its rapid growth,
and the brains will catch up to pubescent behavior and change it
or

Maybe America can be the best country in the world...
one day

or

Maybe I'm drunk...
I was wish that was the case...of Pabst.

   What many hacks forget is that materialistic BS is finite, but the only thing that truly lasts is Memory. And John Lennon is immortal.
   The reason certain artists are remembered is because they stood for something. Justin Bieber will be forgotten in a Milli Vanilli hiccup, but John Lennon is still important. Lennon's music had a certain truth to it. A Man of his Time and all time.

   An important artist is that rare intelligent whirlwind that represents righteous rage against injustice. These Inspirations are generational and usually killed before they reach full potential.
   2Pac was the evolution of Angst -- a byproduct of the assassinations of JFK, MLK, RFK, and Malcolm X -- the child of a repressed revolution. MLK preached nonviolence. Gandhi did the same. And both met a similar fate. So what's a young man like 2Pac to think? After all, he was named after a South American Revolutionary that was brutally silenced.
   Nihilism is the only avenue for most people...but 2Pac held out hope 'til he died... Optimism was his Freedom.
   The last pic of Pac was him peering out of the car that was about to drive him to the grave. He had a heartbreaking look in his eyes. So tired, a bit sad, and regret maybe. Tupac could have been anything...he was so talented and charismatic. He took a road that led to that pic. And that road is hard to let go...addictions: fame, women, alcohol, drugs, and the most devastating, bravado. And I'm not judging him. He's my favorite hip-hop artist.
   After prison he fell into a pseudo-gangster lifestyle. He was an artist, but imprisoned desperation hurts. So Pac portrayed a gangster better than DeNiro ever could...and it cost Pac his life.
   Sometimes I think, and wrongly so, that John Dillinger and 2Pac were the same souls born in different times and different bodies. Organic Mumbai Kush has this effect on my brain. I take another puff and admire their brazen rebellious natures.
   So I blaze another one while jamming Pac's song "Krazy" -- the one lyric that sticks out: "You ain't got to be in jail to be doing time."
   There are lost souls in prison, but even more working demeaning jobs that they hate. A prisoner of what? Expectation? Conformity? Like a Papa Roach lyric: "the possessions you have start possessing you."
   Life is too short to deal with forty hours a week of misery.

I wonder what great things Tupac could have accomplished if he had the chance to grow up. Maybe he'd devote himself to filmmaking and been a great writer/actor/producer/director. Or he'd be involved in politics and be the mayor of Oakland.

"How Do You Want It?"

Bill Clinton has proven that no man or woman is fit to lead until they've spent an afternoon in a strip club...also known as the Oval Office. Might be crass and offensive to some, but if I ever ran for election then strip clubs would be my official campaign offices throughout the country. The best song to get a lap dance to: "In A Gadda Da Vida." Might as well get your money's worth.

I'm not a chauvinistic pig. Overally, women are just as smart as men, excluding the genetically defective Palin and Bachman...and most white women residing in the confederate South. Their crossburning-breeding practices have produced an evil sort of insolent pig who derives satisfaction from lynching black men like Emmett Till. Benevolence has been bred out.

I used to naively think that if more women were in positions of power then the world would be a better place...but then realized women are no different than men. No worse, no better. And mothers are wild cards. The pain of childbirth can create either Empathy or Hate. The blood countess of Bathory enjoyed a sadistic lifestyle. Would southern Confederate women be any different given the chance? The female Hitler could be waxing her mustache in some small Texas town as I write this.

Megalomania exists inside every one of us in varying quantities. Everybody has to be perfect except for Me. This sort of unchecked hypocritical sanctimonious attitude breeds cult leaders and demagogues who peddle ethnic cleansing & genocide.

What gives a person empathy, and what makes a person cruel?

Not even fifty years ago black people were sprayed with fire hoses in the south...and Vietnamese people were being bombed with heavy ordinance that made other people rich. Not even ten years ago Iraq was bombed for oil. Why? God is not the reason I believe in doing good. And the Devil didn't create GW Bush. The only fictional demons are the ones Hollywood peddles to the peanut gallery starring Bruce Willis. The scales of justice are about as fake and distorted as the American legal system, but what cosmic force doles out the imbalance of Bad and Good? And why are the good ones always struggling? Only the Strong survive, but only the rich prosper. And only the rich hold power. For now...

An evolution is coming and They don't even know it. Too busy checking balance sheets and burying money. And it won't be Che Guevara leading the charge, but collective conscience. This book is just another rumble to build the wave... not just a weak wash that recedes, but a tsunami that changes everything.

Author's note: *Just watched the Woodstock concert movie -- incredible footage & amazing bands. And an interview with one of the promoters really resonated with me: "It doesn't have to do with money or tangible things."*

Of course this man was a bit wasted, but that's when the truth comes out.

Las Vegas is a different town. A big loud drum that beats for a buck. A different ethos. Life is Beautiful...if you have at least $170 to gain entry. Chefs, music, and booze to those who can afford it. And so life is beautiful to the new Yuppie, the Hipster. A mass of self-entitled bores wearing bowler hats and skinny jeans too busy texting to sing along or dance to the music.

Life is Beautiful, so long as you can afford it.

The pretty people will salivate over the Killers.
I'd rather be ugly.

21.
Atmospheric Skull Sodomy

I grew up wearing fresh hip-hop gear, not because I was hip & cool, but because my Mom had great fashion sense. She isn't rich, just a generous letter carrier who worked so hard lugging around a fifty pound bag of mail for decades she was forced to have two hip replacements. And she never listened to rap, but she still surprised me with birthday & X-mas gifts of Nike Airs, Jordans, shell-toed Adidas w/carpet stripes, and a triple fat goose jacket my freshmen year in high school. The only people wearing triple fats were a handful of cool black kids, and me. Maybe that's the reason preppy white kids disliked me...they smirked at me with an intestinal sort of hate that they didn't quite understand but just knew that I was Wrong and their hate was Right.

Hip-hop music was my sanctuary those horrendous high school years. 2Pac, Digital Underground, NWA, Run DMC, Geto Boyz, and many others were my constant Walkman companions. Eazy E was a legend because he was honest. He had an attitude, personality, and a cultivated identity built from observation that culminated in the Ice Cube-written classic "Boyz-N-The-Hood".

"Don't quote me, boy, 'cause I ain't said shit."

Hip-Hop had many flavors back then...a spectrum of styles and attitudes. Special Ed, Das EFX, Brand Nubian, Ice T, Paris, KRS-One, and Slick Rick were some of the personalities dotting the auditory landscape. Then Capitalism took over...where the main aim in life became owning a thousand dollar suit.

Now I never buy a rap cd. I remember going to Sam Goodies and buying EPMD and Too Short tapes. And if I didn't have any money then I stole MC Breed and Spice 1 albums. Wear a black Chicago Bulls jacket with the razor blade hidden up the sleeve. Make one slice, and bam, the cassette tape is stolen. Leave the lil' white alarm strip on the carpet. Stealing was my hobby back then and listening to rap music was a passion.

Poetic wordplay, rebellion, sex...all one big middle finger to authority & mortality. The perfect soundtrack to youth.

The music stayed with me through the college years. I introduced E-40, Wu-Tang, Jay-Z, and Bone to the Immoral Towers at Ohio State. Wherever I went I had hip-hop with me. Columbus, Sandusky, Dayton, then Manassas, then Philly for a week, then back to VA then back to Dayton, then to Las Vegas. The music travels.

I even wrote and recorded hip-hop songs...the art had seeped into my bone marrow. Reckless Youth was something to be celebrated. And nobody got hurt...for the most part. Property damage doesn't count. Possessions can be replaced and it was my moral imperative back then to teach that lesson to people who could afford to learn.

The only thing I regret was breaking a certain car window trying to steal a radio, only to find a factory deck...and to later find out at the police station that it was some young woman's car who was just trying to make a living working at the mall. I paid to replace the window...and vacuumed the car in shame. That was the same night I got sucker punched and kicked out of the Erie County Fair.

Now I'm living Better Days, and realizing life isn't about fancy cars, jewelry, or new clothes. It's about being happy, chilling with fam & friends, and *sharing* good times. Making the world better.

The older I get, the more I recognize how fucked up I was back then, and how fucked up our society is now. Rappers iced-out, driving hot rods with 25 inch rims, packin' heat, and glorifying murdering their brethren.

Back in my ignorance, I bought diamond earrings -- a karat in each lobe. Stupid. The most valuable jewels in the world are the words you speak to another human being, not some bullshit you put in your ears or wear around your neck. Thomas More wrote in *Utopia* that jewels are worn by children who finally give them up as they mature, and slavery is reserved for criminals who are weighed down by chains made out of gold.

I finally realized that my ignorance aided the exploitation of Africa. Rockin' a gold chain & ice in my lobes was a materialistic status symbol that signified I was a dumbass. Even if my jewelry didn't come from a murderous regime in Africa, my vanity still enriched another man raping the Earth. The Fipkes swill Capirinhas like a pack of pigs at strip clubs off that blingo bingo.

Those diamonds just don't wash ashore and happy kids pick them off the beach. Nope. Transnational corporations that make Nazis look timid travel to countries, set up shop like Spanish Conquistadors, and do whatever it takes to get what they want. Start wars. Bribe the government. Enslave the populace. The locals are just tools to be used. It makes it more palatable to board members that the locals' skin color is different and darker. Shee-it, the mining companies in Nevada have low taxation laws written into the state constitution, what the fuck you think they do in Africa? Or South America? Or Asia? Funnel blood diamonds to the sheep and have them pay interest on the marked up rocks. Lev Leviev & Africa Israel made a billion dollars exploiting war-torn Angola. That's a lot of greenbacks speckled with red. Good ol' Lev used some of the plunder to buy NYC landmarks like the old

NY Times building. War profits are diamonds that turn to condos. Lev is just one billionaire making bucks off the black backs of Africans. And the severed limbs of children. An African black life is worth maybe one penny to the diamond profiteers.

And maybe less to the American hip-hop idiots rockin' ice and gold. Is this excessive flaunting of jewels some sort of ironic payback to the Africans who sold their ancestors to slave traders? Or just brainwashed assholes hypnotized by the soul-sucking appeal of Capitalism? A black man's community is to be exploited, not to be uplifted. A diamond or shoe made in Bangladesh is worth more than another life.

An entire people have been tricked. Chuck D said it best: "History is His-story." Your American ancestors went through Hell to get equal rights and it wasn't for capitalistic bullshit that instigates gang warfare over turf. And you were partially tricked by your own people. Jay-Z, P Diddy, and other asswipes who pray to Benjamin Franklin...and Mr. Franklin was an Atheist. So fuck off.

Leaders are in short supply these days. A leader uplifts everyone else. Puffy ran Bad Boy, and the only person who profited was him. What happened to Biggy Smalls? Or G Dep? Or Loon? Even Lil' Kim served time. Puff's leadership skills rival that of Frogger crossing I-95...only he had someone else do it for him and reaped the lily-padded benefits. Suge was no better. Maybe worse.

Rotten sewer water under the bridge

And roaring over the bridge is some souped-up muscle car piloted by some brain-dead rapper. Burning fuel at 12 miles per gallon if they're lucky. Stunting is great, but war is bad. But why do you think America is bombing the Middle East? And what did those American soldiers die for? Your gas, ya stupid louse! Just so you can look cool and rap about being so rich. TI is one such idiot. Dude saw his boy gunned down on 75 South outside of Cincy yet still raps about guns and being a gangster. Boy, talk about being dumpster dumb. Heavy is the head? Why? Nothing's in it!

I'll drive any little car if it would save one soldier's life. I don't need a car to make me cool. I'll roll a POS to the club, step out, and be cool because I am...not because of what I drive. Honestly, I couldn't give a flying feces if I'm considered cool. I'm happy, that's all that counts. A car won't make me more so. Automobiles serve a purpose, not masters to be served. Work shitty jobs just to afford an SUV? No thanks. A fact of life is that anyone who drives a Hummer is a Cunt.

A One billion dollar cleanup in Nigeria goes on while Amerikans stunt. Who's laughing now? Let's ball 'til we fall and get high 'til Africa dies. Shell shits on

African citizens for 50 years. And Black Americans have diarrhea...a byproduct of car fascination and fuel consumption. Fuck the darkies says Shell, and Blak Amerikans agree.

Black Americans have no problem killing each other. A dark Adams apple is to be sliced. Africa is a litter box for Heathcliff. And community is clientele. The man who looks like me is somebody I don't like, so it's easy to exploit him. The mirror is my enemy.

Why?

A substantial percentage of crime committed in cities is the result of two decades of rap music glorifying violence and crass commercialism. Unlike Talib Kweli, I believe that rap lyrics are more a cause than a symptom. If all a young person hears are violent tales & braggadocio lyrics about excessive wealth then that young person will crave that...and the reality is that not everyone is gonna be wealthy, thereby creating a psychosis in that young person. Rap music breeds egocentric sociopaths with no respect for community. Young people, whose minds are impressionable, have their values perverted by this nonsense music. At the very least, this sort of music degrades American culture, and in turn, transmits globally like a virus.

Jay-Z is damn near fifty and rocking Slick Rick chains. Just another puffy-faced prick whose brain was corroded by drinking too much sewer water. He was the brain behind Beyonce lip-synching Obama's inauguration...and the horse-haired hurricane blew the electric grid at the Super Bowl last year with her Nano-tech girdle keeping everything in its place. It takes a crew of hundreds to make sure the lips match up with the karaoke. Shake it, fake scream it, and be barely talented. Bunch of horseshit that rivals the Lehman Bros routine. Jay-Z's kid will never be Trayvon because the kid will grow up in private school and learn how to exploit Trayvon. Jay-Z is not progressive. He's a black Mitt Romney that knows the dope game. But unable to change and evolutionize the game. A selfish little boy in a man's body. That's why there's a Z in his name and not an X.

Reasonable Doubt was a classic, and the *Blueprint* was even better. The rest of his catalog is filler. I might bump *The Holy Grail* while on a beer run to buy a case of Hamm's just for irony. A polite way to define Jay-Z would be to label him a dichotomy. Though any man who wears a Che shirt rapping about materialistic bullshit is obviously insane and/or Ignorant. Jay-Z supported prejudice companies like Cristal and Barneys. He gave love to companies that hate his own race. The epitome of self-hate. What do you call that type of hater?

Back in 1994 the Coup made a song called "Pimps" that satirized Rockefeller and Getty. Then, a couple decades later, Jay-Z and Kanye *became* that satire...much to the chagrin of the black community. Kids now grow up believing their bullshit and Jay-Z profits from this un-ironic sham.

His blubbery boy Rick Ross, another fat fake, rapped about date rape. Any man who rapes a woman should have his penis chopped off and be forced to eat it. I'm all for civilized society, but there's nothing civilized about rape, and the penalty should be just as savage as the crime.

Kanye cries about bumping up against a glass ceiling of fashion...and above him are snooty white rich people dancing to his music. While below him, on real Earth, reside his people desperately needing direction and help. Yet he wants to yap about Fendi & leather jogging pants. What about Chi-town gun violence? "Bush doesn't care about black people." Does Kanye?

His idea of helping is sewing a Confederate symbol on his clothes. Southern white slobs in rocking chairs are smiling right now thinking, "That nigra is okay."

All these mentally challenged brainfarts flourished because Pac's demise left a vacuum and scum infiltrated it. Some people are just happy havin' pussy on the couch. And that's all they know.

I love Hunter Thompson, but I hate guns. Why can't rappers love 2Pac, and hate guns?

Tarantino played a 2Pac song during the big shootout in *Django*, even though Pac was gunned down on Koval and died days later. The only life the queef-faced Tarantino has seen is the b-flicks on a movie screen. He has nothing to say... but trivial comments on pop culture. And both are now done. He is done. He may hang around, but unless dude progresses then he's a *Heaven's Gate* waiting to happen. The American public is not a young sparrow...regurgitation is repulsive.

The rap game is like the Game's newest album: No progression. No evolution. Just amplified ignorance with percussion. Every other rhyme ends with the exanimate term "Nigga." A word that is supposed to "empower" the user while resuscitating racism to be used interracially.

"Nigga" perpetuates ignorance and a Stereotype. Other white people hear black people say that word and think, "Hey, if they call each other niggas, then they must be niggas." Riley Cooper would agree.

Nigga keeps an ugly legacy of hate & racism alive. The word still has power or else black people wouldn't get mad when white people use it.

Why use the word freely then get mad when someone else tries to treat you like one? Nigga is a horrible word and it's time to let it die. You don't hear other ethnic groups calling themselves racial slurs. What up, my slope? Hey Spic, pass me the wire cutters. This Gook is trippin'!

All horrible words, but none worse than nigga. That word is almost unprintable because of the psychic damage it has done to a generation. Rationalizing hypocrisy is heavy duty, straining the medulla oblongata 'til it snaps, but the solution is simple. Whatever happened to "What up, man?"...Or if you want to signify your ethnic pride, "What's going on, Black Man?"

Because a nigga is not a man to the masses. Just an ugly term for a lower class of people to be beaten, repressed, and treated like scum. Privatized prisons are printing money because of the term.

A man is a man, no matter the color. A man should be spoken to like a man, not like a second-class citizen or slave. Respect is Respect. Love is Love.

The best revolution of all is a revolution of the mind. And one of the ways a mind communicates to other minds is language. Learn that, and you have keys to the palace.

Author's note: *You can't hang back in the shadows wanting to be the sun. You have to become the Sun.*

And the only way is to burn off enough fuel to illuminate the world around you.

Where do suns get their fuel? From inside. Within. No one gives it to them.

Use your spirit, and if you're like me, you were born with a surplus and have enough fuel to share for a lifetime.

Rap Lyrics

Rap Lyrics used to be the profane poetry of the proletariat.

Now, lyrics idolize money, but screw that, every writer should write rap lyrics about what irritates them.

Iron Man 3 rocked it? Stop it,
I'll put Squeaky Fromme in your closet,
on Xmas eve, instead of cookies,
chew on my nuts like I'm shittin' Ghoulies,
Belching better lyrics than Kanye, come out my ass when I sit on the john, hey,
Happy Birthday, let me wrap this
with a cactus, sit it where you shit,
your practice like a mattress, get paid for movin' wrists,
3 act structure, a huckster,
gettin' paid juicin' youngsters,
fill in the bl_anks,
cookie cutters,
Every script similar, have 2 good lines & destruction
War, Violence, and Explosions,
this combo got minds erodin'
An industry of rodents chewin' cheese
These movies more like propaganda for Nazis,
Who won WW 2 or Z?,
we watch Fritz Lang's nightmares in 3D
My Metropolis is swallowed in your esophagus,
Intellect awareness higher than a Rasta spliff...

22.
Murderer's Row

The NFL is the celebration of an American Fantasy dreamed up by rich white men (alright then) who are the moral descendants of southern slave owners. Art Model was no different than Jefferson Davis. Instead of whipping naked black men and making them pick cotton for free, these Owners dress up muscular mahogany specimens in Milli Vanilli biker shorts and force them to run 40's for homoerotic entertainment.

Damn that Abraham Lincoln!

Owner's philosophy: Let the Darkys play sports -- there's no power in that. Besides, they'll just squander their salaries away while stimulating the economy in the process.

Despite the vitriol, the National Foosball League is a good idea. The Blacks in Amerika are still broke, but at least they're entertained by athletes with the same skin color. Pacified to the point where they'd rather shoot each other over pairs of Air Jordans than work for equality.

And the Saltines go absolutely batshit crazy rooting for their respective plantations. Our slaves are better than yours! Fuck the Environment, Wars, Wall Street, and anything Else that matters. Go Bears!

Buy the ticket & a jersey, and take the ride.

Get money, get money, get money, get money, motherfucker, get money!
   An anthem found in a Jeezy song, a mantra for the poor and downtrodden. Beat into their heads like a drum by their peers. Superficial supermen with Rolexes and white Tees. Say you live in a shack with your pappy and make 300 bucks a week; it might be cool to see someone on TV who looks like you who makes 300 G'z a week and wears a diamond watch. But you can't rap…you can't write or flow, but

you can run a 4.4 40 and catch the pigskin with no problem. Eazy Street is your destination.

But what if you're paid and cock deez? The American Dream is boring. So what do you do for kicks?

I wanted to know so I spent a day with the NFL's most dangerous.

A '64 Chevy Impala with the wood grain steering wheel was rented for this rare occasion. Mike Vick drove under the influence of a motley crue of Quaaludes, and Ben Rotgut rode shotgun…he couldn't be trusted with wood. Two twelve-inch subwoofers pounded against the back seat, vibrating the backs of Marvin Harrison, Ray Lewis, and Pacman Jones. The only person smiling was in the trunk, Rae Carruth, clutching an Uzi and sucking a pacifier.

Vick kept making bets on how many animals he could run over, and drunken-ass Ben kept calling and kept losing. A hundred a Rottweiler here, two hundred a Pekinese there. The Impala never did less than 90 MPH down the highway. Pacman loved throwing dollar bills out the back window, exclaiming, "we're ahead of the rain."

A mile past El Paso is when the journey turned bumpier than Terrell Suggs' chin. Ben kept telling Vick that his dark skin was ravenous. Whatever that meant. Vick was cool 'til Ben pulled out his pecker. Vick jerked to the side of the road. Looked at Ben. Not knowing what to do…yeah, Vick has herpes, but it's one thing to give it to a groupie, but plain wrong to give it to another Pro Bowl QB.

Before Vick could decide, two gunshots rang out: head shots both. Marvin Harrison smoked Vick and Rotgut point blank. Execution style.

Harrison is one ruthless bug-eyed bastard. He'd rather smoke somebody than catch spirals. I was terrified. A witness. But he liked me. (Later on Harrison told me he had a propensity to shove Lincoln Logs into his orifices. He didn't know why…it was funny. Even to this day he carries around a Lego in his asscrack.) Happy we shared a moment he ruffled my hair then got out the car.

Harrison tossed out the two overrated QBs and sat in the driver's seat. I knew we were in trouble when he let Carruth ride shotgun. The drooling psychotic bastard hung his Uzi out the window, spraying at anyone who looked pregnant, which was pretty much everyone in Houston. Just when I thought it couldn't get any worse, we ran a red light and hit a pedestrian, who flipped over the hood, rattled against the ceiling, and smacked the pavement behind with a jaw-rattling crash that spewed broken teeth like a broken Pez dispenser. Tires squealed as we braked.

I got out, traced the skid marks & gold teeth and found a drunken, mumbling dreadlocked Fool clutching a Patron bottle. So we threw him in the car. Stallworth was his name, and he said he was a really great driver. Marvin believed him. The plan was hatched.

We would rob a bank.

Why not? They already did it by playing a simple game. How hard could it be robbing a real bank? I almost believed it was a good idea…but realized their reasoning was influenced by wearing a silly uniform and bulky helmet that was more cosmetic than protective against concussions…injuries that must've damaged their brains beyond repair.

So I agreed. A bank heist seemed like a logical continuation of a night spent sipping Patron and swerving on the highway. Hours steam by faster before the crime than after. Every con said that. Probably because they had the rest of their life to think about it. Not us. Everything was out in front, a thing called destiny: a life of mayhem that was worth rejoicing only if you had the stones and steroids. Soon, the sky was soaked with orange. The bank underneath seamed inconsequential, so stupid and worthless that it should be robbed just for the sake of normalcy.

We parked the hooptie against a piss-stained curb and got out. Stallworth stayed at the wheel with a 5th of tequila…the getaway driver. Marvin carried a 9 milli in each hand, followed by Ray Ray holding stilettos, Pacman on his ass like pimples on Gasol's back. Carruth hiccupped with glee.

Shit, I'm not Patty Hearst; I watched from the curb, puking my Fruity Pebbles up. When the gunshots POPPED, I curled into a fetal position and prayed to Roger Goodell.

Curiosity killed the cat. It's never killed me, but has caused me to see some things I wish I hadn't. The sounds of manic mayhem pulled me inside. The walls looked like Jackson Pollack painted them high on PCP using only the color red. It was a slaughterhouse of slasher film proportions. Ray Lewis ran around ripping arms clean out of their sockets then chewed on 'em like drumsticks. Marvin Harrison made the chubby bank tellers dance by shooting at their feet, intentionally blasting the big toes off everyone. And I don't know where Carruth got the chainsaw. He seemed to derive gleeful pleasure from slicing off bloody kneecaps and tying them around his legs like Roy Campanella shin guards.

Bloodlust was in the air, turning everyone into raving cannibals. Everyone except for Pacman, who was filling a garbage bag full of cash. Bank bills, dye packs, transponders. Everything. Fuck it.

When Harrison had no more big toes to shoot off, he motioned for everyone to leave. We hauled ass and hopped into the Chevy. Stallworth screeched off…his bloodshot eyes barely open. The Getaway was filthy and took us a whopping seventeen minutes just to get around the corner and onto the freeway. The Impala's dented grill was covered in ripped flesh and scalps, so much so we nicknamed the car Leatherface.

Stallworth was a madman. I'm not sure if he intentionally aimed for people to run over, but he seemed to derive some sort of perverse pleasure out of hearing the sickening thump a skull made underneath the spinning spokes of Dayton tires.

The official tally of our getaway: 3 bloody baby strollers, 4 joggers, 1 rabbi, 14 elderly swingers who were merely minding their own kinky business practicing bikini Tai Chi in a park, 2 girl scouts (Stallworth was able to nab a box of thin mints when their shopping cart of cookies went tumbling over the car), 3 Mormons on unicycles, 4 hot dog vendors, 1 and ½ winos (a bum and his double amputee cousin), a crossing guard that forgot to look both ways, and last but not least, a blind man and his seeing-eye dog who never saw it coming.

We escaped clean. Everyone was elated and wanted to celebrate our good fortune. There's nothing like snorting a fresh line of Peru's finest after a heist so we stopped over at Jamal Lewis' house to pick up a kilo of party favors.

The house was a mess. A thick mist of ash was floating around like they had a volcano in the backyard. Dumbbells and bags of cocaine were strewn on the floor. A throbbing pulse permeated the house. Not music, but a banging. It was Travis Henry in the back room having unprotected sex with ten women at a time. As soon as he busted a nut the women became instantaneously pregnant. Good thing Darrion Scott sat in the corner with a plastic Krogers bag. Henry would hand Scott the crying newborn, and abruptly, the crying would cease. Forever.

Scott then tossed the slimy youngster out the back window where Braylon Edwards stood wearing a #23 Cavaliers jersey. No matter how many infants were tossed his way, Edwards always found a way to drop them…blaming his butterfingers on the placenta and membranes coating the offspring. He would pick up the nine-pound mistakes and toss 'em into the roaring bonfire in the backyard. Woodburnin' babies. If that wasn't enough, Edwards roasted marshmallows and wieners over the blaze. A bulldog going by the name of Incognito was chained up outside and would occasionally sneak away with an infant and wrestle around on the ground with it like a new chew toy.

Back inside the house, Pacman Jones sat in the corner catching snowflake-size pieces of ash on his tongue while Jamal Lewis sprinkled steroids in a crack pipe and hit it. He passed it to Ray Lewis, who took a long toke, causing his pupils to permanently roll back in his head, the result most unsettling – Lewis stared around with large white orbs where his eyes used to be.

Ray Ray turned to me – cocking his head. "I need some pussy." Then he tried to sniff my crotch.

I squirmed away. Told him I knew the best whorehouse in Texas. Crab-free and you can slap the sluts for five bucks.

Ray Lewis leapt from his chair. Roared, flexing biceps as big as my legs. That was the signal to mount up and move on. So we did.

We drove all night long. Drinking and taking every drug imaginable. The only way to travel. It wasn't fate, but an empty fuel tank that led us to our Destiny. That was the name of the whorehouse we pushed the car to. All my heathen companions piled into the bar, leaving me outside to enjoy the moment.

In the middle of a dusty desert sky, a bright star shone down. Magnificent. A perfect glowing pentagram. I breathed in the fresh air, enjoying the silence...short lived. A wheezing Winnebago pulled up. A couple of Mexican immigrants shuffled into the ramshackle bar. I followed them.

Our merry band of thieves was drinking inside, arguing about logistics. There were only 2 whores available, old, sagging, but friendly, and a fierce debate erupted about who gets what hole. Gunshots rang out -- bullets peppering the ceiling.

Time slowed. The air was sucked out of the place, which was good because the only thing I smelled was ass, jalapenos, and rocket fuel. A grenade explosion rocked the door where it used to be. We all turned to look.

The Hombre smiled even though he carried an AR-15. A sheisty man going by the name of Aaron Hernandez. Ready to tell a lie and reap the benefits. He spoke Spanish, but I could translate: They needed a place to stay; his wife was giving birth to a savior & prophet.

Her freshly broken water dripped from her thighs. Carruth put his head underneath like an oil pan, and savored every drop.

So I volunteered the backseat of our Impala. It was already covered in body fluids, a few more couldn't hurt. I showed her the way outside as Hernandez compared his assault rifle to Carruth's AK, seeing which one was bigger.

The mother was grateful to be away from the prying eyes that all seemed to suggest gang rape. She smiled as I led her to the car. She squirmed against the leather seat, grunted, moaned, and when I was done sodomizing her she was ready to give birth. I spread her legs, and clapped...thinking that applause would entice the little bastard to expedite the process.

Finally he showed himself and said "hi" and "hola". A prophet indeed. The world was his oyster, and why not? He just poked his head out of one.

I grabbed the cute lil' bastard with both hands and yanked. Easy as scooping out pumpkin seeds from a Jack o' Lantern. He smiled, puked on my leg, and then settled into his mother's arms. The Umbilical Cord hung there, mocking me. The father was inside drinking with the killers so it was up to me cut the gooey thing. I don't like knives so I burned it off with the Impala's cigarette lighter. A pork belly scent lingered awhile, like Hannibal Lecter invented his own brand of incense.

Then it separated. Smoldering. A perfect moment. I lay against the steering wheel, watching the stars above as she nursed her newborn. Thinking the whole time, that cord might make some good beef jerky. And I'll wash it down with some fresh milk after the baby's finished.

Author's note: *My sense of humor is normal and the world is warped.*

23.
NFL Football

The Steelers lost the Super Bowl a few years ago: A satisfying sentence to write for anyone living outside of Pittsburgh. RapistBurgler had a chance to win that game at the end, but couldn't close the deal. He tried to force passes the same way he tries to force himself upon unsuspecting college girls…both endeavors yielding the same unsatisfying results. His stat line resembled his Ngata-nose job. That was the same Super Bowl an annoying slut forgot the words to the National Anthem. Only thing uglier than Rotgut's nose was the half-time show. The Black-Eyed Peas resembled a glorified Karaoke band performing at a Las Vegas Halloween party. But that is the type of Corporate shit shoveled our way…feces being branded as Muzak: a combo of Music & Wack. How can the Peas be cutting edge? They have no edge! They are a non-threatening Pop Band who rely on synths and studio computers to sound halfway palatable. Their live performance was a train wreck…speaking of wrecks.

The Cleveland Browns 1.0 have won a couple Super Bowls. Art Modell threw keg parties south of Dante's Inferno with his buddies Joe Pa, Nixon, Kenny Lay, and David Koresh (who tended the BBQ grill).

Baltimore fans rooted for the Ravens with no sense of irony, history, or pride. Just a pack of raving lunatics who only reinforced why the city should be designated a Superfund site of toxic intelligence. The Real Baltimore team, the Colts, fled the city during the dead of night for Indianapolis. The team that Unitas played for left for the bright lights of Indiana. Then Art Modell stole the Browns away from the loyal fans of Cleveland, moving it to Baltimore.

Now, the same fans of the Baltimore Colts root for the Baltimore Browns. Irony is too nice a word. This is a sterling example of the utter stupidity of the average American: a deranged populace looking for something to cheer for, even if it's for their own exploitation. Shuffle the cards until the dumbass is too mesmerized to care. Equate civic pride with rooting for a football team.

Football. The Ultimate team sport. A "window" into American Society. Sociologists and Anthropologists probably had a field day watching the Super Bowl and its Commercials. Organized violence mixed with crass commercialism. Better drink that Pepsi Max – what better way to wash down all those fatty

Doritos? Zero calories meet empty calories. A fine way to define our culture. Or lack thereof.

Everything is shoved down our collective throats and Defined by corporations. Gives new meaning to the term "Corporate Culture". The Super Bowl is just one example. The 4th of July, Thanksgiving, and Christmas have all been co-opted by Corporations. Holidays that should be celebrated for their ideals are now just opportunities to consume & buy. Every kiss begins with a "K"…so does Kunt.

What better way to show your love than to buy a Lexus and park it in the driveway with a big fucking bow on top? Work twenty different jobs so you can afford a status symbol…and don't buy just one but two. You're not celebrating the Holidays correctly if you're not buying. At least that's what we're told. So have a Coke and smile – and don't bother to think or wonder why Coke privatizes water for profits while polluting the same water supply from which they get it.

I find this all to be fascinating & disturbing in a macabre way, but it's not a Stephen King novel, it's the society I live in. An American one. 'Tis the world we spin on. Rotgutberger can rape at will. Ray Ray Lewis can stab at will. James Harrison & Ray Rice can beat women at will. Donte Stallworth can drink Patron and drive like he's in *Death Race*. And everything will be forgiven on Sunday. Football is the Catholicity of American Sports.

Society allows its gladiators legal leeway when it comes to violent transgressions. Otherwise, where would the masses get their kicks? The beer and nacho chip industries would suffer dire consequences.

HTTR

Hell To The Redskins…for their insistence on using a racist name for a football team. I don't think white people would like it if there were a team called the Cleveland Crackers…or the Houston Honkies. Black folks would be furious if there was a team named the New York Niggas. Hispanics would despise the Sacramento Spics. Chinese people would hate the San Diego Slants or the Chicago Chinks. Europeans would be rioting in the streets if the names Mick, Limey, Kraut, or Frog were used.

So why is it okay for a team to be named the Redskins? What makes Indians any different from anyone else?

And why is the team named the Redskins anyway?? When I think of Washington DC I don't think of Indians. I think of corrupt politicians, teeter-totter legislation, and pimpish lobbyists with red-hot clothes hangers. So the football team should be named after the political process itself: The Washington Gridlock. Or name the team after the majority of people who conduct business there: The Washington

Whoremongers. Catchy. I'd buy a jersey.

But the Redskins' fans squawk about the team name being tradition. As if tradition is something to emulate. What they fail to understand is not all traditions are worth keeping, specifically the racist ones.

In all honesty, the way the Redskins play football they should be called the Washington Squaws. Pocahontas knows as much about football as Daniel Snyder. What's up with that "Hail Redskin" horseshit anyway? Sounds like some sort of Nazi salute.

Sports mirror the society it resides in. Ours is a Nation of Megalomaniacs that cheered Ray Lewis, the self-proclaimed vessel of God's glory. If God was real, I don't think She would give two shits about a slimy football game. And She isn't Beyonce...despite what you see on TV. What is Beyonce even good for? She doesn't sing anymore. Just a lip-synching automaton swirling extensions around. A role model for young girls at Half Time. Pom-poms and sexploitation. James Brown said it was a man's world, and he had the backhand to prove it.

And that is why Football entertains me. Guess I just have a warped sense of humor. During football season I used to have an indefinite reservation on the TV all day Sat, Sun, and most Mon evenings. It was my solemn duty as a brainwarped American Man to act as a dictator in the fall. There is a stereotype to embrace. If my wife so much as glanced at the remote during a Bears game then all Hell shook loose. Once she had the gall to change the channel during a commercial to *America's Test Kitchen*. Suffice to say, she didn't appreciate my use of a Super Soaker indoors.

Speaking of soaked egos, I was kicking it with Orlando Pace one night -- before he was picked #1 in the NFL draft. And he was boning some ugly chick we all called "Goose" because she honked like one during intercourse. Afterwards I was cracking on him and he got mad and took my Atlanta Braves hat...the nice one I stole from K-Mart. He had no intentions of wearing it...just waved it around asking what am I gonna do? Well, dude's six foot six and weighs over 330 lbs...And I wanted to slug him. But I didn't, and I still regret it.

Instead I went to 7-11 and bought the biggest Slurpee they had. Then rolled over to Pace's crib just as he was getting out of his car. He walked over all tough like Deebo from *Friday* and demanded the Slurpee. So I gave it to him -- threw that red sugary shit all over his Mr. Potato-head lookin' ass then drove away. He stood in the middle of the street dripping Slurpee with his hands out like, "what just happened?" But he knew he deserved a Slurpee drive-by.

Later on, Orlando said the NFL was just Entertainment. Which explains his balletic false starts in Chicago...But the cannonball-headed clod makes a good point. The public holds the athletes in high esteem for their athletic prowess -- their ability to entertain -- surely not for their beliefs or intellectual abilities. Yet,

Tim Tebow still gets media play because he's a good church-goin' white man with a strong chin, big arms, and a ball sack with room for commuters. Tebow is God's player, but if God actually existed then why would a supreme being who disregards human life in such a malicious manner in Haiti, Africa, and every place a tornado touches down in America give two flying fucks about football? Self-righteous Caucasic egomania runs amok like Tebow on the two-yard line in Gainesville. Those Gators were God's chillun. Tebow, Hernandez, Riley. Such good boys.

It's all entertainment. Tebow being screwed over by the Elway. Hernandez proving he's a gangster. Riley being another racist billyhopper.

The reality of the situation is that football is fun to watch. And the players get paid fairly well to participate. But it's not that serious. The sport is a diversion. And the self-important asses who think they are God's gifts in eye-black need to understand that while they still can. Before the concussions kick in.

James Harrison admits trying to hurt people, but not injure them. Think too hard about that logic could cause a concussion. But I know it to be true. When I played football with my buddies I always tackled them hard, but never tried to hurt them...except for one time. This asshole named Chad lived around the corner...the home-schooled son of a preacher. And he Always talked trash whenever he came over. One day he was talking madcow sort of feces when we were playing football. So I whispered to his QB to hand-off the ball to Chad up the middle. Hut hut hike, and sure enough, Chad got the ball and I hit him low and blew up his leg. He stopped talking trash real quick, immediate-like. He rolled around on the ground, clutching his cracked femur...pleading for help. We all ignored him, walked home, and left the shit-talker there with a broken leg. I found out later he hopped home cursing the same deity his father adored.

I didn't see Chad again for about a year, when he came over and started yapping shit yet again. So I threw a haymaker at his eye and sent him crashing to the ground, with a cut opened on the side of his face. He wobbled to his feet, slightly bleeding, and proclaimed it a lucky punch. Some people just can't stop talking shit. A disease of the mouth.

The moral of my digression is this: It should be okay for NFL players to hit someone in the head only if the opposing player talks shit. I have no problem with Trent Williams socking Richard Sherman.

"Progress or decay."

Good advice given to Clint Eastwood by his father that went unheeded. Will the NFL make the same mistake and speak to empty chairs in the future?

I used to play football, but quit after 8th grade. Got tired of comin' home with bruises every damn day. So I didn't play in high school. Instead of football practice, I'd go home and whack it. Pleasure over pain. Grab a Vicky Secrets mag and practice for the gridiron mattress. (Gil Scott-Heron would like that line)

I prolly played a 1000 playground/sandlot/backyard football games and never got hurt even though we had no reservations tackling on the concrete sidewalks. But put on those pads & helmets and have old guys coaching you and shit's different. I never minded getting hit in a game-like scrimmage; I just hated the stupid practice drills where the idiot coach had you run head on to another guy like bighorn sheep. If it weren't for the brain-dead drills I would've played football. Now I'm glad I didn't.

Author's Note: *The NBA banned Donald Sterling for life over some racist talk yet Daniel Snyder trots around town rocking Redskins gear. This just proves that anyone who spends a billion dollars on a sports team is more than likely an asshole. The Sterling "controversy" is a humorous bag of shit lit on a neighbor's steps for amusement. The neighbor being us. The lighter the media. And the feces being professional sports in general.*

Sterling is the only racist owner? C'mon, the NFL owners make Sterling look like Joe Biden. We all root for teams controlled by assholes. That's what makes us assholes.

Rooting for an NFL team is like rooting for your favorite corporation that exploits the same state you happened to be born in.

24.
Cleveland Bolivia

The craziest city in the United States is Cleveland, Ohio. Convicted sex offenders bury women in their backyards. A bus driver uppercuts a cunty loudmouth. Another bus driver entices three slow girls to a decade of rape, torture, and even worse, salsa music. Then there was the brawl at a kindergarten graduation party...which will be the last thing the kids graduate from.

Cleveland is the panty liner of the United States. Our crotch is bleeding, but it's better to hide it with a thin veneer of plastic...Cleveland.

LeBron was the genital herpe that got away. He made everyone forget about the Torso murders of the mid 1930s. Serial killing has always been a hobby of Clevelanders since I can dismember.

Sure, work at the docks, unload some crates, and then saw a hooker in half. Why not? There's nothing else to do. The polluted lake water drives a person mad. And now the jobs have disappeared. Bootlegging is out of the question. Booze is legal. Drugs are an option, but all of the corners are taken. Instead of flipping keys, a man could always flip burgers.

Bolivia has no McDonalds in its country; Cleveland breeds Mickey D workers.

A solution: Smart, brave, and mobile Clevelanders mount up and move to Bolivia. More jobs, cheaper living, and safe coke. Put down the energy drinks and pick up a life.

Coca Cola used to have cocaine in it...now it's full of high fructose corn syrup. Which is worse?

"The only Americans are Browns fans."

I read this on Facebook somewhere. Obviously the statement is an ignorant one…more than likely brought on by too many wine coolers or Boones Farm bottles. A more honest comment would be: The average American is a Browns fan.

This may ruffle some feathers and twist some satin Care Bear panties, but if you root for a Cleveland-based sports team there is a good chance you are an idiot or masochist, or both.

Here's why:

Cavs – The worst team in the NBA. Responsible for creating the monstrous ego, LeBron James. Cleveland citizens worshipped this man-child like he was Jesus Christ with a basketball...despite his obvious character flaws. He never displayed class during his Cleveland tenure. But what can you expect from a child in a man's body with the IQ of a grapefruit? It was a stunning paradox that a blue-collar city like Cleveland would idolize such a selfish and arrogant athlete. Then he fled the dying city seeking sand & sunshine. A fitting end to an ignorant city that values building football & basketball stadiums over fixing up schools. The education system crumbles, who cares, it's almost tip-off time!

When the going get tough, the weak get going. LeBron's gone now, but don't worry, the noble Mr. Gilbert built a casino that will erase all of Cleveland's economic woes. Drink the Jim Jones flavored Kool-Aid, chew the Jimson weed, and place your bets!

Everyone shook a fist at LeBron's abrupt departure, but no one makes a peep regarding public education, jobs, and crime. Cavs fans idolized a fake savior so they deserve the heartache. The NBA is no different than organized religion -- spend money and time on fake bullshit that doesn't better the community, or the world. It's all just a delusionary recreational activity to make people forget their mundane reality. Cleveland is a prime example of the basic American instinct to support an illusion in order to "win".

(Miami is guilty also. A city of frontrunners...just like our entire nation. "Love it or leave it." People love to say that, even though their ancestors fled their obviously hated home countries. Better to run than face the forces that be, but when there's nowhere else to run, it's time to face the music. Twenty years from now LeBron James will have the cultural significance of an empty soda can. An idea doesn't mean anything if nobody knows about it. And accomplishments mean nothing if you sell your soul to get it. HST had a noble Ali as a sports icon. My generation is stuck with Gucci-couchie LeBron and they love it. Sniff your finger and smile. You're an American.)

Indians – To root for the Indians you have to be either an eternal optimist or blind ignoramus. They always – ALWAYS – trade their best players. ALWAYS. Without fail. Wonder how good that rotation would be with CC & Cliff Lee still pitching to Victor Martinez?

And why shouldn't the Indians trade their best players? It's good business. Cheaper this way. The Idiots keep coming back for more no matter what...filling Jacobs Field, or whatever corporate name it has now, and paying nine bucks a beer. The slow drag of the game and the inept play of the Indians cost the average beer drinker approximately a hundred bucks a game to stomach nine innings. Cuyahoga County has the largest mentally ill population in the state and most of 'em are Indians fans that enjoy showing up at games in racist red-face with painted seagull feathers stuck in their bonnets. Cheering for the Tribe is the favorite avocation of the abnormal.

Browns – Piss on a Browns fan and they think it's warm summer rain while the yellow ring of snow around them is melting. Browns fans have a Buddhist-like devotion to suffering 16 weeks a year because the bellyaching it induces creates a collective joy that lets the numbskulls know they exist. A greedy, profit-driven owner took away the Browns. Moved them to Baltimore. No loyalty or allegiance to the community, this move was a perfect example of what happens everyday in Corporate America. Browns fans were irate, but they eventually got another team. And another greedy owner who built a new stadium (while the city decays). And the fans root on…for the same filthy thing…with no sense of irony.

Capitalism at its worst – make people search for self-worth in things that are bought. Define them with competition in which they play no part, and have to pay bundles for.

But what are people rooting for? Pampered Millionaires to beat other Pampered Millionaires so BILLIONAIRES can make more money. College Football is similar where people root for exploited athletes to beat each other to make their Corporate Plantations millions of dollars.

It's sad that people need to root for a sports team in order to show pride for a city. If you really want to show pride for a city then *do something* that benefits it. Shouting at the television doesn't cut it. Being a sports fan is a mind-numbing exercise of futility that benefits Corporations and Greedy Owners.

I understand people seek out sports to derive joy, but it's pretty pitiful that people define themselves by who they root for. I might derive enjoyment from football a couple hours a week for seventeen odd weeks in a football season, but that it is an infinitesimally small percentage of where I derive joy. So small that I can do without it. Especially if my team moved to another city and some mutated team was created in its absence.

I am not a miserable person who hates to be happy. Just the opposite in fact – I find joy & happiness every single day…just not in the accomplishments of others.

People may view my assessment of Cleveland sports as overly harsh. Maybe so, but it is an Honest assessment. Stupidity is stupidity no matter how you cut it, define it, or try to defend it. And I have seen the results of stupidity. What It can do. And it's happening now in Cleveland. A Slow Death.

Cleveland cursed itself when it built new stadiums instead of rebuilding the schools and community. People refuse to wake the fuck up. Grown men rooting for other grown men throwing balls in hoops. Pro Sports have mutated into twisted self-aggrandizing charades whose fans are the duped and disappointed. Consider me neither.

Maybe I shouldn't analyze things like sports and other trivial pursuits that people like, but unfortunately I cannot just turn my brain "off". There is no switch. And even less of a filter. If you, the reader, do not agree with my opinion, so be it. Wave your pretty flags and shake your foam fingers while the ship sinks. I used to think that cemeteries and golf courses were the two biggest wastes of land. I have now added a third: Football Stadiums.

The Roman Empire declined, but not before leaving us with crumbling artifact of the Colosseum. We have made considerable progress since then; there are several such structures dotting every state in our country.

Play Ball

Author's note: *It's rumored that the last year Art Modell was alive he chartered a private jet to the Mid-East during the NFL draft and slayed every Egyptian newborn in celebration of a new Ravens season. Many people saw him drink the blood of brown-skinned babies, remarking, "I'll live forever" then wiping the viscous red fluid under his bloodshot peepers like eyeblack.*
Five months later Modell was dead.

If any Cleveland fan is feeling spiteful then take a road trip to Druid Ridge Cemetery in Pikesville, Maryland. There you will find a nice quiet place to take a righteous shit.

I have it on good authority that Modell now watches every Ravens game in Hades while suckling on crockpot-cooked fetal pigs that were once sinful Browns fans.

25.
Pigskin Plantations

American society is steeped in capitalism like my balls in the mouth of a woman who made the mistake of taking out too many payday loans to the point she relegates herself to gobbling soft hairy smelly nuts while lying on her back humming "This is the End" by the Doors.

After the initial explosion of fun for the few who can afford it, all we are left with is a lukewarm teabag that has gone soggy. The buying and selling of goods supposedly drives this great country of ours (though I would counter that the stealing & re-imagining of wealth is what drives Wall Street & Capital Hill). Websites like eBay and Amazon flourish. Hell, there is a garage sale every other weekend in my neighborhood...Estate sales every other day in Sun City. So it boggles my brain and boils my platelets whenever the NCAA decides to punish college kids who play football. Especially kids who sell THEIR property.

A few years back the fascist pricks that run the NCAA decided to suspend Ohio State quarterback Terrell Pryor and five other teammates for selling rings and other football memorabilia. Pryor hocked some of his personal property for tattoos and cash, so he'd have a little money in his pocket. That sort of action reeks of desperation...and that's sad. Pryor shouldn't have to sell his Big Ten championship ring because he's broke. Not when 100,000+ people attend EVERY OSU home football game. Not to mention the lucrative merchandise sales. I own half a dozen Buckeyes jerseys, a few hats, a sweater, shirts, jacket, etc. And how much money does OSU make from going to a BCS Bowl Game? Yet Pryor was broke and forced to sell cherished personal property...and then got punished for doing so!! The NCAA plantation owners branded Pryor with a scarlet letter then sprinkled salt in the wound by making Pryor and pals pay back the money they made, effectively forcing Pryor to turn pro a year too early. Now that is a real education in the dildo-ish ways of American Capitalism.

NCAA Football is slavery with benefits. Athletes get exploited while the corporate universities and slimeball coaches make all the cash...even though it's the players who really earn the money and risk personal injury. Though rare, players risk paralysis...not too long ago a Rutgers player was paralyzed, and an OSU player from my hometown was paralyzed in practice. More prevalent are the detrimental concussive effects of playing football. These young men are still growing even though their brains are being shredded in the name of Entertainment.

Worse still, the players are not financially rewarded...and no, a scholarship doesn't cut it. Not in a multi-million dollar industry that flourished on the backs of broke college kids.

The height of hypocrisy is NCAA football

OSU had a decent coach in Jim Tressel, but he was raked through barbwire in a highly publicized Witch Hunt.

It means two things when you start a witch-hunt:
-You are jealous
-You are spiteful
That describes the slave masters known as the NCAA.

Auburn got a pass with the merc Cam Newton, but the Bucks went straight to jail without passing Go. Bama makes a habit of paying recruits and players. And the NCAA punished Pryor more than an Oregon running back that smacked up his bitch like a Prodigy song. Selling personal items is worse than domestic violence? According to the NCAA, selling something you earned is worse than choking a young woman. Their rulebook resembles the Bible.

Witch Hunt

Point the periscope at any college and you'll see a geyser of whale shit. Come on now...grow up...Ohio State was bad?
Jim Tressel may not have always called the right plays, but he pointed his players in the right direction. He was the best coach in college football and the sport kicked him out like some hobo on the midnight train. Why? Avarice?
Greed.

Brian Kelly recruited Teo on Craigslist

I met this really sweet girl online, but unfortunately she died from choking on a Pringle.
In lieu of flowers, please send donations to:
Heattwave Productions
Anon Man short movie Kickstarter fund
Las Vegas, NV 89135

Whether it's Heisman votes or crowdfunding projects, fraud has never been easier.

C'mon Man!

The media should have known something was fishy when they asked Teo for a death certificate and all he could give them was an Ice Cube album.

You don't have a girlfriend unless you go on a date and kiss her...or what inmates at Folsom call "lights out".

My hemorrhoids are a hoax. I met them online and found out later that I was just itching a figment of my imagination. But boy does it feel good!

The Catholic cunts spun the story with a PR firm -- basically two vaginas ramming a double fisted dildo into each other until the media lapped up the droppings. Whaddya expect? Sportswriters have way too much time on their hands and lack the creative inclination to write anything new or insightful. They make a living scrambling for the crumbs coaches leave 'em.

Brian Kelly has created the Lehman Bros of college football...a bunch of self-involved sheisty assholes that will do anything to win. Kelly has resided over a rape scandal that ended in SUICIDE, negligent manslaughter in the form of a kid getting killed during a thunderstorm, and the Teo fiasco. Rudy would disapprove...or maybe not. Kelly is a redheaded troll that passes for a leprechaun only because he promises the pot of gold to idiots with wide eyes. Kelly should be sharing a cell next to Aaron Hernandez. Both have multiple bodies on their souls to account for.

Tressel has been long gone, but the weasely ND coach is lauded...even though he was responsible for the death of a student, and didn't even receive a slap on the hand. Insane!

Rake a good man over the coals, but Joe Paterno was allowed to "retire" at the end of his season. I never liked Paterno -- he was nothing more than a whiny mascot -- a Nixonian man who turned a cross-eye at pederasty. At least I finally know what a Nittany Lion is: a sodomite carnivore that preys on the young & weak. Raping young boys was a Penn State sanctioned perk from 1994-2009.

After the King Troll's demise the Paternos wanted to sue the NCAA. That's like the Dahmers suing the FDA. And most PsU fans still see JoePa as a hero...yet my perception differs. JoePa is currently being penetrated in every orifice by crustacean-like creatures in Hades everyday. My perception of Penn State is that it's a second-rate university whose only claim to fame was a sordid football program. And I perceive Penn State fans to be a bunch of hilljack hypocrites who prefer to perceive themselves as being unfairly persecuted victims denied of a competitive football team instead of showing contrition for their roles in allowing a morally depraved culture to permeate the sport. Their blind acquiescence to iconography would have pleased Mao Zedong.

Despite the humdrums of child anal penetration, State College will Erect a Joe Pa statue in 2015. In other news, Chicago middle schools will commission murals of R Kelly overlooking all cafeterias and gymnasiums.

The fans and players both prayed in Happy "lap" Valley after the scandal. What exactly were they praying about? That they wish Joe Papa reported the crimes to police? Or were they merely trying to recreate the pederast experience by dropping to their knees, bowing their heads, and to quote *Deliverance*, "pray real good."

Campus war protests in the late sixties have given way to Penn State protests for pedophile's rights. Riots, candlelight vigils, and prayers on the fiddy yard line make forcible anal penetration tolerable. Rabid sports fanaticism is soluble so long as the media dilutes it. History may not forgive, but no one cares anymore so it's forgotten. Yesterday is a year ago in our ADHD age.

College Football
1875 - 2009
RIP

My favorite sport is dead. Suffocated by controversy, corporate greed, undisciplined players, and molluscoid coaches. Oh sure, there are college football games every year, but they're lifeless zombie-like affairs stumbling towards insignificance for the non-betting public. The kids on campus whoop and holler, but that's what kids do, especially now that they've been taught to Submit and Conform. Throw on a big blazer with a bright U stamped on the middle and lose yourself.

Recruitment is the name of the game. 5 star slaves, I mean athletes, are coveted in the Confederate SEC. And the young black men ignorant of history flock to these crackerfied schools where the students have no problem regularly using the N word in everyday speech yet still root for their favorite team. Not too long ago women in Montgomery, Alabama screamed, "Kill the niggers!" at the Freedom Riders. These southern women held babies in their arms while yelling invectives in 1961. Now them babies all growns up, yelling Go Tide!

The SEC is a last-gasp gloat fest for the South. A chance to prove they can do something else effectively besides slavery.

Is irony lost on these athletes? Instead of performing for the 2-faced crackers, these athletes should play football in the enlightened North where their talents will be appreciated without the blatant racism. I advise young black athletes to avoid playing college football in any state that had multiple lynchings in the 1900s...because the white people who hung Negroes are the ones cheering at the stadium...or at least their seeds are. Are the offspring of Emmit Till's killers Ole Miss fans?

A Superfund site is polluted by chemicals, but there are college football superfund sites polluted by history. Google 'Tulsa race riot' or 'Black Wall Street riot', then ponder about playing football for Tulsa, Nebraska, Arkansas, or a host of other racist hillbilly colleges. A recruit should know the tradition they play for.

History is a living and breathing entity unlike the brain cells of a concussed college athlete who sacrifices future critical thinking for no pay.

The demise of college football is not mere hyperbole shouted by a bitter fan...the sport is dead because of an imperfect system that does not reward athletic excellence. College football's flaws are many, and none more aggrieving than the bs BCS system. This corrupt system takes away the sport's vitality and replaces vigor with a popularity contest that decides the champion. Yeah, there will be a long overdue championship tourney, but who decides what teams get to compete in the playoffs? A cyclonite computer and a bunch of voting vermin with the objectivity of Nucky Thompson's ward bosses. Condoleeza Rice being a member of the College Football Playoff selection committee is an example of everything cruel and disgusting about college football. I would expound on this further, but I'm too busy shopping for shoes at the moment. *Selah*.

The game has evolved into a sickening tug-of-war between overpaid coaches and pampered players. Carpetbagging coaches jump from team to team with no concern for loyalty. Saban started the trend and is now followed by Rich Rod, Brian Kelly, and Urban Meyer. Their sluggish trails of slime have stained the face of college football. Money cancels away integrity. The economic recession has severely impacted academic budgets throughout the collegiate landscape, but Texas paid their millionaire coach a five million dollar bonus to keep the fat cat content...then fires the old demented bastard when he proves incompetent.

Urban Meyer is a perennial Drama Queen, as he loves to pry the spotlight away from his players by announcing retirements, heart attacks, and other important things. He loves his players, and his coaching is the reason his teams win...yet, when a player is arrested, and later commits murder, then Meyer is not culpable, but not only that, what ever happened to responsibility? Meyer takes responsibility for his own health, but had no qualms about playing Tim Tebow one game removed from a scary concussion. Why not? The coach knows his pay is dictated by brainless brutes banging each other on the football field. Psalms painted on eye black make it all better. Tebow can waltz on water, cure jock itch, and turn turds into wine. Let him play. Speaking of feces, Meyer is merely a pompous piece of gator poop now wearing a buckeye necklace. O-H!

On the flipside of that equation, the good coaches have to tiptoe around their coddled players in fear of getting fired. Mangino and Leach were victims of the modern day pussification of players. Those coaches committed the grievous sin of not being PC: a microcosm of modern day America where we hate to extend full rights to the entire population yet enforce a harsh brand of PC. Our society barely tolerates divergent ways of life...yet tolerates freedom of speech even less.

The Texas Tech incident was particularly distasteful as a superlative football coach was fired because of a Spoiled Brat's boo-hooing. The James family is the bane of college football. The father was a part of the SMU scandal, and his sniveling son brought down Tech's successful coach. ESPN lost all credibility when it stuck by its blowhard sportscaster and let him spout off burro shit on live television. Now this swine is suing Fox Sports, claiming that they fired him because of his religious beliefs, which are staunchly homophobic.

Football is a tough gig, and if a player can't hack it then they should quit. There's always lacrosse. And so these inner city kids are taught and trained to be tough wild venomous animals able to run 4.5 40s and tear the heads off quarterbacks. Forget about starting businesses, and learning history. I've heard the inherent racist sentiment uttered by many a white guy, "It's better these black kids bang each other's head on the football field instead of banging away on the Crip and Blood infested streets." This is stupidity propagated by people with low expectations and zero morality. Combine the two and you have a dead sport.

College Foosball won't be alone in the graveyard...it will be joined by MLB, NBA, College Basketball, Boxing, Golf, and cricket. I didn't include Hockey because I'm not sure it was ever alive.

MLB was killed by Steroids and the lack of salary cap. If a player is caught taking roids then the 1st offense should result in a one-year suspension & being ineligible for the Hall of Fame. 2nd offense should be a lifetime ban from baseball. Pete Rose and Shoeless Joe are both suspended from the Hall, yet baseball pats the hands of A-Roid, Ryan Braun, Peralta, and other misc Roid Freaks. A-Roid gets a 211 game ban, but plays the night of the announcement. And the sports fans hound him for autographs after the game, a rabid pack of ball-sniffers worshipping the worst of Man. And there, Nixon's great-grandson stands, A-Roid signing memorabilia, besieged by a desperate wave of inhumanity. Yankee and White Sox fans alike. Outside of Boston & LA, MLB fans are a boring lot, and disinterested at best. Young kids go the ballpark now with smartphones instead of mitts. Maybe it's not such a bad thing that cellphones cause brain cancer.

Like most sports, integrity is rare. The Yankees will win at any cost. And all costs. Play a cheater. Employ whiners like Posada who begged out of games because he felt disrespected. The poor baby got paid over $70k per game, but he doesn't feel like playing because he's batting 9th. Well, the fans should repay this sort of asinine attitude by not paying for any more tickets. Girardi doesn't care. And neither should you.

Ballplayers being paid 200 million dollar contracts is the end...and the beginning of the awakening.

The NBA was done in by selfish spoiled overpaid athletes posing as thugs (the retirement of Air Jordan didn't help things). Players named weird disparaging names like Darko make twenty million dollars. Getting paid that much lint normally meant that you invented something, but in the NBA it's equivalent to robbing someone. Anyone who pays to see an NBA game is a mental midget because that loot goes straight into the coffers of those arrogant pricks with pituitary problems. You are to blame for LeBron.

College Basketball used to be quite exciting when players stayed for more than a year...now it's only breathing in March, the rest of the season it's comatose. And nowadays, with the excessive foul-calls, flops, and ref baiting, college basketball has morphed into a cheap crooked spectacle that passes for a sport.

Boxing was done in by scandals, Don King, and athletes avoiding the sport in favor of football and basketball (a financially wise decision and better on the ticker...and this sport migration will repeat itself in the future as athletes flee football for basketball and baseball...maybe even soccer). Golfing aka Tiger Woods was assassinated by the media...which loves to build a person up only to viciously tear them down. How dare that Black Man poke his pecker in White Women?

Sports have overstepped their societal importance. Instead of being minor diversions, they are now major timesucks that too many people derive identity from.

The only sport still breathing is the NFL...though this is only temporary as the dangerous game of violence damages brains. The Frontline documentary *League of Denial* compared the NFL to Big Tobacco, which seems plausible because the NFL denied that the brutal sport caused brain damage & covered it up. I'm a Huge football fan, but knowing the adverse health effects the players face leaves me feeling guilty.

There are 2 sides of thought:

1 - If the players are still willing to play then why care? Enjoy the game.

(but the side I'm leaning towards)

2 - Empathy: These athletes are bashing their brains for my amusement. That is sorta sick.

   These players have families & children...and every week I see crushing hits that kinda disgust me. Should I keep watching? is an honest question I really need to think about. Some scumbag players like Brandon Merriweather act like human battering rams and try to bash the defenseless players' skulls in. How can I root for that?
   At least the pros get paid for their risk. The College Kids suffer for their deceased sport. College players should be paid for risking their brains. The school corporations & NCAA make beaucoup bucks and will fight to protect their profits.
   Football, if you give it serious thought, is really a violent reprehensible game and there's no way to change it. It will ultimately wane in popularity like boxing did...so long as society evolves and progresses. The fans are just bloodthirsty louts who like to see big hits. The average NFL football fan is an NRA member, Fox News watchin' blowhard like Jonathan Kinson from Odessa, Texas who called Jermichael Finley a lazy drunk after Finley was carted off the field on a stretcher. These heathens have no problem cheering even when one of their own players gets hurt. Texans fans cheered while Schaub writhed in pain on the turf. And KC fans cheered the year before when their "beloved" QB Matt Cassel suffered a concussion. And when they're not cheering injuries, they're scuffling in the parking lot, punching women, and shooting & stabbing other fans.
   Football is an endeavor that takes impressive physical specimens and runs them headfirst into a woodchipper. A modern version of the violent swill Roman emperors used to entertain the masses with at the Colosseum. Fans cheer on an accused rapist with the speaking skills of a sloth as he guides his team of academic misfits to a BCS championship. Reggie Bush proclaimed Jameis Winston a role model. If that's true, then no wonder the black community has an identity problem. Our country's future will further recede so long as egomaniac manchildren are put on pedestals. It's a sick twisted world when the Assholes continue to win, sing, and grin about it. And if you don't like it, then you're the hater.

Since I'm a horror enthusiast I find zombies to be slightly entertaining. So I'll still follow college football because I'm a Buckeyes fan. As the years pass, and the moral decay found in our financial institutions continually seeps into the athletic landscape, I will care about sports less and less. The only real sport anyway is finding a way to live a happy life. I have about 30-40 years left and I don't want to waste them on the couch watching football. But the thing about life is you never know. I could have 30 years, 30 days, 30 hours, or 30 minutes. Pablo Picasso said, "Only put off until tomorrow what you are willing to die having left undone."

26.

The Dark Ages

I have no tattoos. You wouldn't spray paint graffiti on the Taj Mahal would you? Beauty is skin deep. Las Vegas is no different. Underneath its silicone-enhanced Botox allure is an inner fiber of desperation. The Strip is the veneer, Downtown is the skeleton. Instead of keeping it in a closet, Vegas prances it around with a laser light show overhead... To keep overweight drunken tourists distracted while crackheads waddle in their midst. Are these crackheads the problem, or the symptom? Is Vegas the anomaly of American Leisure, or its depraved future?

It's a sunny Sunday afternoon when I wheel into the parking lot of the Gold Spike...a refurbished casino/hotel downtown (that no longer operates and has been overtaken by Zapponians). The first thing I see is a Drunk passed out on the sidewalk, cops around him. The poor bastard's obviously lost his match against the tequila worm. I fare no better later...

False Advertisement. That's how I sum up Downtown...but it could also summarize Vegas in a nutshell. There is no Louvre, there is no Central Park, and there is no real skin left on Mr. Wynn's cheeks. Yet there is the illusion, the facade of everything in the world worth visiting -- right here in Vegas -- right before your eyes -- it looks real -- but it's not -- just a Hollywood set to disguise slot machines. And you, the tourist, are the mark...an insect to be bled. And you love it! Don't fuss about winning. Like HST said, "Learn to like losing." Or you're a flea, and the big cat -- the strip -- will shake you off to the fleabag downtown area, where anything goes, especially shadiness. Anyone who has lived in the desert knows that a palm tree doesn't give much shade, but what little it throws, the shade is pronounced.

Tightwads are lured downtown with promises of cheap beer, cheap food, and deep-fried Twinkies. Those deals are fluid and change depending on the time of day. The Plaza and Vegas Club rescind those offers when they matter most. Those casino owners inhale money and exhale the grime that coats Fremont Street.

Now I feel comfortable in grimy hole in the wall bars. Warm waters that sooth so long as the Hipsters are not around. I've been Downtown before...drunk even, chugging green beers out of plastic footballs, so I knew what type of environment it was...and is...cheesy but enjoyable.

Crackheads roam freely inside casinos beggin' for bucks. I shrugged one off and he called me a "bitch-ass". Before I could counter with an uppercut he shuffled off looking for a nice dumpster to take a bath in. Another bum tried to sell me weed -- which is fine, I'm always looking for a nice dimebag of herb, but his sorry ass wouldn't let me smell the product. "Daddy don't lie." He kept repeating. But this daddy don't buy oregano. So I refused the offer and tipped him a buck because it was obvious he was a desperate wreck fiending for a fix. Like the other tourists...

See, we are all tourists here in this bright part of the desert. Nothing grows here but promises. And most remain unfulfilled. Humanity shuffles in and out to experience a brief respite from guilt. Confession for the masses, but instead of priests, there are slot machines and hookers with mascara dripping off plastic eyelashes.

Downtown is Dodge City. Adapt, and do it quickly. Gamble. Play slots and blackjack...maybe come out slightly ahead. Spend it on food & alcohol...alot of alcohol -- light beer, craft beer, draft beer, mojitos, and Tequila...Binions had pitchers for pennies on the ounce...another place had PBR by the bucket. Drink it all and use the metal bucket for a hat to protect against the raging horde outside.

Then the trouble begins. It always does. A full moon rises...the dirty dusty street plays games with my booze-addled mind. I start to become my surroundings. My wife's fears come true...I become a belligerent asshole...or was the outcome a self-fulfilling prophecy? Semi-constant nagging is like pouring kerosene on a drunken pyro. I'm gonna drink...excessively. Deal with it or don't, but shut up about it.

Every casino blends together. The only thing that matters is following that zigzag line to the next bar. Then the next one. Another bartender smiles, I'm not interested in flirting, just pour the shot...and don't forget the lime. I have a long night ahead that is becoming shorter by the second.

This harsh path of agave leads back to the Gold Spike. It's late and the cafe is still open. And the asshole waiter won't take my American Casino Guide coupon. I can still read the fine print, and the coupon is valid. But the waiter has the nerve to call me "bro". Indignant shit pops off. A mean-faced ghetto queen at the next booth judges me with a sneer. I can tell she hates me...probably because I bought her boyfriend a shot earlier and now he's nowhere to be found.

I get thrown out of the tiny grill. Great. I don't like slop anyway. The amused security officer helped me find the elevator, and so I find my way to my room where I pass out -- on a mattress instead of the sidewalk...because I had the foresight to make reservations.

Drinking Problems: Maybe you have one when you're too grimy even for Downtown. When you threaten and scare the people who threaten and scare normal people then you either have a problem or a gift. Depends on your disposition.

The next day I went home, grilled a feast, drank even more, and listened to Led Zeppelin...an informal celebration of surviving the real Vegas. Tourists usually do, but I'm a Local. And that means something. To keep your head above water in this cesspool is truly a remarkable feat.

What about the others around the country? The other people who have no idea what is coming their way? Casinos are being built everywhere...which will turn their environments into economic deserts. The only oasis is the bank account of the casino owner while their plebeians tend sheep around the moated castle.

"My fate is to live among varied and confusing storms. But for you perhaps, as I hope and wish you will live long after me, there will follow a better age. This sleep of forgetfulness will not last forever. When the darkness has been dispersed, our descendants can come again in the former pure radiance."
-Petrarch

Modern day society reminds me of the Dark Ages. An intellectual darkness that follows the collapse of an empire. Mankind has evolved and devolved at the same time. Our technology may be more sophisticated, but we are still saddled with a Dark Age mentality. Humanity has thrived to the detriment of the environment. We've become a scourge on the best planet in this solar system. Our planet is a diverse ecosystem that is being destroyed by the beast of humanity. Courageous men who once dreamed of democracy started the United States of America. Why? Hummers and McDonalds? And what do we live for? To put a dollar bill in a slot machine and bet our lives away? The privatization of our government has ushered in new era of feudalism. Till the master's field, and spend the pittance earned on games of chance. Culture has deteriorated to capitalistic casino fever.

Ohio has casinos but no high-speed railway line. Detroit has a casino, yet it filed for bankruptcy. New York just voted to build seven casinos in their state. Hurricane Katrina was merely an opportunity for Mississippi casinos to buy battered land to cultivate more casinos. Missouri wants an MGM casino because they're Missouri. Wave signs and welcome the machers to town. I hope the bites on their asses don't become infected with poverty and crime. A form of rabies that puts Old Yeller to shame. Gambling is good, just like greed. Tuck your ticks into bed and try to get rich. Isn't that what matter$? Sheldon Adelson, the vile pudgy possum of a man who runs Sands Corp, builds casinos in Macau & Singapore, China in addition to his casinos in Las Vegas. He wanted to expand into Spain, but they denied his greed. These casino developments are billed as job creation projects, but what these projects are really creating are casino-connected communities that only churn out profits for the few. Education will suffer. Crime will be a problem. And resources will be over-consumed. These are facts. Just look at Las Vegas.

Author's note: *I turned on the television for a minute one evening and caught Tony Hsieh talking to Jon Ralston. Hsieh seems to be a visionary, and he may be able to make downtown Vegas better. Ralston reminded me of the guy who never shuts the fuck up. You know the type: the obnoxious asshole at dinner who doesn't stop running his mouth even while he's stuffing it. All the while spewing safe, bland opinions. Un-insightful like marrying a blind woman and asking her what a rainbow looks like.*

Ralston almost had my empathy a couple years ago on Thanksgiving when he televised an adoption special. At the end of the program he recited a touching monologue about adopting a child then he immediately advertised the next day's show about massage parlors & prostitution. Now when I enter a bordello, I don't know if I want to adopt or screw someone. Ask Woody Allen...

What Would Woody Allen Do? Both.
I need one of those bracelets: WWWAD. Sounds like a slow hillbilly asking what? Or what GW was looking for in Iraq.

Even if you're not gay you still wanna stuff your cock in Ralston's mouth just to quiet him. Cut to Family Guy...and Peter Griffin has his cock balls-deep in Ralston's mouth while he mumbles something about the city council...or was it city tonsil?

27.
Bad Will in the Savage City

Living in Las Vegas is dog years compared to normality. I close my eyes and a series of feelings & thoughts flash by like the astronaut in Kubrick's Space Odyssey. Sensations. Vibrations of pushing the vehicle as far and fast as it can go. The check engine light reminds me to rev it even further. Go. Never stop. Not even when the checkered flag waves. Drive through the stands and hit the highway. Find another speedway to race through. Burn rubber 'til it curls black onion rings on the median. The engine smokes only when you use it properly. Make the coroner's job tough. No sense in leaving pretty corpses. I'm getting cremated anyway. Selah.

If you see a *pos* Taurus racing through the backstreets of Summerlin at night with the windows down blaring the Rolling Stones' *Sticky Fingers* then I suggest you proceed with extreme caution and give that maniac a wide berth...his erratic driving is no doubt the result of an insane bender of epic proportions and he won't hesitate to play Chicken with anyone who strays in his path. A future urban legend leaving a wake of shattered silver Natty Patty bottles and BMW smoke.
   The best way to roll BMWs is on Jack Kerouac's mustache. BMW being an acronym for Black & Mild with Weed. *On the Road* was used for a practical purpose -- a solid foundation to roll sleek blunts.
   Now I know how Bruce Banner feels...or Lon Chaney in those werewolf movies -- waking up half-naked, not knowing were you are. I'm just lucky I woke up in the living room and my wife is the one who found me. She helped me to bed as I mumbled something about starting a male escort service/dance troupe called Rug Cutters.
   The next morning is bright light shining through every slit in the drapes directly into my bloodshot Georgia roadmaps. I'm sipping coffee, fortifying myself for the colossal bender ahead. It's always best to approach a balls-out scrotum-smoking bender with caffeine and a lil' TLC & THC...and massive amounts of food. So I had a tasty free breakfast buffet at Red Rock Casino -- ham & cheese omelets with tomato and jalapenos. Nutrition mixed with spices to work the perspiration system. Practiced Lamaze on the way home so I wouldn't soil my shorts in the car...

As I waddled into my house to deliver shart missiles to the porcelain god, one of my Gypsy neighbores two doors down gave me the Evil Eye as she shuffled to check the mail on a Sunday afternoon...yellow vodka stains around her potato eyes. I kept my distance; afraid she will try to whisper "Thinner" in my ear.

Opened my front door and walked into a haze. By the way my two cats were shedding you'd think I had grizzly bears for pets...hair swirling around like funnel clouds. I'ma wait 'til the Gypsy grills her dinner later then sweep the hair outside. The wind is blowing just right.

I can brush both cats multiple times a day and their hair pops back like they're some mutant chia pets. The only solution is to ask Dr. Desai for a vial of feline leukemia and feed it to the bastards with their Friskies...or introduce the Cure through pixie-stick colonoscopies while they nap. Blow the chemical solution into their puckered pink poop chutes with a flexible drinking straw. That'll teach 'em.

As I jogged to the bathroom the tone-deaf mongoloid next door started playing his drums. His drum kit consists of a snare and some cymbals that he plays in the same pattern over and over again. I'm sure that Van Gogh had a similar neighbor...

His father tries to drown out the noise with work. If you live next door to billyhoppers don't plan on sleeping in...cuz they're always banging & hammering away, fixin' shit. And if shit ain't broke, they'll break it just so they can fix it. Those inbred suns-of-ticks work with their hands gundamn it, they're not happy unless they're clanging away like a deaf monkey fuckin' a drum set.

No time to stick screwdrivers in my ears, Nature called collect. Crapped 3 times. Felt like a Ghoulie crawled up my ass and did jumping jacks in my stomach. Mike Tyson's tiger must've raped me in my sleep! I don't remember drinking rocket fuel last night.

The only cure is Miller Lite washed away by Seagram's Gin. 'Beer before Liquor never sicker' is bullshit. That's just a euphemism written by some old hag who never ran out of beer. I'm a biological anomaly with a cast-iron constitution; I have no need for superstition. But the house is not a safe place to drink -- it smells like a mixture of a cow barn/monkey cage at the zoo/meat packing plant/YMCA locker room/Smithfield Farms chicken processing center/Fat Bastard's sumo diaper/roadkill carcass/Kirstie Alley's curdled ass cheeks/laxative testing facility/dumpster outside a colostomy clinic.

Flee is the instinct. I heard that Firefly reopened, but if I wanted salmonella then I would ask my wife to cook dinner. The only option is to Fire up the grill in the backyard and chuck some brews in a steel bucket with ice.

It's only 90 degrees -- and all day long I hear the neighbor's AC belching and belching. If you're from Norway or Greenland then don't move to Las Vegas! Why move to a fuckin' desert if you need cool air? Stay home. Shit. I can barely hear my Neil Young cd over the rusted-out monster they call an AC unit.

Invest in some ceiling fans. Or transplant your sweat glands. Guess what? Perspiration is normal.

It's a nice day. Palm trees sway. I smell rosemary roasting. The grill is lit. But all I hear is some industrial-strength infernal fuckbox breathin' away monoxide fumes as it cools off a ranch house. Why? Are they keeping corpses in the garage?

Later tonight, after the gin kicks in, I'll fry up some bacon and pour the grease in the rotating fan on top of their AC unit. Smoke 'em out. They may ruin the day, but the night is mine -- those weird hours when you're supposed to sleep. Rest up. Shut your eyes 'til they hurt. Train your wayward soul to fetch, roll over, and play dead. The best way to really get under someone's skin is to strike at night like the Viet Cong. Rattle their Pavlovian habits. Teach 'em what Fear is.

Fear is not knowing what's gonna happen next. Fear is the uncommon, though the feeling is quite common. Water your grass, take out the trash, and find your roof littered with piss bags.

How'd those things get there? And who would piss in a sandwich bag, secure it, and then toss it on another person's roof? And why does my house smell like bacon?

And why does anything happen? Sometimes for a reason. Most times for none at all. You deserve nothing you get. You only live. Like a snowman in a snow globe...and some get shaken more than others. And some people deserve to be shaken, and that is what night is for.

A balance to the madness. The superstitious might call it Karma.

...

Went to bed late and woke up early, courtesy of the annoying Mormons ringing my doorbell. Too bad these missionaries are always men because my morning dog was poking out its boxer window wondering what was going on.

I answered the door in a cursing tornado of invectives directed towards the BYU football team. Then I asked why the hell they were standing there with their stupid looks on their stupid faces telling me about their stupid God when I have never rang their doorbell at the unGodly hour of 11am only to tell them that there is no God? The only thing Brigham Young was good at was popping the hymens on the 11-year-old daughters of his followers stupid enough to believe in his cultish ravings.

That sort of truth mixed with a stone cold hard penis poking out a boxer pocket is enough to convince young impressionable men that Satan is real. They ran to their ten speeds and peddled away leaving behind their black bike helmets. I scooped 'em up; they'll make good bedpans.

Slammed the door and sat back in the living room, smashing the plastic hats together. Trying to focus.

I would never bemoan a hangover -- it's one of those things, like "if you can't do the time, don't do the crime." A hangover is a state of mind...a mental endurance test that separates the weak from the foolhardy. The best thing to do is have another beer. Or pizza & Dr. Pepper. Or Toft's ice cream. Who am I fooling? I don't get hangovers anymore. The last time I had a hangover was a few years ago when I projectile-puked ectoplasmic green vomit all over the shiny pristine bathroom at the In & Out Burger down the street.

When I came out of the bathroom, my eyes were watering, face flushed, vomit spittle dripping from dried lips. I stumbled over to place my order. The poor girl behind the counter forced a smile and asked what would I like? My eyes felt like bloodshot marbles that wouldn't stop rolling. I felt bad breathing in her direction, but I didn't want to be rude. "What kind of food do you have here?"

The girl tried to explain that since it's an establishment with the word "burger" in its title that they specialized in juicy burgers. A burger sounded like the worst thing in the world at the time so I ordered one.

SMASH

The bashing of the yuppie brain protectors woke me from stupor...samurai swords and nunchuks were strewn about the living room. The ghost of Bruce Lee must've broken in and ate Doritos, drank Bud Ice, and watched *Phantasm*...

Then an inkling of walking to the gas station shined through the moss. Brief glimpses of 40 bottles accidentally dropped on driveways, tall cans tossed in bushes.

No surprise. Ice-brewed lagers are my weakness. Feels like my entire body is coated in adamantium. The drunkenness lasts for a finite amount of time, and turns the average man into Borat, where your wiener will crave the small hole even though your cranium feels like Tony Spilotro put it in a frickin' vice. The result is a sloppy focus that strengthens overnight. A realization occurs that an average man may not have survived the previous night.

No time to waste on sentimental superstition. Luck only happens to the tough. Wake up you bastard, there's work to be done.

I need to requisition much-needed provisions. Books and beer are essential tools for every writer. First stop is the library. There I notice a disappointing trend...many of the books I check out are in worse shape than James Woods' pockmarked face. Some movie stars get plastic surgery, Woods opted for taxidermy.

Warren Zevon's biography looks like someone puked their spaghetti dinner in it. So I go to check out another copy and the same puker barfed in that one also. *The Boys on the Bus* by Timothy Crouse was soiled like the Brundlefly read it while in the midst of a drooling bender. And *The Proud Highway's* pages were stuck together in an amalgam of snot, Cheetos, and pubic hair. Either there is a deranged pervert on the loose that loves to destroy library books, or Las Vegas readers are a disgusting lot with no regard for other people. I take the books and bounce-pass 'em back at the librarian in disappointment. A buzzkill is pending and no beer is in sight.

So I go to Albertsons and discover that some people are the walking, living, breathing embodiment of hemorrhoids. This one particular pain in the ass wandered aimlessly down the aisles like he was auditioning for a George Romero flick...constantly getting in my way...acting more like an obstacle course than a human being. When it was time to check out there was only one line open and Mr. Silver-Haired Hemorrhoid beat me to it. Then the wait began...

His birthday card was wet and they needed to get him a new one. His credit card wouldn't scan properly. And he needed cigarettes, sending the poor cashier to walk the length of the store again. And just whom was this scabby seventy-year old pasty-faced clusterfuck buying a greeting card for? His beloved poodle?

While the cashier scrambled for his lung cancer delivery sticks I had the gall to give the douchebag a dirty look which he returned while typing on his smart phone...probably checking his E-Trade app to figure out what happened to all of his Enron stocks. A barely-functioning Neanderthal checking out before he checks out. A smart phone is called a smart phone because it helps dumb people look smart.

And so I go home to write...

Ten hours later my house smells like someone's been conducting a chemistry class on the varied uses of sulfur. You too can make your house smell like a limestone quarry. Take 12 parts Buck Range Light and 2 parts Clif bars, and then wait a half hour and voila: odoriferous results.

Side effects may include singed nose hairs, green eyebrows, nausea, memory loss, and divorce.

Escape the aromatic oppression and head outside with pineapple yellow bud shipped straight from Hawaii. Light it, puff it...Out in the atmosphere like the Millennium Falcon...watching the stars twinkle, and the moon shine, and the clouds pass by waving bye. Being alive is being outside at night. The air is crisp, rejuvenating the destruction of the day. Anything is possible. Everything is in front of you. Sit back and enjoy the night sky -- the plasma screen for cavemen...and just as entertaining now. Even more so. And so I smoke...

Cloudy eyes, I tried to walk into the house...the only problem being the screen door wasn't open. So I ripped through it with the constitution of a musk oxen only to collapse on the floor.

Woke up to carne asada fries & a chorizo burrito from Roberto's Taco Shop. Washed it down with ginger ale and tequila. Time to go hiking.

Trudged up a mountain at Red Rock Canyon. Found a solitary tree on top...stretched out underneath its shade and listened to the wind whisper through the canyon. Offering advice. And so I took it. To always live in the moment.

On the way down, I sat on a cliff; saw something beautiful, and thought about my Grandpa. Reminded me of a Warren Zevon song, "Keep Me in Your Heart for a While". If awhile is forever then I can do that.

The days we went into Buds off W. Madison are set in stone. Him drinking beers at the bar and me playing shuffleboard for a quarter. We both had our habits. Never talked all that much, but real friends don't have to. Small talk is for small people. Being together was enough. Whether it was stringing Christmas lights along the basement walls or being the Best Man at my wedding, my Grandpa has a permanent place in my heart.

Zevon's song evaporates right along with my thoughts. Red Rock has a therapeutic way of temporarily reliving memories. And you wake up to see beauty in all directions. Blue skies and red floors. So I step closer to the cliff's edge to get a better view.

Watched birds fly underneath my feet and really wondered why there is war on this planet.

Then I saved a desert tortoise...karma is on my side...

28.
Red Rock Canyon

Most people end up where they're supposed to be. Destiny is a result of an individual's personality and temperament. Many people may not like where they live -- some may even hate it -- but they are the reason they are there. The common excuse to not move and find one's lot in life is Family. Granted, family and friends are an invaluable part of a person's life so long as their love births bonds of identification & understanding, and not the bondage of ignorant beliefs.

Most people in their youth dream of moving away from home and starting afresh on their own. Either these dreams fade away from lack of inspiration, or they move only to return home shortly, unable to break away from the tethers of comfort-induced monotony: that small tinny voice in the back of a coward's neck quivers and whispers, "Nobody's anyone in a big city. Everybody's someone in a small town." And soon enough everyone knows which cemetery that person is buried in.

An active intellect may motivate the person who strikes out on their own, but I believe courage is most responsible. Courage and Belief. The belief in one's ability to find direction and happiness. To find a place called Home.

After nomadically bouncing around for the past twenty years I have found home...It may not be Nevada, but it is the West. I came to this realization after hiking many times at Red Rock Canyon. The mountains seep into your subconscious without you even noticing -- until one day you realize that you are where you're supposed to be.

I'm not a rugged frontiersman or cowboy, but I feel at home surrounded by mountains (and palm trees). The more I go outside, the happier I am. Human beings are not tuna fish to be stacked in tin can cities. It's in our primal nature to explore. Sitting on couches cultivating beer bellies is antithetical to our biology. Living in a concrete jungle long enough would turn any animal mad. Any chance I get, I head over to the maroon mountains. Hiking at Red Rock can take on a slightly spiritual dimension, knowing that pioneers and Indians traversed the same paths hundreds of years ago seeking a new life -- a new home.

Will my home be here in Nevada, or California, or Colorado? I don't know, but I'm willing to find out. So long as it's in the West. When I was a young pimple-ridden kid in Ohio I told a buddy that I wanted to live in Las Vegas. And now here I am.

As for the future, I can see myself living in three places:
- LA - making movies
- Palo Alto - creating websites
- Somewhere in Colorado - living a dude-like existence smoking reefer and hiking.

These three options are equally appealing so why not try them all? If I fail at making movies and as a tech-startup entrepreneur then I can move to Colorado with no regrets. Because I tried. Life is such a precious thing: a person should do what they want to do, and that includes living where they want to and experience new things. The majority of stress results from expectations. Shift your focus from the results to the process, and life becomes more pleasurable. Like Kansas sang, "we're all dust in the wind." Some stick and make a mark, other's don't. Regardless, enjoy the ride. We're all lucky to have taken it.

Author's note: *I was outside listening to Tom Petty and realized I'm living the American Dream. I'm not successful yet, but I'm still living comfortably. Plenty of food, beer, a woman than can tolerate me (most times), freedom of speech, and the freedom to pursue my dreams. And I'm thankful for everything. There are people in other countries without those freedoms. They're not even allowed to dream, much less pursue them. Whether I'm takin' number ones in a casino pool, or just taking a leisurely stroll through Summerlin, I'm living the American Dream. Where else can you live so great? Sure, there are problems, but there are smart people who can fix them. Maybe I'm one. Maybe you are too. I'm not sure if I'll ever be successful, but I am sure that I will have a fun life, here on out, for as long as I desire to.*

So, don't sweat any personal petty worries. A Petty Worry is insignificant bullshit that Tom Petty wouldn't worry about, and neither should you.

29.
My Favorite Affliction

We all have our crosses to bear (And mine's sports gambling) so I chopped off the bottom and made it a plus sign.

A bulbous harvest moon hangs over the Las Vegas strip spelling certain Doom for every sports book in town. An ominous symbol resembling an illuminated liver spot on Art Modell's forehead. In less than twelve hours the Minnesota Vikings will battle the Cleveland Browns and the only people who care are the Gamblers.

Inside the Action

Polynesian gangsters are out in full force tonight...driving the Vikings spread up to 7 yet keeping the payout Even via inside sources. These Hawaiian hopheads have brains as big as their bellies and they make me weary. Hang back in the book. Survey the area. See who is really Who. Sketchy characters with blatant ulterior motives have infiltrated the books. Find out what the play is and strike like a Cobra.

Sweep the Leg

The Browns just hired Jim Jones as coach and will be giving away free Kool-Aid at every home game as a part of the new "Get it over with" promotional campaign. Haslam even bets against the Browns in order to help subsidize his Pilot Flying J defense. Cleveland fans deserved to be fleeced and I take up the cause as if I was born for it.

A sleepless night passes -- visions of defeat keeping me awake. The hype of today's seemingly innocuous Vikings-Browns game has been driven up to dizzying Super Bowl-like heights. Bloody Mary fueled pomp is buzzing throughout town and the circumstances are dire for anyone caught on the wrong side of the spread. Dreams will be made and souls will be crushed. Some people will skip town & flee the shylock while others feast on BBQ & guzzle margaritas at Lucille's. Never before in the history of the NFL has there been a matchup of two 0-2 teams that has caused such mass panic & hysteria.

The Browns Backers of Las Vegas have collectively re-financed their mortgages in order to properly bet on the game. As a matter of civic pride. Everyone else (83%) is wagering on the Vikings with house money. A few perspicacious rogues known as the Smart Money are taking the Browns...which immediately cause heart palpitations and cold sweats under my balls. Did I bet the wrong team?

This is a football game for the Ages. And the only way to watch is going All-In. Bet enough cash to pucker your lifesaver. Each down will be a life-altering event. Even the extra point kick can make or break a gambler's spirit forever. A minute will seem like a week. Seconds last for days. And a yellow flag fluttering to the artificial turf means the whole world is Against you.

Sports gambling is a zero sum game. "You lose some, You win some" is a brainless euphemism uttered by habitual criminals with drug addictions. You win or quit. There is no other way when betting vast sums of money.

A Few Hours Later

The Fix is in. All hope is lost. Never bet against the Smart Money. 2013 is the year I quit sports gambling forever. Betting on NFL football is for speedfreaks who like to flip coins. I'm finished. This heathen game took 7-9 months off my life today.

My public gambling image is now shattered beyond repair. I'm hesitant to cash in a couple winning college football tickets from last night. The book will be swarming with swarthy syndicates. Cheshire grins mocking my every move. Bug-eyed lemurs uttering sarcastic comments and sozzled soothsayer wisdom that will turn out to be untrue this time next week. My only saving grace is that I don't live in Cleveland. Yet I will punish myself tonight and eat a downtrodden immigrant meal of corned beef & cabbage.

Unlike most sports pundits, I did Browns fans a frickin' favor and made an ordinary game interesting with obnoxious trash talking. And the game *was* exciting. Though it is a splotch on my soul...and will take a decade or two to erase the damage.

An expert on the subject of gambling told me that having an opinion on athletic contests could be costly. More so on your sanity than bank statement. I will heed this wise man's advice and focus my efforts entirely on screenwriting while I still have some scruples left.

But football betting has been profitable, and there's still a mostly-whole season left... If only the crooked refs hadn't called holding. If only the quarterback's mother never had a child. If only I bet on the other team. *If only*. Two words that the seasoned gameblur whispers to himself while his intestines bleed. 'If only' is the mantra of a sucker.

If only I hadn't bet on the games and saved my money.

At least I don't have much cash to lose. There are rich Longhorns fans who bet their 401k on their overrated team. I lost pocket lint compared to most of the degenerates at the book tonight. I watch these discolorful characters rant and rave while the games play, and I think to myself...that could be me in ten years -- unless I wise up. Maybe I'll only bet a maximum of ten games a season. Sure, that's the ticket. I'll start tomorrow.

Streaks in gambling are a real phenomena...and what separates the successful gambler from the loser is the ability to recognize when the streaks begin and end. Every bettor is just another Buddy Guy and wants champagne when he's thirsty and reefer when he wants to get high. And so gambling is that means to the high. A high in and of itself. Losing is almost as extreme feeling as winning...but taking that drug is a spiraling heroin-like habit. Winning is, and has always been, better. Gambling is Skydiving with everything on the line...like letting your ex-wife pack your chute. Sometimes the ride is a blowout settled by halftime and you can enjoy the scenery. And sometimes the chute pops out 100 feet above the ground late in the 4th quarter. But if you're half bright, knowledgeable about sports, and disciplined, then sports betting is a better risk than the stock market. My eTrade account is worth about as much as hobo dick cheese.

Football gambling is an obsession -- a trance into injuries, stats, and point spreads. The only way to win is to live it. Try to use caution. Take a break every now and then. Watching too much football is like staring at the sun -- it leaves a stain on your brain. Rooting a 7-team 6-point teaser to victory is a fragmented experience only rivaled by an epileptic who spent the entire day playing Xbox.

Autism is the norm at sports books. Abnormal behavior is not only encouraged, but subsidized with free drinks.
Cursing/Berating/Ranting/Raving/Imploring/Deploring and finally, Accepting the futility of it all. There's nothing more off-putting than manic desperation, and nothing more American than spending a Sunday at the sports book.

The Iceman Cometh early

Sports Gambling and the Play are both a depressing yet insightful meditation on Dreams. Take away a man's pipe dream and you're taking away his sanity...even his humanity and will to live. A pipe dream can be that lil' swig of fuel left swirling around in an old piece of machinery long forgotten. That fuel might rust it from the inside out, but at least the machine keeps running.

None of my dreams have ever come true, but they have kept me livin'. They have gotten me through this monotonous bullshit we call everyday life. The thought of being someone...that has kept me going. Then I realized my dreams were not set in stone. I could change them. Mold them. Make them me.

In modern times it seems the desire to dream has been replaced with the gambling impulse in order to Consume and Buy. Americans suffer from hunger pains of which they know not.

Peel back the husk of humanity on the average American and you'll the see the corn has gone rotten with apathy.

2014 should be the year Americans dare to dream again. Dream to make our communities better (and) Dream to make ourselves better.

There are only two types of people who don't dream: Cowards & Zombies.

Sun Belt, Baby

The average college football fan has never heard of the Sun Belt conference, and only the degenerate gambler or sharp bettor actually wagers on the games. I probably fall somewhere in between.

The pride and joy of the Sun Belt used to be Troy. A buddy of mine from OSU, who gave me the nickname No Hoes because of my lack of dating skills, was a defensive tackle who was considering a transfer to Troy State. And Coach Larry used to interrupt our Madden games with recruiting calls. Well, that coach knew what he was doing as my buddy put down the OE bottle long enough to transfer to Troy State, then went on to play for the Cleveland Browns at nose tackle for a couple years. Now Troy is a bona-fide bowl team that regularly churns out NFL players.

The Sun Belt offers decent value, but bet the Big Money on the big conferences and big games...that is the meal ticket...but the Sun Belt is the avenue to make "Kickin' It" money during football season. Kegstands, buffalo wings, burgers, pizza, tequila, rum, chronic -- The Sun Belt provides; as the bookies never ever get a good grasp on the games, and so, the point spreads resemble a kid that resembles your next door neighbor: something to be whipped and tormented. When I see a weak point spread I'm all over it like Oprah on a corndog.

A couple hundred bucks of profit per week should subsidize any Man's game-watching needs. This type of frivolity attracts attention...so when your neighbors hear & smell the Bob Marley drifting out of your backyard, they will ask how you can afford to kick it so intolerably happy every weekend...just smile and utter three magic words: Sun Belt, Baby.

Last season I bet against the Texas Longhorns. Mack Brown changed the team name to Roadkill. After giving up 550 rushing yards to missionaries, Mr. Brown thought the name change was Necessary. Like Wallace Hall, Brown blames the loss on his insatiable appetite for reading. It seems the coach was busy reading the funny papers instead of his playbook during the game. Brown remains proud of his defense, which has earned a fitting moniker: the Maginot Line.

This past season was a revolving door of misery for Texas. Karma finally caught up to them from the time GW Bush kept flashing the "Hook 'em Horns" satanic symbol during his 2nd inauguration like he was a wasted frat boy on his 4th beer bong. Oklahoma State treated Texas the way a thoughtful Cleveland neighbor treats a hitchhiker. Though Texas was only abused for four quarters, it felt like a lifetime for Brown. Then Baylor blew 'em out, making Texas the Face of football futility. The BCS Bowl committee obviously had a sense of humor matching Texas up with Oregon in the fitting Alamo Bowl. History repeated itself as fleet-footed brown people massacred Texas. Mariotta, the Oregon QB, had a calm weird satisfactory demeanor the entire time he sliced the Longhorn's jugular. The Texas defense sulked around like they'd rather play lawn darts with Michael J. Fox. Big strong steroidal brutes heaving with silent tears are distressing entertainment. So much so that Brownie Boy got fired even after he fled the scene under the pretenses of recruiting.

The Texas Longhorns have turned into the tepid white accountant with butter fingers in the prison shower. Teams took turns sodomizing the fraudulent steers. Brown should be shipped off to Rikers Island for massive embezzlement violations. Mack daddy Brown made $5 mill per year coaching, and this salary was siphoned off for other reasons that are not quite clear at this time. Sports commentators are quick to come to his defense. Brent Musburger specializes in Brown ball-licking.

During a Saturday night college ballgame I was chit-chatting with a powerful syndicate scumbag at the sports book and the slimeball swore up & down and all around that Brent Musburger is a renowned twat hound with a predilection for ovulating teens, and steals their intrauterine devices with his teeth while they sleep. Musburger is rumored to have stashed these treasures in a storage unit strategically located adjacent to a Bumble Bee canning facility in San Diego.

Conversations at a book can be just as intellectually draining as the games, and Monday nights are the worst times to watch a game. Monday Night Football is what I call "the Bermuda Triangle for sports betting." Avoid wagering on these games if you can. A dog covering a crazy game is a given, sending the gambling junkies into rages too bleak to recover from. Brawls break out in the weirdest places. Opposing fans taking pisses side by side have been known to slug it out, dicks waving, urine streams soaking everyone else in the restroom.

The only people who regularly bet on these games are degenerates desperate to make up for losing weekends. I once bet $2000 on the Ravens years ago when Kyle Boller outplayed Brett Favre...which reinforces my point that the MNF games are unpredictable and wacky. There's nothing more dangerous than sports bookies that take a beating the previous week. Prepare to feel the wrathful scorpion sting of impatience if you don't lay off the inflated spreads that typify MNF.

Now I'm an overly cautious bettor who only likes to wager on the Sure Thing. The excitement level has gone Down, while my bankroll has gone Up.

Author's note: *Unlike the good, I believe that everything bad must come to an end, and I will quit sports gambling once I move away from Las Vegas.*

30.
Living Las Vegas

Las Vegas is a meat grinder of a city with a two-day shelf life. As it stands. Without proper leadership it will funnel into the Mojave and be a decrepit landmark next to the Yucca toxic waste depository.

Like any city in the United States, living in Las Vegas has its pros and cons. The negatives outweigh the positives, but I recommend living here for at least a year before 2020. I feel lucky to have experienced the city while it was in its prime. But always cast a weary skeptical eye at a city whose visionary founder was a degenerate Mobster. The water will run out. Not a matter of if, but when? Until then, enjoy.

Vegas is a dreamland for young adventurous adults, and an oasis for the elderly with retirement communities everywhere...though make sure to swallow cyanide tablets before entering a nursing home as every establishment in the state was cited by state health inspectors for deficiencies. Bedsores are not limited to the bordellos here. Speaking of...

If you're single, stay single. If you're married, get divorced, and move to Las Vegas before you turn forty. Thank me later. No disrespect to northern Cali, but Vegas is the silicone valley. Big and fake.

Overall, it's the best place to party, but the city is afflicted with serious maladies that threaten its future. Las Vegas is not a place to raise a family. And I'm not talking about the strip, casinos, or hedonistic atmosphere...I'm referring to the horrid state of its education system. There are many facets, but two major ones:

-Education is not valued by the Politicians or the Nevada Power Structure.
-There are serious flaws in the school system at the administrative level.

Clark County recruits teachers on a nationwide basis as they slash teacher salaries, freeze teacher pay increases, and lower health care. There is always a budget crisis in Nevada, but taking a hatchet to education solves nothing. Maybe having a state income tax would help as well as raising taxes on the casinos and mining. The average class size in Clark County ballooned to over 35 students, almost ten kids above the national average. Instead of raising taxes to adequately fund education, the Governor and his state minions rather flush the future of

Nevada down the drain. Hey, who needs an education to fold towels and cut slabs of prime rib in the buffet line?

The few tax dollars that drip into the state coffers are unequally distributed between the North and south. Carson City and their ilk demand a disparate share of the plunder. Why feed the democrats down south? Up North is where the action happens and the deal making is sweet as buttermilk. The Transnational mining companies operate with impunity and care less about Nevada than they do some rural area in Chile that they've already destroyed.

If you're not a teacher, or if you don't have kids and will never have any, then Vegas is a great place to live. Or if you're a comedian, singer, dancer, magician, or entertainer then living in Vegas is a must. Circus Circus is currently taking applications for a net maintenance facilitator for the polish twins who perform their trapeze act wearing ice skates. It's a busy gig.

Besides the occupational opportunities, you can go out & drink a bunch, eat a brunch, gamble a bit, and come home with more money than you left with. One night my wife was comped a room at Red Rock Casino. I went there with 20 bucks in my pocket...and had dinner at a Mexican restaurant, played slots, video poker, and bingo, drank copious amounts of Bud Light, Mich Ultra, Amstel Light, Jager bombs, and Patron, then had a breakfast buffet in the whirlwind leftover of a morning. When I got home I found out that the money in my pocket had doubled into 40 bucks. A phenomena native only to Las Vegas.

Other people save up for vacations to visit here, while a quick trip to a casino is just a normal routine for locals. Palm trees sway in my backyard -- Mountains are five minutes away to hike. Las Vegas is The hedonistic destination. A respite for the wary soul. The meteorologists sure have tough jobs out here in Vegas...just come up with different adjectives to put before the root word "sun". Abundant sunshine, mainly sunny, insanity-inducing sun, etc. The off chance that it's cloudy, just wait for dusk -- the night sky is always illuminated by neon. When it's overcast and the air sucks the clouds down into a still fishbowl, the entire city smells like a dingy pool hall. And when it rains the smell is the Earth burning. Thankfully, a rare occurrence. But then...you start to like it. That musky earthy scent. Organic incense.

Stay on the Strip

There's something to do no matter the time, just make sure to bring enough money for coke and escort fees for whores of various ethnicities...otherwise the vacation becomes a wasted opportunity. These neon lights aren't advertisements for moths. Grow up or go home. We have enough fat cowards sleepwalking the strip. Fuck or flee. Leave your inhibitions with your regrets. The fact you're here means you're unhappy with your home life. So drink elderberry cocktails, sniff a rail, snort another, down the hole goes a shot of Jager, and guess what? That hooker who looked cute playing slots in the lobby is now gargling Scope to wash your cum out of her mouth. Good job. You have balls. Keep it up and maybe one day they'll drop.

There's something about the heat out here. It boils the fat off your brain. Making it easier to think. Like, a thousand bucks would just be wasted on the mortgage when these innocent young Taiwanese triplets want to play yo-yo on my mu-goo-gai-pan.

People deserve to have fun and this is the place to have it...but the locals deserve a decent education system for their children...something that Steve Wynn likes to juggle, trade, and execute in Communist China. There's a rumor floating around Macau that Steve only sodomizes pre-teen girls that don't wipe. He likes to flick his dick so the shit sticks to the mirror...teaching the maid to get a better job.

Just another example of a Vegas education...

The major con of living in Las Vegas is the sustainability. The citizens can't just drink conventioneers' cum forever. The water supply will dry up in the next fifty years, unless the Southern Nevada Authority sips northern Nevada's milkshake. That proposal is to take away the water that sustains agriculture and give it to the greedheads in the city. A better solution would be to build solar-powered desalination plants on the west coast and pipe the sweetwater here. That's the only way the city will survive. And even that major project would be iffy at best. Twenty million people in the southwest rely on Lake Mead for water, and that water will be gone by 2060. A university study out of San Diego just predicted a 50% chance that the water dries up before 2021. Home prices will be worth a penny on the dollar then...

All Vegas needs is an evolution...the river is drying out. That's a fact jack. Why else spend hundreds of millions of dollars building deeper straws into the Colorado River? Soon the brown stream will be sucked dryer than me at a Shanghai house of table baths.

"I'm a freedom man"

To some, Evolution is just a word or idea. To me, it's a state of mind. I wake up thinking Evolution. I go to sleep dreaming the same thing: Evolutions leaping over fences. Once you start dreaming of sheep you become one.

I walk down the street in Las Vegas and wonder -- why the hell am I walking on concrete in the desert? I should be walking on Plexiglass-protected solar panels that power the city. The sun should power every house, business, and casino in this town. The only casino currently developing solar power is Mandalay Bay.

I'm always thinking of ways to improve things. Now, the genius is finding ways to implement those ideas. And the people currently in power only have one genius -- making & retaining money at all costs. Even if the cost is hurting their community. And this malice goes uncontested because there is no stable activism.

Las Vegas is a transient community that is not close-knit, and the neighbors can be, and often are, snoopin-ass Mormons or other Christian scum that will report you to the HOA or constable for minor infractions...like not having the right license plates or for having a couple drips of oil on your driveway. They ignore the barking dogs in every neighborhood that like to defecate on your front lawn. At least there's smog to wake up to in the morning. Another day working for somebody else.

The HOA's are the new mob in Vegas. Racketeering, extortion, and sodomy are just a few things they're good at. They are legal tools of harassment and discrimination designed to weed out "undesirables" (i.e. Anyone not old and white). A few weeks ago I received a notice about brown grass in my front yard...yeah, that shit's gonna happen when it's 117. The yard was dead when I moved in, they're lucky there's any grass regardless the color. Then I got a notice about a couple oil stains on my driveway. It's a driveway! Where should the oil drip? On a young girl's lip? I'm not R Kelly.

Then a couple hours later my slimy Mitt Romney-supporting neighbor came by, ringing the doorbell, then knocking, telling me important news about my sprinkler system. Dude was wearing khakis and a button-up long-sleeved shirt in hundred-degree desert heat even though he's unemployed. Sheisty-ass Mormons -- strange fruit. This dude was sniffing around like he's some sort of bill collector, or a self-appointed neighborhood watchman.

My wife and I pay $1200 a month to rent this house. I'd think that would afford us a little bit of privacy from snoopin-ass Mormons knocking on my door like they're the police at 9 o'clock at night under the false pretense that there's something wrong with a valve on my irrigation drip system. Makin' me get dressed to answer the door. Craning his neck, looking in my living room expecting to find a grow house.

I informed him that I too abide by a strict Mormon moral code. There will be no alcohol in this house unless I imbibe it. There will be no sodomy unless I initiate it. There will be no blasphemy directed towards me. And there will be no taking the Lord's name in vain, for vanity is only reserved for me. I thought taking the moral high ground and declaring that he and I are the same person would solve the problem. Turned out, I was wrong. Punctuating my protestation with a devout "Goddamnit" probably didn't help matters.

And so the Mormon harassment continues...

Received another letter from the HOA -- just a friendly reminder to trim the bushes hanging over the sidewalk area...the sidewalk area that ends in my cunt neighbor's yard. The sidewalk no one walks on but the khaki-camouflaged Mormon imbecile who has nothing better to do than pick trivial fights with the wrong person.

I went outside to see the bush on about one inch of sidewalk. I didn't notice this serious transgression earlier because I possess a fucking life. So I trimmed the sinful bush and noticed the neighbor's front yard lacking holy cleanliness. The law works both ways, bubba. I emailed two complaints to the HOA regarding the sinner's lawn: a trash violation, and unsightly articles on his property. Tomorrow I will file two more: Nuisance Rubbish, and landscaping violations. Triviality is the Clark Count way of life.

Rodents are on the loose and Las Vegas is out of mousetraps. Rat on your neighbors. Rats everywhere. Fine, the Mormon has my attention, so I'll give meaning to his life. This sort of pissing contest is to be loathed, but when confronted with harassment the only recourse is to fight back like an alleycat-eating rat with rabid fangs bared.

Hatfields & McCoys this is not...but a writing man riding a three-month bender is not the type of person to poke a stick at. Especially a nocturnal creature prone to unconventional means to get its point across. I have no problem shitting in a grown man's mailbox, or depositing a toxic pot of detritus in the offending burgher's backyard. An easy recipe is to cook a couple pounds of corned beef & cabbage, then let it sit for 3 months in the fridge until barnacles fester. Biological decomposition of rotten meat is the oldest trick in the book...and one of the most effective. Wake up to horseflies and desert rats running rampant in the backyard will cause a man to lose sleep. Not to mention the odor. Psy-ops 101.

I love normalcy...because it's a rare thing. I wouldn't fuck with me, knowing what I know. And what I know is the whole damned area stinks.

The truth is, the state has been sold. Nevada is one big blinking Vacancy sign.

Out of state investors and foreign consortiums buy up all the cheap property then rent it out to the Locals. Bidding wars ensue. This creates another false real estate bubble that will pop in another ten years. Locals get shat upon...they don't receive preference from the banks, and so they rent. Indentured Servants are known to be susceptible to the crabs in the bucket syndrome. Their lifestyle breeds resentment and even worse driving habits. Everyone for themselves on the highway of Cunt

City. Your insurance rates increase, but at least there's a blinking slot machine to spend your last nickel on.

It's open season on pedestrians in Vegas. Whether it's drunk drivers, Fed Ex, or old geezers who forget which pedal does what, people (especially children) are getting clipped way too often. Even school bus drivers are outta control, clipping civilians, and speeding. So I propose a new initiative: If you're a pedestrian in a crosswalk and have the legal right of way and a car gets too close then kick the offending vehicle as hard and as many times as you possibly can. If the driver wants to beef then feel free to kick them also. The only Effective way to combat ignorance is by showing there is a consequence for it.

An old lady ran over three little girls in a crosswalk, killing one after dragging the poor girl several feet. The hag didn't even get out of her car to check on them. Obviously this old bat spent too much time in Selfish Central.

Grocery shopping here can be just as dangerous as crossing the street. Keep your head on a swivel or the self-entitled Botox Bitches will run you down with their carts. All in a rush to buy some quinoa or muesli that they'll never eat, but brag about buying. Note to Botox Bitches: Yous don't look like younger human beings, yous look like well-groomed zombies. A petrified perfumed fossil with glossy Pinesol cheeks that sparkle in the moonlight. A grocery store is the last place I expect to find your sort.

Dinner at Terrible's

Change the name of a pig, but it's still swine. The worst casino in Las Vegas is the Terrible's Casino aka Silver Sevens aka grimy sweatpit of a hole that earns its name. I won a hundred bucks in a free slot tourney so while I was there collecting my money I noticed my stomach rumbling...so I figured, why not try the buffet?

A lousy decision...as I waited in line for a slice of leather brisket a severely wrinkled bum in front of me farted so loud I thought his colostomy bag had popped.

The clientele of Terrible's is composed of bottom-feeding dirtbags, crackheads & their wino cousins, and blubbery hags with cigs permanently attached to their corrosive lips. Now if you like hobnobbing with hobos and rubbing elbows with the jet set of skid row then Terrible's is your casino.

I haven't been there in years, but I can still smell the players club...a crowded purgatory with the aroma of a burlap sack of sweaty balls...with a touch of Lysol, urine, and ten week old body odor wafting off street creatures wearing tattered purple sweaters. The sort of thing you smell sprawled out on your kitchen floor after breaking your hip right before the housecats start gnawing your nose off. And that would be a welcomed relief...

Everywhere I go in Vegas I am confronted with outright rude behavior. It's almost like I'm the Invisible Man, and people are entitled to butt ahead of me in line, not stop at stop signs, even walk into my path and expect me to move. Now when I go out, I give people 3 strikes. The third person to act in a rude manner gets the righteous pent-up anger that would be better spent spread out...but what's the fun in that? I'm doing the asshole a favor by flipping out on them; otherwise they'll never change their asshole ways. This sort of thing gets tiring, but is necessary in order to retain any self-respect.

It takes a granite-like constitution to stay sane here...and dumb luck to make it out alive. I don't recommend more than a decade living in Vegas. This desert jambalaya may not be here in fifty years, so enjoy it now, at least once, while it lasts. Just remember to buckle up.

"When the music's over, turn out the lights."

Author's note: *Las Vegas really is Cunt City. The neighbors are consistently bad. HOA's consist of overzealous fascist swine that use their petty power to routinely harass young people with trivial complaints. The atavistic education system is a wretched stack of bricks unable to progress due to too much inbreeding. A young adult who moves here is not made to feel welcome. And I wanted to like it here. The only way to cope is to live in a constant state of numbness. A city built for sociopaths.*

As soon as I can shoot my short movie Anon Man, I'm outta here. If I can't afford to move then I'll just act crazy and have myself committed to the local mental hospital. They're giving away free bus tickets to San Francisco.

Update: My Summerlin neighborhood has a higher turnover rate than Mark Sanchez. The neighbors I wrote about have all moved out for various nefarious reasons. A couple new ones lasted a few lunar cycles then took off, fleeing misc bounty hunters. I still see a Boba Fett here and there hoping the Canucks come back.

Guess I'm the last one left. The 7th letter of the alphabet.

A racist still lives on the corner, sun tanning all day long. Ironic: He despises blacks but spends every day trying to look like one. A black friend of mine visited for a week to shoot a book trailer. The day he leaves is the day I get 2 HOA complaints. One for my grass being too long. The other for not having enough grass.

31.

Aye, Aye, Captain Queef

CCSD announced today they have hired Steven Brooks as their new superintendent. Brooks' first executive decision is to reinstate corporal punishment, and he will personally paddle the bad kids...and even some of the good ones too...

If you're a go-getter with an IQ below 50 then you're in luck. Clark County School District needs Principals without principles. Sign up today, and you too can be the incompetent Billy Bob Briggs in *Casino*. Home Ec teachers are encouraged also, because who knows how to run a school better than someone who can bake brownies?

  Other attributes sought:

-Be not only willing, but be begging to engage in a Machiavellian mixture of nepotism, cronyism, racism, and/or affirmative action exploitation.
-Be petty and vindictive. These are necessary traits to succeed.
-Have dead nerve endings in your ass, as you will be spending most of your time sitting on it.

  Apply today. Incompetence is a valuable attribute, for it isn't something that can be taught, rather, it is a common Clark County characteristic that is inbred into a person that shifts the afflicted mind towards a tendency to intimidate, bully, and hold their school & staff in a stoolish state of tyranny. God Bless, Las Vegas.

"The American educational process prepares those with second-rate intellects to thrive in a bureaucratic environment. Obedience, rote memorization, and neatness are enshrined as intellectual achievements. Just as the SAT measures the ability of the applicant to take that test, the bureaucratic rigors of the studio system probe the neophyte's threshold for boredom, sycophancy, and nonsense." -David Mamet

Intelligence & common sense is pushed aside for memorization. That is the key for the Establishment: to teach young people to remember what is good for them, and good for Capitalism. Filling in an oval is akin to circling the hamster wheel. And it's only getting worse now with the emphasis on standardized testing. Listen up and learn to love it. No account for instinct, ethics, and decision-making. Follow the pack mentality is rewarded. We're heading towards a cliff. Care to follow?

Classes are designed to teach mundane facts to the lower classes instead of philosophies that could upset the balance. Truth is dictated by chalkboards and bored teachers.

Cheating is a common byproduct of the emphasis on test scores. The remedy is obvious: Revert back to the days when education revolved around the actual education of children, instead of teaching to a test that does little to prepare kids for the real world. And the test is implemented for a reason. To ensure that schools fail so they can be privatized for profit. Or to create a system that labels schools as "failures." Another reason is to fracture the teachers' union. The Cons-ervatives clamor for test scores to dictate the merit pay for teachers. Though no one mentions the fact that principals divvy up the classes and favoritism plays a dominant role in who teaches accelerated classes. Dump the ELL kids and problem children on the Latino teacher and give your white (or black) buddies the accelerated classes.

Society isn't color blind, and that's unfortunate. Institutions of learning should be...even though standardized tests only discriminate the poorer populations of America. As if we didn't already know those schools were failing. And why not? Property taxes play a part in funding schools and so the affluent neighborhoods have better schools. And the poor "niggerhoods" are something to be exploited by insects like Michelle Rhee. Bounties are put out – an eight grand bonus for teachers and 10k for principals. And so abnormally high erasures on standardized tests become the norm. Students are not to be taught properly, but to be exploited like cold-calling clients in Glengarry Glen Ross. It is safe to assume that Rhee is a Cunt's Cunt.

And it is no better in Vegas, only worse. The school board pays a carpet bagging tick over $350k a year to be superintendent...which damages forever any word that starts with the word "super". The flea flees before his four year contract is up...taking the money and run is a common refrain for this town. Politicians and school admin treat the town just like a slot machine to soak up all the cash they can.

Las Vegas is recruiting teachers; they need 200 more, yet hate to pay the ones they already have. Teacher layoffs are Always feared at the end of the year.

Pension and healthcare benefits are besieged, and teachers have to incrementally pay more into these benefits. Classroom sizes constantly increase. But at least there is no state income tax. Hurray! Internet companies would love to set up mobile teaching labs here and force kids to stare at computer screens all day long, and then get paid untaxed profits for performing a public service. Andre Agassi would be the first to sign up. He's always looking for a fix now that meth is illegal. Another major player, Tony Hsieh, is entrenched like a tick downtown with enough influence to have the City Council pony up over sixty grand to pay for Teach for America teachers. These fresh college graduates with no background in teaching or education will be a 2-year Band-Aid for the Zappos crew. Dollar bills always grease the squeaky wheels here in Vegas.

Charter schools are touted as the answer to the languishing public schools, and public school teachers are constantly vilified. It's like sending an army off to war with no boots, no helmets, and only one bullet in their rifles, then criticize the cowardly bastards for getting beat.

Sure, there are some bad teachers that take advantage of union benefits by consistently working 4 day weeks, but what about my wife? She's a teacher with six years perfect work attendance in her first six years, and would've had seven, but had emergency surgery with seven days left in the school year. She has no connections here in Las Vegas...just another recruit to be abused like an addict sniffing Elmer's Glue. And these things happen everyday here. It's a hard dry dusty town built on the backs of others. Fall down a sidewalk shaft here and your surviving relatives get a saran-wrapped set of teeth that were fished out of the sewer drain. And just like the local news anchors, they clattered after each flush.

CCSD reminds me of the schoolhouse that Daniel Day Lewis' character sets up in the movie *There Will Be Blood*: An artifice to keep the help happy. The illusion of progress is powerful, especially to those too blind to see the truth. Pretty soon every state will be like Nevada as casinos are spreading like pubic lice in a whorehouse basement. Mines and fracking operations will follow. So pay attention. What happens in one state affects every other state. The country is a body, and nobody wants an organ to rot. Brain Drain is fine so long as it doesn't happen here. Spend tax dollars only to seed another state's growth. So long college graduate, don't forget to write! 30% of college-eligible students plan to stay in Vegas, and that percentage is optimistic at best.

Steven Horsford's face was plastered on local papers years ago yapping about merit pay and firing underperforming teachers. Sure, so long as that underperforming teacher's face is the opposite color as his. Racial politics have a harsh way of undermining democracy and causing the population to divide lines based on ignorance. Whether it's Nevada or Alabama, it happens everyday in America. Black & White spite is still alive on both sides, much to the detriment of the neglected children forced into an inadequate education system that really doesn't give a shit about them. All of this merit pay talk is just another smokescreen to detract from the only real solution: Raise taxes (on gaming and mining).

And the real reason the powers that be (Gaming, Mining, Politicians) don't raise taxes, outside of greed, is because 71% of students in the Clark County School District are non-white. The lily-livered rich can afford the $10k/year tuition to send their kids to private schools. Prejudice people don't pour money into educating minorities. So instead of financially rectifying the situation, the common refrain is misplacing blame. CCSD is the nation's fifth largest school district, and only 29 percent of the students are white...and what exactly is the percentage of white casino owners? and mining companies? The Las Vegas population is treated like the Help. At least there is 30 seconds of silence each morning in the schools to mourn public education. Surely there is separation of church & state and this time is not for praying. If it were, then I'd recommend praying to the deity of rationalism to sway your parents to either move or constantly picket school board meetings.

Public policy has turned towards demonizing the teacher. Bullshit movies like *Won't Back Down* reinforce negative public opinions. Eliminate school funding, then eliminate teachers, then what do you have? Set up a few tables with computers dictating the lesson plan from the Matrix. Teachers are now the scapegoats, compensating for poor public policies and lax taxation. I'm not a fan of taxes, but I'd rather live in America instead of Guatemala.

I was at Suncoast Casino one day and observed the epitome of Republican behavior. This older white dude wearing a polo shirt was playing the Wheel of Fortune slot machine and bitching about the taxes on the jackpot that he was *trying* to win! I remember muttering, "If you don't like taxes, then stop making money."

These swine want easy money. They care nothing about their community so long as there's a golf course or two. Kids are caddies, undeserving of a tax-sponsored education. This is the mindset of the rich & entitled. Robin Leach is the Benedict Arnold of the American Dream. He merely sucked aristocratic balls for a living. He exists on 2 knees. The middle class walks on two feet. An education enables us to sprint, and rich pricks prefer a fixed race.

It's no fun to be shart upon. Remember that if you go to college wanting to be a teacher. Pick your spots, or a better major. Because education has been relegated to a minor. Fishing for anal fissures is a more rewarding endeavor than teaching in Las Vegas.

Some Wynners are really Losers

The Wynns & Adelsons have no loyalty or home. They exist on the wire, pangolins with low morality. Finance is a foul-smelling secretion from their anal glands. Stevie-boy is worth $2.9 billion and Elaine's snatch was worth $1.9 billion, yet they both want the public to believe that the casino industry cannot afford to pay a higher tax rate for schools, even when they pay over double the NV rate in Macau to a corrupt Chinese government. Adelson too. The evil-looking maggot rolls a hundred million dollars on a no-win prop bet like Gingrich for Prez, but no more cash can be spared for education. He's really quite a kind man, just visit his hospice. They pump in morphine aerosol to smell like the Venetian.

Elaine "sparkles" in an interview with her favorite gay flunky reporter so she must be caring. Not really.///just enough to satisfy her rich liberal conscience, but not enough to endanger her divorce settlement. She's just another set of whitened teeth smiling on the circuit of mediocrity. Elaine wormed her way into the position of President of the Board of Education. Every Clark County job is for sale. And what exactly are Ms. Wynn's qualifications? Fellate a rich guy and she magically knows what is right for the rest of us. A bachelor of arts & sciences goes a long way when you swallow the richest guy in town.

Stability in this town is a smokescreen. Stay and play for a day...but if you bring your family, teach 'em how to fold towels or de-bone fish. Or toss cards at Dracula's bordello...uh, I mean Encore. Stevie Wynn has a taste for the plasma of others. It keeps his cheeks icy.

"Stay Frosty"

Station Casinos freeze out unions, but maintain a positive public relation with the locals by running frequent ad campaigns touting their beneficence. I hate to complain, as I take advantage of their generous promotions on a weekly basis: Money in the bank, courtesy of Red Rock Casino. But I can't help to think the money in my pocket they gave me could have been better spent on wages. I chalk up my political passivity for sloth and general public curiosity. A person can learn quite a bit about human greed by regularly visiting a casino. Or lust. And gluttony. If a man was on his deathbed then it should be in a suite at Red Rock Casino with the yellow pages opened to "Escort".

But if you're merely sick then go to the Orleans casino. The Friday night crab leg buffet is a big draw for midwestern hillbillies. Regurgitation is a common occurrence. Some billyhoppers do it on purpose so they can feed it to their babies without fear of choking the youngsters...who usually have just as many teeth as the fathers. I ate there once and noticed a retarded lady wearing a Michigan Wolverines sweatshirt vomiting cream-colored crabmeat all over her table. Crustacean splatters created a nice contrast to the navy blue shirt. The dribbles down her chin were dabbed by the people sitting with her. Their Walmart wardrobe was is in desperate need of dry-cleaning. Once the lady's chin was wiped clean she puked again. Loud. Sounded like someone tried to open an umbrella in a yak's ass.

Now you would think this lady would be taken to the bathroom by her family. But no, this is not a venue for civilized people. She just sits there. Dabs at her chin with a wet napkin. Tries to smile. And asks for another plate of food...and her party immediately accommodates this wish. Up-chucking mongoloids are not only allowed here, but fed repeatedly until everyone else around them pukes as well. The smell makes you want to sniff lighter fluid then set your nose on fire. Even the waitresses, crusty older white women with matching eighties-feathered Winger groupie hairdos, encourage the madness by giving retards doggy bags to puke into on the way home.

These sorts of deranged behavior can trip-wire a fragile mind. A couple years back a Navy Seal tore off a drinking binge on the Strip that resulted in multiple assaults. I have no problem with an Excitable Man running around the Las Vegas Strip smacking random people with a metal pipe for no apparent reason. It livens things up.

I say drop all charges, expunge his record, and give the poor bastard two pipes and tell him to beat the shit out of the Mario Brothers, My Little Pony, the Joker, Captain Jack Sparrow, and the rest of the degenerates dressed up like Halloween and beggin' for change. Have the Seal tune up a couple dozen of those escort peddlers while he's at it. The Strip is overrun with bums. No, I don't want a bj, bottled water, timeshare, tickets to the club, or to be serenaded while I walk from Caesars to Bellagio. All I want is to gamble and drink a couple 7&7's. Is that asking too much?

The last street performer I saw on the strip was dressed up like a Jewish Nazi outside the Venetian and every hour on the hour he killed himself in exotic ways. He stuffed uncooked bratwurst in a trash bag wrapped around his stomach and disemboweled himself onto unsuspecting gondoliers who floated by. Another romantic moment on the Strip.

There may be a "mayor" of Las Vegas, a figurehead to pose for pictures, but there is no real political leadership on the Strip. Navy Seals excel in such a vacuum. It's time to bring them in and let loose for the greater good. And when they have completed the mission, send 'em to Carson City. Bums are known to reside there in even greater numbers.

Author's note: *My wife's a good person and qualified teacher with a Master's degree, but I guess some of her middle school students just don't listen. It's hard for me to identify with those students because in the 6th grade I attended the Glenwright Academy for accelerated learning. And I respected my teachers.*

But maybe the problem is having 36+ kids in a classroom, or maybe, just maybe, the parents don't raise their kids to respect the learning process or teachers.

A novel idea: Parents, raise your kids instead of letting television & Xbox do it. There's only so much a kid can learn from watching a Disney DVD, or a FPS videogame.

32.
A Few Bad Apples

I had a couple bad teachers before college. I hesitate to use the word "bad" because their incompetence sprang from old age, but their teaching methods were the opposite of good so what other word is more appropriate?

There was the old middle-school biology teacher with torpedo titties who always gave out homework, but never checked the answers when she graded the papers. So I always wrote profane non-sequitars in the blanks. Like: The duck-billed platypus has a [12 inch cock] and webbed [balls full of purple cum].

I'm not sure that answer was correct, but I still received a perfect score.

Then there was the high school French teacher who had a habit of crying when other students made fun of her. Despite the weeping she was a good teacher because she gave me the passing grade of "C" even though my average hovered around 50%. Plus, she didn't bust me when I brought in a two-liter bottle of cherry 7-Up spiked with Tanqueray. She sniffed the suspect bottle, shook her peacock head, and said I disappointed her.

Now the ancient English teacher with droopy eyes was more sad than bad. He still had enough spunk in his 90-year old engine to march back and forth through the classroom extolling the virtues of proper grammar and Metamucil, but he gave out vocab tests every week and was too blind to see that the entire class cheated on them. He always said to never end a sentence with a preposition...but I never knew what to end a sentence with. But enough with all that.

I even lived next door to a teacher for a time. A middle-ages math teacher who tried to regulate the neighborhood like he was still in school. I ran through his front yard one day in the midst of a water gun fight, and he charged out his front door, demanding me to give him the water gun. So I squirted his pasty freckled face and ran away.

He took such obsessive pride in his lawn that I tried to cure his compulsion by pissing on it every chance I got, leaving brown patches polka-dotting the greenery in demonic cursive patterns. Then to expedite his expulsion from the block I initiated a daily dose of psychological shit warfare. Human feces bearing my DNA would turn up in unexpected places. One morning it would be curled in his sidewalk rock salt coffee can. The next day the feces would be steaming on his front steps. Nothing was off-limits. The stranger the place, the better. He moved away soon after, thus teaching me an important lesson. Pranking is alot like life. In order to succeed you have to be willing to do what other people won't. If that means shitting in mailboxes, so be it.

    Looking back on all of the teachers I had, I'm surprised that so few were incompetent. Most did a pretty good job. This is amazing, considering they deal with kids all day long who, for the most part, are rotten little bastards. Going to school is almost like going to prison. Animals surround you and if you show the slightest bit of weakness then you're hauled down by the hindquarters and ripped apart for dinner. More so for students, but still not easy for teachers.

    This brings me to the new mythology of demonizing teachers. People latch onto the fallacy that it's the teachers' fault that students are doing so bad because it's easier to digest. It's the teachers' fault. Not the undisciplined Kids' faults. And surely not the Parents' faults.

    There may be a few bad apples teaching, but what do you expect when the orchard has gone rotten?

Author's note: *Two English teachers in high school tried to reach me, and get me to apply myself in school...especially the wrestling coach. Such an intense demeanor and stare. When he said something you believed it. One day in the hallway he asked me what would it take for me to be serious, and concentrate on writing? Being a dumb kid who grew up in America I answered "money".*

Two years after graduation, and one of the worst feelings was being a cashier at Meijers when he came through my line with groceries. He didn't say anything. Just a look.

Maybe this book will make him happy. I'm just makin' up for lost time.

33.
A book is really written at Midnight

My next book is about a community of blind people whose only hobby is origami. The title is Crumpled Balls.

That morning buzz you feel is a reminder: To start early and don't stop. When you open your eyes, it's time to wake up. I don't care how many hours of sleep you got, or what time it is, it's time to go to work.

   The circadian rhythm is nature's way of testing your fortitude. Only God can judge me. Tupac once said that. And God hates a coward. So get up and be something. At least curse the wind while pissing in it. That's God's inside joke. And I read the novel so I know what God thinks.

"When in doubt, tell the truth."
-Mark Twain

   Any man with a reasonable brain and working car is heading south on 93 towards Lake Havasu. Since I have neither, I'm stuck halfway between Death Valley and Laughlin...in a dusty, downtrodden town strung up with blinking lights trying to find meaning in a manuscript.
   The desert does something to a man. It fries away the reason. You start to believe there's gold in the mountains. The Lost Dutchman gold mine is full of believers. Skeletons smiling, holding pickaxes and manuscripts that were never read...
   And I wonder, why are they smiling? Was the search just as fun as the find?

   Writing a book is even more fulfilling than reading it. Taking scraps of thought and trying to make sense of them...and life while I'm at it. People have been doing that for thousands of years. Trying to make sense of mortality. The knowledge that death is whistling, waiting around the corner has inspired great art and horrible superstition. My book is just me whistling back...not sure if I'm afraid or not...but one thing's for certain, the clock is ticking. Faster for me than most so I'd better collate my thoughts together...if not for the betterment of mankind then at least for posterity's sake.

My favorite day of the week to drink is Sunday. Celebrate life actually living it and having fun instead of reciting ancient rubbish written by hacks, who if they lived now would be writing for *Mike and Molly*.

A pious person's logic will always be faulty. A depraved friend of mine who became Re-Born said he wouldn't go to strip clubs anymore because he wouldn't want his daughter working there. My response, "But don't you eat Burger King for breakfast?"

Proselytizing demons like to whisper, "Stop Drinking."
Why?
So I can suffer the same necessary horrors of conformity? Where your offspring pick your bones clean before the vultures start the feast?
Or maybe live a life of Masculinity where my Penis is only good for Offspring and Action Movies?
No thanks. I drink beers for the benefit of humanity. I want the whole world to smell my masculinity. Here it is. Deal with it. Or fuck off.

The darker the day becomes, the better I write. Night falls and page counts rise. Pretty soon it's Monday morning. The only people up this late are real people forging a path. To where? I don't know. But at least they're moving.
Standing still is freezing under a cold shower. Might as well dig yourself a plot today. Pick out a casket. Mahogany, Cedar, maybe Cardboard. That seems right.
Or listen to the World Health Organization and avoid working at night. According to this limp-dick proclamation, the late shift will give you cancer. And so will the sun. So follow the No-Fun club's advice and hole up in a cubicle during the day, then sleep with the covers covering your head at night. Rinse. Repeat...until someone shovels dirt over your pretty well rested face.

Writing a book is the great American excuse to drink, and so I embrace it. A 30 pack of Natty Light is another obstacle to the sunrise...or a conduit to recognizing the real beauty of it. Only a person close to the edge can speak the truth without worrying about the social consequences. I probably don't have much time here so I may as well make it a better place for others. Selah.
There are people who love me and people who judge me. Sometimes I can't separate the two. And it's very rare to find someone who only does the former. It's human nature. The more someone dislikes himself or herself, the more they dislike you. The only three people who will ever like you are your Mom, your best friend, and maybe yourself. If you're lucky to drink enough. I still think I'm an asshole. A

necessary one.

I have problems. I eat too much fruit & vegetables. I help too many old ladies cross the street. And I roam neighborhood-to-neighborhood looking for discarded aluminum cans to recycle. Yet, I see the lucky citizens of Las Vegas flit here and there with the carelessness of a fruitfly searching for a moldy crate of pluots. Maybe we're all just an insect that has a day to live, and so we live it up. Sure. But what about the ones after us?

Bad Dreams of Mortality

A normal night is getting to sleep around sunrise. Maybe I can catch enough winks to wake up around 10-11am. Imagine my disappointment when a bad dream interrupted my slumber around 6 am this morning. I use the word "bad dream" because Nightmare is associated with Newtown and happens in broad daylight. Normally I can sleep through bad dreams, but this one was different...more vivid than usual.

I was competing in a bike race alongside a highway that wound itself through a series of twisting mountains with steep embankments along the edge. A difficult course for sure, but the bicyclists also shared the two-lane highway with traffic, mostly consisting of semi-trucks...the big bastards with two sets of wheels and jagged mudflaps.

To make the race even more harrowing, I was surrounded by old ladies who pedaled their bikes in a haphazard fashion with a blatant disregard for the other racers around them. One old hag cut me off, causing me to go careening off the road and down the mountainside.

I bashed into a stream, wet, but no worse for wear. Infuriated, I scrambled along the ravine, vowing to get back up into the race so I could exact a little revenge. There were huge jagged concrete pillars in my way, sticking horizontally out of the mountainside creating a treacherous passage.

Dragging my bike, I ran hard, trying to navigate my way through the outcropped maze...then I realized the Earth below was unstable and the pillars started moving. I tried to crawl below a pillar when it sunk, pinning me against the cool dirt. An unbearable sensation of claustrophobia arose...waking me up!

Now if I had to interpret this dream, I would come to two conclusions:

1 - I don't want to die. (no shit, who does?)
2 - I don't want to die before I finish the race...fulfill my dreams...which is kinda weird having a dream about not fulfilling dreams.

So now I drink coffee, cognizant of the fact that sleep is where dreams go to die. Even when I get drunk I can't rest the next day. Sleep is for dead men. And I have too much life circulating through my veins to be sedentary.

A word of caution: If you absolutely must sleep then never eat buffalo wings right before bed. It will induce crazy-ass dreams. Once, after gorging on a few dozen wings, I dreamt an epic cinematic adventure about boneless buffalo wings. It was a cross-country Cannonball Run competition where the winner received free wings for life. There were harrowing car chases, Oscar-worthy dialogue, and scrumptious wings. My car was equipped with ranch squirters that made the cars behind me spin out.

Matter of fact: Do eat wings right before bed...it's better than going to Redbox.

Or - if you want to dream while awake then smoke weed. Imagine floating in a tunnel of smoke, too happy to move your arms and legs. Scuba diving on land. It takes concerted effort to write while high. Once started you can become productive. The insights will be the same as sober only weirder. Which, in our society, seems tame and normal compared to reality.

A Dream that is real: Mortality. The ignition of everything is the realization of Mortality. Getting old is probably the worst thing that can happen to you. Walking around wearing diapers and every time you take a step you feel the excrement squish together and rise closer to your waist, ready to soil the new polo shirt you just bought and tucked into your creased khaki pants that reek of bad behavior. So, my advice to young people is this: Live now.

Everybody dies. One day. When I was younger I never thought I'd see death...in fact, I'd tempt it. Whether it was driving 85 mph down route 2 drunk out my mind, or playing with guns, I thought I'd either live forever or die young...both fantasies eliciting the same satisfaction.

Now I'm a bit older and see death creeping over my face in the form of a wrinkle or two. The mirror is a constant reminder that we're all slowly dying. And most people are judged by their reflection, not for who they are or what they think. That's why I consult the mirror occasionally, but never pray to it. If I eat well and work out I might be able to avoid my inevitable end for another couple decades if I'm lucky. That's a long time. But not long enough...

I don't care if I die...yeah, it would suck and a lot of great movies wouldn't get made, but what I'm most concerned about are my relatives dying. They're getting up in age. And I don't know how I will cope with it. I want to always see them again. I want to take them for granted.

Not seeing somebody you care about ever again is a heartbreaking proposition. I don't believe in the afterlife...a fantasy people concocted to cope with the finality of death. And I can't hate on heaven. I would love to kick it there with everybody I love. Unfortunately, my mind destroys that illusion with reason. So...I embrace every second like a minute. And I appreciate everyone close to me. I want to hold them and say I love them. But I don't because that would be corny.

Fuck it. Consider me corny. Starting tomorrow I will display my feelings more readily. I'll say, "I love you" when I want to say, "screw you"...now this only applies to family. If I'm not related to you then go fuck yourself.

Death is promised...but it can be prolonged. I remember my Grandpa hooked up to multiple tubes in a Cleveland ICU room...one of the strongest men I've ever known, and somehow he pulled through. He must've wanted to see the sunrise. Then one day he wasn't strong enough to put off the inevitable. Those around him sealed his fate with bad decisions in tragic fashion. What happens to a tribe when it is responsible for the death of its chief? Persevere and pull through. Learn. Live. Not forget...maybe not forgive even, but still love. What other choice do you have?

My grandparents have always been the foundation of my family. The roots of the tree. And no matter what wind or weather surrounded them, they always held firm, steadfast. Something to lean on. They balance you, upright you, steady you, revitalize you, and make you feel like it's alright. And you know what? It was, so long as you felt their love.

Through the tough times that inevitably befall anyone who has ever lived a life worth living, my grandparents were always a safe harbor that I could count on. The eraser that cleaned the slate, pumped air into lungs, in short, my grandparents were life...until one died. And he didn't have to...at least in the horrible way that he did. Suffering for the sins of others is a biblical tale that shouldn't be repeated by a devout follower who lived an admirable life.

I didn't pray. I learned from my best man's mistakes: Be careful who you surround yourself with. Your life is not a committee decision. No one lives it for you, and no one should decide what happens at the end of it. Medical decisions are an inconvenience to others, a fork in the road to life and death for you. The only counsel to keep is your own.

I used to think that crying was a self-indulgent act for attention, but now I think it is a natural act that means a person cares. And I shed a tear or two when I remember my Grandpa, who always smiled like he meant it. Because he did. And that is the key -- live life like you mean it!

A reason to live is a powerful defense against the grave. A zest for life is an antioxidant. To see what tomorrow brings is a curiosity that never fails to intrigue. Whether it's the sunrise or the morning paper, it's a new day.

However virile a person can be, death will still knock on their door. And most times that knock will be fatal. Some people succumb, others survive. Why? Sometimes the allure of the final slumber can be enticing to a person in pain...yet they travel on with the aid of good weed. Why?

Family. The only thing that matters. My Grandpa's a part of me that carries on. He didn't live forever, but he will last as long as I do.

Everyone dies, might as well die believing something...something tangible -- not a myth, but a belief in mankind. Or even better, die seeing something beautiful. Hobble up to a mountaintop and take the scenery in for one last time. Regardless, the important thing is to look back on your life and be proud.

Treat every invaluable day for everything it's worth! When it's my time to kick off 3 decades from now, my odometer is gonna have more miles than the 1961 Ferrari GT in *Ferris Bueller's Day Off*. And I'll be proud that I tried.

Life is a constant process & struggle to improve one's lot, be it intellectually, socially, financially, physically, and/or emotionally. Some of these goals are connected and interdependent. The complete person strives for all of them. And this striving is the journey. This is what makes a person good. Not what they are necessarily, but what they *want* to be.

Every man has a bit of wildness to him. And he has to run wild long enough to settle down...sort of like an untamed mustang. But the rare and lucky man has a reserve of wildness that will never be tamed. I am one of those beautiful beasts -- I have a voracious appetite for living that extends throughout every aspect of life: work, play, food, sex, booze, music, Everything. I'm only on this planet for a finite amount of time and I intend to enjoy every minute of it! My wife is one of those stubborn cowboy/women who gets bucked off, but holds onto the saddle & is dragged along on a bumpy and cactus-riddled path. I try to slow down enough to pull the prickers out of her resilient ass every now and then.

So far I have found out that we should treat people right on this ride and not worry about another side that may not exist. Though I feel I'm incapable of dying. My organs are forged in cast-iron steel and the brain attached is derived from an ancient tradition of Scottish highland magic called Willpower. I plan on being the sad man at everyone's funeral because I'll never have one.

I'm passionate about many topics and try to figure out a solution to the problems I criticize. But the inherent problem of mortality really has no solution but Humor. You have to maintain a sense of humor...and chuckle at the absurdity of it all...

I have Life figured out: One day I'm gonna kick off, so I'm gonna have fun 'til that day comes.

It's that simple...most things in life are simple. We're all gonna kick off, so might as well enjoy your time here.

The most important thing is that when it's time to kick off to make sure that you leave behind a clean conscience. Don't screw anyone over. And try to leave the world better than when you found it. (Like, don't run Enron, or start wars, or kill people, self-explanatory etcetera)

"The seasons don't fear the reaper,
we should be like them."
-Blue Oyster Cult

If you understand that Death is an inevitability...that it's going to happen no matter what, then you stop fearing it.

And when you no longer fear death, you can start to really Live.

We can treat each other better. Because everything is temporary. Everything is precious.
We will not always be here, enjoy the rarity.

At the same time, life is too short to tolerate assholes. So treat people the way they deserve to be treated. (Shower cool people with love, and give cunts golden showers)
If you're having fun then you're probably doing the right thing.

If I get to 60 years then I'll be happy.
If I get to 70 years then I'll be ecstatic.
If I get to 80 then that means someone invented a titanium liver and had the generosity to hook me up.

Have fun. Enjoy the ride. Some people close their eyes on a roller coaster...others raise their arms and yell.

Author's note: *I almost felt guilty when I looked at the clock last night and saw that it was 3:40AM and I was still drinking Sam Adams like a champ. But then I thought: would my Grandpa regret drinking beer 'til the morning sun while listening to Bob Seger? Would anyone? So I embrace my "flaw".*

We all have to check out one day; at least I'll have fun doing it my way.

Drinking beer and having fun is not a last regret, but a last wish.

34.
High School Horror

This morning I was checking Facebook and came across a topic on the discussion board in my high school class group. "Where are they now?" Not many people posted, but the few who did treated the forum as a confessional. I felt uncomfortable and a bit giddy reading it. Their lives were just another common block on the buckeye brick road back to boring Ohio.

Where am I now? Well for starters, I am a porno star, deep-sea diver, ice road trucker, Dean of gyniatrics at UNLV, and hot air balloon enthusiast. Who cares? I'm me. The same person despised back then.

Looking back on high school is like trying to remember a bad dream that has finally started to dissipate. Why bring up those bad yellow streak years? Uncontrollable acne, dandruff, uneven grades, bullied, teased, and the occasional black eye. I didn't grow a backbone 'til senior year due to self-esteem issues. I could stand up to a grown man in my own house but not a punk boy in high school. Two preppy white guys picked on me for a couple years. A toothpick with the face resembling Qbert, and another rich kid with a last name that sounded like a Nazi throwing up sauerkraut whose daddy peddled Lasik.

Public Humiliation was in abundance; inversely there was no sex life to speak of outside of jerking off to Sports Illustrated swimsuit edition magazines. Kathy Ireland's smiling photo is stickier than most.

My self-esteem was nonexistent, berated away at home so I didn't defend myself at school. And bullies can smell it like sharks in a bloodbath. Low times on Hayes Ave are a blink now, yet it seemed like forever back then. But I survived High School without ever being high. And much to my own surprise, my will to succeed was somehow left intact. Those were rough days. Friends were in short supply and the few I had then, I still have now.

A survey conducted by Clemson University found that 1 in 6 kids get bullied in high school. High school should be a learning experience that prepares kids for college or entering the adult workforce...not a miserable sentence that rivals prison. Teachers need to get their collective heads out of their apathetic asses, and parents need to raise their kids right. Many high schools have become wastelands of conformity and havens of Bigotry. The truth about life is that Being Different is Awesome. And these kids who get picked on need to know that. High School isn't the end of the road, but just the beginning. The people who are Different are the ones who do great things. The asshole Stepford preps fall off eventually, succumbing to the dull lure of suburban mediocrity. The Different kids have interesting lives.

William Golding's book *Lord of the Flies* still resonates. His book should be incorporated into every freshmen high school English class and studied. Too much of the current curriculum is focused on having students fill in tiny ovals on a scantron instead of learning how to critically think for themselves...but maybe that's the point of No Child Left Behind policies. To breed a nation of Automatons who nod, put pencil to paper, and do what they're told. Grow up and be a Congressman or drone pilot. And knock the books out of the hands of whole villages. And get a silver star for each kill. Good job!

I take solace in the fact that most of the "cool kids" peeked in high school, while I, the nerdy outcast, am progressing. To where? Who knows? At least not to normal as They know it. The truth is, I'm a writer barely scraping by, hopping one lightning bolt to the next, be it bottle, book, or script...trying not to be defined by untapped potential or neglected dreams. Avoiding the monotonous nine to five sentence and multiple mouths to feed. Haven't accomplished my goals yet, but I can see them upon the horizon.

A high school reunion beckons. I don't understand...do people just attend them to brag, or just hook up? It might be fun to go only to see the many fat suits people have climbed into. Bright smiles with helium-inflated cheeks. Reaching out with a shaking hand, the same hand that used to smack your books. Only reason it's shaking is because your bicep is a bit bigger than theirs now...

Have You Ever?

Have you ever had a friend that hated your guts because he hated himself even more? The Cool Guy in high school. But you're the Nerd. Time changes and so do both of you.

The Cool Guy is now a loser. Joke of the whole town. The Nerd might still be a nerd, but he's living a cool life in a cool place.

before That...

One man dips, one man rises, and they meet at the intersection. And become Friends. The craziness of immortal youth clouds each other's vision. Fooling each other -- to the point where they think they can be business partners.

But what's the business?
Actually
WHO's the business?

   You got it. The Nerd. And his abilities...which are formidable. One man will be the writer/director, the other will be the exploiter...not producer, because the exploiter doesn't produce shit but lies.
   So the Nerd (who is now slightly cooler than the Cool Guy because the Nerd has been on Jay Leno and written cool scripts that have placed in contests) fires the Cool Guy.
   That partnership is over and so is film school. Good riddance to both. What else to do but succeed and wright tight shit? The Nerd's hometown is a memory and his former friends cling to the Cool Guy...blind to the truth.
   The Nerd embraces who he is -- gets a lil' crazy, buys a gun...thinks it might make him cooler, but all it does is make him crazier and brings him closer to the edge...he mistakes being a nerd with being a bitch. So he tries to prove how tough he is. Lucky he doesn't die.
   Meanwhile
   Like a wind-up toy -- chattering teeth with legs -- the Cool Guy spreads false gossip about the Nerd to the "friends" back home. They cling to every word...out of proximity. The Nerd is out of sight, out of mind. The Nerd accepts this...knowing that time will tell the truth.
   Years Pass
   Out of the confused haze of stunted manhood the Nerd emerges. No longer confused. No longer haunted. No longer Mad. Just determined. To hone his skills. To fulfill his potential...a potential that has always hung heavy on his shoulders like a demonic shadow.
   Calm. Now Rational. A brick on his shoulder instead of a boulder. The Nerd understands both the light & darkness in his mentality. Embraces the dichotomy. Knows it as Truth. Instead of shying away from the fear madness of survival, he vows to use it to inform his writing.
   The Nerd makes progress. His old life left behind...except for a few friends who realized that the Cool Guy was a fake fuck.
   Now the Cool Guy wants to re-connect. A dirtbag who really hates the Nerd and his family, but is desperate for resurrection...wants to see his scumbag face in the Sandusky Register even though it was the Nerd who was on the Tonight Show.
   The Nerd deletes the Facebook email from the Cool Guy.
   A week or two later the Cool Guy makes a generic rap song ten years past his prime that calls out the Nerd. Promises to put the Nerd "on blast"...a threat being a false one, a lie that insinuates that the Nerd has been sodomized. Which has never

happened in the physical form...maybe that blast referred to a metaphor? So the Cool Guy throws a hail mary of lies that fall short...off target...now he is exposed for who he is: an infant in an adult's body.

A baby boy. No longer cool. Probably never was...

Nice Boys

Guns N Roses screeched a creed back in the day declaring, "Nice boys don't play rock n roll." Nor do they write books. Nice Boys.

I can't be nice and spoon-feed you Gerber's baby food bullshit. That's a disservice to you, my soul, and humanity as a whole. If you want a fairy tale while you while away your demise watching Disney movies then so be it. If you want the truth then fasten your Pampers.

Nice Boys are the ones who smile while they pluck the wings off Butterflies. The boys with fat daddies and fatter wallets. The ones who smack the books out of your hands in high school hallways. The ones who grow up to be insurance salesmen, preachers, and generals in Vietnam...or Iraq. Same thing.

Nice Boys shit with the door closed so no one sees them wipe their ass with the American flag.

Nice Boys hate you because they dream of skullfucking you.

Nice Boys think it feels funny.

There was a fat redheaded Nice Boy on my block who people liked. He was trustworthy because he smiled. And so he babysat a young boy across the street from my house. A young boy that the redheaded Nice Boy made lick his dick.

When my buddies and me confronted the scarlet-haired Nice Boy about this. We asked Why? His only response was, "It felt fhunney."

And so it does.

It feels funny. So is perception. Here was a redheaded hero who turned out to be a sex offender...while I was the public enemy #1 bane of our neighborhood because I liked to spit loogies, Curse, and raise hell with toilet paper. Still do. And it doesn't feel funny to me. Because it is funny.

And that my friend is a microcosm of how to get elected. Smile. Even if it feels funny.

The Nice Boys are nice because everyone says they're nice.

The Nice Boys drop the bombs and make other boys lick dick.

The Nice Boys buy the ballot. The Nice Boys pray with bullets.

The Nice Boys are the inbred offspring of genetic failures whose inherited wealth exceeds their stunted intellect.

The Nice Boys are always above the law.

The Nice Boys aren't nice boys at all...

You Can Never Go Home

   Does a wolf ever go home? Or a bear? Spend too much time somewhere and the shedded hair & shit is off-putting. Maybe home is for the birds -- visit on a seasonal basis then leave with the setting sun of summer.
   Sandusky, Ohio is, and will always be, a part of me...a postcard of my past. Scribbles on the backside of public posterity. My family, and a friend or two live there. And a friend from Sandtown is equal to ten friends in Vegas. Or twenty in Hollywood.
   My hometown is a small blue-collar city that I respect. It builds character, and those who excel don't suffer fools 'cause they grew up with them. The few people who make it out become the best at what they do.
   I remember being drunk, freestyling in the parking lot of the Drink at 2 AM. To the outsider eye I would be an anomaly...a nerdy white guy rapping in a circle...but I knew most of those dudes since the 3rd & 6th grades. My type of behavior is like playin' poker or tossin' horseshoes with your friends.
   Sometimes it was violent. One time I had to sock a dude's face -- the doorman at the Cedar Point bar, Louie's. Matter of fact, I had to sock his face twice...he was a slow learner.

Ohio is a combative state...I've never been in a fight outside it. Took inventory of my life and realized I've been beat up three times:

1- High School -- Scales, a six foot five dude who I thought was my friend.
2- Perkins -- Hell's Angel biker, but I got the first couple punches in.
3- Columbus -- 2 coked-up dudes, I punched their brother over a botched hot-wire gig.

I take solace that I've took the hard lumps early. It stiffens backbones. Prepares you for the real world. If you want gravy then go eat some mashed potatoes because life in Ohio is served with several slices of humble pie.

Want to move to Ohio? Fine. Just don't forget your low expectations. Down some dark and twisted country road lies a shack full of skanks all too willing to give lapdances for ten bucks a pop. A sucker for a bargain, I shelled out a couple fivers while intoxicated. A trailer-trash stripper tongued the bills and swallowed them...saying she'll pick 'em out of the shitter later. She drank ex-lax with her coffee...I could tell by her smile -- a grill only a hockey player could love. A tooth here and there haphazardly jutted out of her gums like an amateur's attempt to mold a Jason Voorhees mask.

No time to talk as she grinded my kneecap like it was a hemorrhoidal scratching post. The more she gyrated, the more Long John Silvers flared my nostrils. Back and forth, back and forth, the woman moved like a weary zebu that hadn't eaten in a month.

I gritted my teeth, held my breath, and silently prayed for the song to end while Crotch Crickets chirped and leapt every which way.

It seems Eternity is a five minute long song. Afterwards she licked my forehead, which still has a psoriasis stain to this day. I inspected my favorite pair of jeans expecting to find a Chlamydia crab monster to be perched on my knee, but to my relief there was only a fresh skidmark and a few dingleberries.

Later I lit my pants on fire with leftover Jim Beam and hung them on the mayor's clothesline. And that was the worst ten bucks ever spent in the history of strip clubs. I'm not even sure that place was a club...it was more like a lemonade stand of flabby old whores looking for enough money to pay for the next bus out of town.

Most ambitious people born in Sandusky look for a way outta town while tourists pour in. Cedar Point is the draw: the best amusement park in the country. My buddies and I used to cavort up & down the midway shouting the lyrics to the Onyx song "Throw Ya Gunz" much to the chagrin of the terrified tourists. Their looks of dismay all seemed to convey the same thought: Next year we're going to

King's Island.

Sandtown is a place a person goes to *after* making the money. The summers are great on the Lake. Cost of living is affordable. The city may lack leadership, but a few ambitious people could change that.

I used to visit Sandusky every chance I got. Distance didn't matter. So long as I had the time, I made the effort. Sometimes nature intervened:

HE WAS A MAN

A travel noir

A late model Corsica barreled down the highway like a bat fleeing Hades. The bat didn't pay Hades her twenty bucks, and Hades was pissed. She gives great euphemism, and she'll be damned if she does it for free.

Anyways. Back to the Corsica. A middle-aged white man hunched over the steering wheel staring intently at the road ahead. Maybe too intently. A fart leapt from his ass without warning.

Now this man was faced with the decision of a lifetime. Keep driving and deal with the situation when he got to his destination, or face the ugly truth now.

It couldn't wait. The fart was wet, disgruntled, and on the move.

Turning off the turnpike, the man scowled. Time was being wasted. All for what?

A shart.

He should have known better. Never trust a fart.

He wheeled the Corsica into a rest stop straight out of the Dark Ages. Sweat beading on his forehead, the man quickly shuffled into the restroom like Charlie Chaplin hiding J Edgar Hoover up his ass.

Once safely entrenched in a stall, the man removed the egregious offender: a soiled spot resting on a red and black pair of Tommy Hilfiger boxers. His favorite. Knitted out of a fabric that felt good all over his manhood. Like wearing a pair of Viagra.

So he was faced with another dilemma of a most delicate manner: Leave the waterlogged boxers in the stall, or take them home where they might be salvaged with a little warm water and love.

A lesser man would have panicked. But not this guy. He stuffed those boxers in his pocket faster than Pee Wee Herman hiding summer sausage in a movie theater. Damn the consequences.

Now he could deal with a more pressing issue. A monumental task that was sure to leave emotional scars. And that was wiping his ass.

Mudbutt strikes unexpected. There's no pattern to the destruction. Call it tornado of the ass. And the man was forced to wipe with rest stop toilet tissue -- which is about a quarter ply...a delicate fabric designed for constipated midgets.

Rigging a wipe like a rectal MacGyver, the man attached toilet tissue to each finger on his right hand utilizing paper clips.

He was ready. So he wiped.

And came up with a nightmare resembling a Rorschach inkblot.

In it he saw his fear. His past. His failures.

So he flushed it. It's better to look ahead than behind. Especially his behind.

After wiping another five dozen times, the man deposited the soiled detritus in the toilet, flushed, plugged it, stood back, watched the flood rise, satisfied and not a little bit proud, left, soiled boxers safely secured on his person.

The Corsica roared back onto the highway. A smile eased over the driver's face. He faced a crisis. Not of his doing, but of nature's. A crisis every person faces once in his or her life.

Mudbutt.

The driver shifted in his seat...his smile faded away, replaced with a thin lipless crease of consternation.

Another fart was on deck. Ready to be released.

Should he risk it? Should he live in fear and let his life be dictated by bowel movements?

Never!

The joyous sound of released gas filled the car like church bells on Sunday.

Not a drop leaked out. He walked the trapeze wire of life wearing ice skates and didn't flinch. He sniffed the air once. Twice. And knew it was all worth it.

Everything was fine...in a sulfuric roadkill type of way.

He was a risk-taker. He stared into the abyss of mudbutt and smiled. He wasn't afraid anymore.

He farted the same way he lived.

He was a man.

35.
Internet

With the invention of Facebook, a friend has taken on a new meaning that dilutes the essence of really having a friend. The only thing I know is this: the litmus test for true friendship is their reaction to your success. If you accomplish something positive, a real friend will make you feel good about it. A fake friend will passive-aggressively make you feel bad about it, someway. And if you fail, a real friend will help bury your mistake and move on. A fake friend will help bury you.

Now that I have Internet I can watch my Bukkake porn without people peering over my shoulder at the library. Good riddance. Spending an hour surrounded by these hacking, sneezing, slobbering scurvy bastards would change even the most adamantly pious Jesus freak pro-choicers' mind into favoring abortion. In fact, they would require it for anyone conceiving under the age of 18.

The Internet is almost synonymous with Anonymous Insults: an opportunity for punks to berate other people without consequence. I prefer insults in book form with my name attached. Write a blog and get skewered by cowards. Read a news article, but be sure to avoid the comments posted below -- any mongoloid with nose pickers can scribble something obscene. Bathroom stall graffiti is more interesting and usually more rational.

Another aspect of the Internet I loathe is the free market of unsolicited advice. Give and Receive without worry. Most times, advice mutates into attacks. There's advice and there's passive aggression. I would tell you which is which, but I don't have time to explain things to slow people.

Discourse has been reduced to 140 characters or less. Woody Allen would've been the king molester of Twitter if it existed forty years ago...now we're stuck with snarky Jeff Fahey, another douche with the shelf life of yogurt. George Burns' burps had more humor.

It's funny, I have a few dozen Twitter "followers" and I only know a couple of them. As for Facebook, the vast majority of "friends" never like or comment on my posts. So what's the sense of having an online Presence? I'm better off opening my front door and yodeling on a megaphone for my neighbors.

It's all a facade. Like the wizard behind the curtain, we're all projecting or protecting an image. Update your status. Static or otherwise. We are a Yahoo nation of yahoos -- uneducated, anti-intellectual, crudely materialistic people praying to popular opinion.

Postconsequence Society

I'm not sure I subscribe to the theory that we live in a postmodern society. Theories sound too much like theocracy, whose adherents follow blindly without regard to any contradictory evidence. Postmodernism rubs me as just another idea concocted by failed writers who have too much time on their hands and lack the creative inclination to write anything new or compelling. But maybe we Americans live in a Postconsequence Society...meaning there are no consequences for our actions anymore.

In this age of social media, men and women can hide behind the veil of anonymity and type anything they want online. Without consequence. Howl, curse, eviscerate with no provocation other than boredom. Heckle, disparage, and berate without a care in the world. Facebook is one such outlet. When people aren't too busy bragging or conforming or posting passive-aggressive missives dripping with self-righteous indignation they have the opportunity to talk shit to anyone without fear of getting their ass kicked. And that's a problem because this type of social interaction doesn't promote intelligent discussion or hold people accountable for their actions.

I'm not a tough guy. I've lost as many fights as I've won. Those losses, or ass-kickings as I tend to refer to them, were valuable because each one taught me something. Don't talk trash Before a fight, or you run the risk of getting sucker punched. Do not berate people bigger than yourself. If you have a disagreement, try to work it out in an intellectual manner. And if an ignorant hoodlum cannot be reasoned with, well then, punch first and fast, and try to get in as many licks as you can before he stomps you.

Life Lessons. I appreciated every one. An ass kicking will change a person's philosophy about shit talking.

Conversely, kicking a person's ass can be an unselfish act that helps make that individual a better person. Because some people just can't help it...it's in their nature to talk shit, and they won't stop unless they are taught a lesson. Humility can only be learned the hard way: Receiving a haymaker to the eye usually does the trick. Even then some people will continue to bump their gums. These are special cases -- born assholes with defective genes, and though repeated thrashings do not correct this genetic defect, they at least quiet the insufferable cuntlicker for a little bit.

The worst type of asshole is the coddled white guy with a patronizing personality that is completely unjustified. A self-entitled douche raised with the moral temerity of a sidewinder and the intelligence of a desert rat, this prick thinks it's his duty in life to disparage anyone who might have a higher IQ. You can't debate with this type of Neanderthal so an ass kicking is the only logical alternative. Some small men with big opinions lack the intestinal fortitude to back them up.

It may sound barbaric but every town in America should have a community boxing ring where disagreeing parties can work out their differences. Why should boxers and UFC fighters have all the fun? Besides, this type of community project would help alleviate the already overburdened justice system in this country. As of now, the shit-talker is protected in this country by antiquated courts. If you knock out a shit-talker and he squeals (which he usually does) then you are the one prosecuted. Yeah, the shit-talker might have a chipped tooth, but you do the time. How is that fair? An irrational consequence.

So make the shit-talker work for it. Implement my boxing ring initiative. If the swine wants to constantly berate people online or otherwise then he better get his sorry ass off the couch and start working out because there will now be consequences...in the form of boxing. If I don't respect a person's infantile intelligence and he insists on berating me, what better venue than a boxing ring to get my point across?

Cyber bulling is just the tip of the iceberg. American society is rife with no consequences. Wall Street is the best example. We don't live in a free-market society, but a free from consequence one. Financial companies screw our economy with their greedy biz practices and when they are about to go bankrupt, what happens? They get bailed out. By the guvment, another entity that never suffers a consequence. If the Prez and Congress decide to go to war they do not suffer the casualties...the American People do.

A law should be imposed: If the President declares war then he/she should be on the front lines leading "their" troops into battle, and their offspring suited up right behind. And Congress should lace up their bootstraps also...at the very least those sloth-like sedentary fat fucks would make good cannon fodder. The first troops conscripted should be white male Ivy League college students. Let them learn a life lesson or two...instead of wasting spare time rowing and playing lacrosse...hand those inbred nepotistic greaseballs a bayonet and M14 rifle, and point them in the direction of the Taliban.

As it stands, Americans live a carefree lifestyle that ignores consequences. Ignorance prevails in the form of SUVs, muscle cars, and reality TV. No one will say they like war, pollution, or oil spills -- yet they still drive gas-guzzling vehicles without reservation...and declare it their American Right to do so. Yes, America is the home of the "free", but it shouldn't be consequence-free. Just because it's your right to be ignorant doesn't mean you have to be.

Facebook

"I have a lot of Facebook friends therefore I am" is equivalent to saying, "My cock crabs keep me active."
  I have neither.
  Facebook is like walking into a crowded auditorium and announcing intimate details of your life with a megaphone. We live in socially irrelevant times. Facebook is High School in Perpetuity (and I fucking hated high school). The only meaning to online life is fake friends. My fear is we are becoming a nation of Neos, connected to the Matrix of mediocrity.
  Facebook is an interactive low school where the popular dumb kids still get Liked: a portal that gives the painfully average person a cyberspace spotlight. A dull candle glow that creates stars. The popularity of the site stems from the fact it gives Everybody a chance to have their own reality show. No matter how boring their life is they can still feel important because a dozen people think they're witty. A wall cluttered with self-important peons who are all in a hurry to do nothing. A drab canvass of baby pictures and affirmations of the mundane life devoid of peaks, lows, and anything of interest.
  Facebook has become an overwhelming blast of Domesticity that numbs the mind and pains the soul. The Sewing Circle Hotline. An empty social nothing. The same thing we see on TV. The 21st century heroin. It's easy to kick it -- Facebook -- sure -- let it go.
  It's less about communication than it is self-gratification or indulgent congratulation. Delude yourself into thinking that life really is exciting even though your only portal to the outside world is the 2x2 screen on your smartphone. A figment of flogging. You may never have lived outside the tiny burgh you were born in -- but that's okay because you have a thousand Facebook friends.
  All one big sham that continues to fascinate me. It's truly a social phenomenon, and I'm interested in seeing the results. Will it be a forum for social change? Or...turn our society into a bunch of conformists who resist individuality in fear of losing a "friend".
  Some use Facebook as a propaganda device. Whether it's a pic of some guy holding up a hand-written piece of paper touting his Horatio Alger story (a favorite fairy tale of the right), or a picture of Obama with a box of donuts (should be a box of dildos the way he screws his supporters), both sides are doing it. Propaganda

used to be spread by the government & its media, now the people spread it for them for free. An example of the dog chasing its tail -- the people promote propaganda to themselves. A brilliant form of manipulation, though this transmission device has the potential to be seized by Evolutionaries and used to promote the truth. Disagreeing with the political processes of the country is an ingrained part of our culture.

At the very least Facebook can be boring. I'll write something funny or thought provoking and get nary a response. But other people's piddling status reports get dozens of likes: My poodle Poppy ate all her food then pooped on the kitchen floor then wolfed down her own feces for dessert. Comments include "How adorable" and "Can you teach my husband that trick?"

I finally figured out my love/hate relationship with Facebook. I love it because I get to write goofball things that offend other people...the site becomes a source of chuckles for me and my family. And I hate it because I sometimes read what other people write. Let's face it...not everybody is a writer. (some people may be thinking this while reading my book) I lose 2-3 friends every time I drink due to the crazy shit I write. So...I figure I can drink a hundred more times 'til I run out of "friends". I'll never be in the "In Crowd" and I thank lil' baby Jesus for that.

Why So Serious?

I've been informed that my profanity on Facebook is offensive. My reply: If you really want to see something offensive then turn on your television. Sure, I curse more often than most...but that's either humor or dispelling frustrations. I've noticed that many Americans are hypocrites...easily offended by profanity yet the majority of their entertainment is violent. So I curse a little, so what? I'm not harming anyone...and I'm not consciously trying to offend anyone's Puritanical sensibilities. I suffer from Sam Adams-induced tourettes. At least my online social portrayal is accurate. My drunken rambling missives invariably offend the people who are really offended by their own lives.

Facebook can be a quicksand of Passive Aggression. I prefer shit-talking directly. I grew up in Ohio where apples are chucked at your head during lunch. My preferred projectiles were pee-bags and feces. Piss & shit. The primal way of showing displeasure with a person is the most effective. Nary a house on Boalt Street escaped the wrath of my summer carpet-bombing pee-bag campaigns fueled by Faygo Soda. Only a diabolical genius would use an innocent object like a Ziploc baggy as a weapon of terror. Just add urine, tie it, and toss. My strategy was to saturate the roofs of the neighbor's houses with pee-bags until they all capitulated to my rule as king prankster. Any resistance was met with me shitting in their mailbox and wrapping a hundred yards of kite string through their front yard. Imagine waking up at 7AM to go to work and not being able to get to your car without a machete.

    This sort of brazen behavior instilled fear throughout the neighborhood. A righteous sort of anxiety that maintained balance. The Kids were to be taken serious. We had a say. Get out of line & disrespect one of us, and prepare to find crop circles in your finely manicured lawn. ET didn't create them...it was urine. Nature's peroxide.

    Pranking is a way of creating an equal society. A lost art form today. Now every crazed adult has a gun, making a past hobby a dangerous occupation. Kids could care less; they are all too busy checking Facebook anyway. I don't prank as much as I used to, so I'm relegated to vent my frustrations in an inebriated state on the social network. Frustration is a natural byproduct of passion. Talking shit on Facebook is a lot cheaper than therapy.

    The dude you have to worry about is the older anonymous man who's bottled shit up his entire life and snaps. The life of silent desperation is the ultimate tragedy.

"Looking at the proliferation of personal Web pages on the Net, it looks like very soon everyone on earth will have 15 megabytes of fame."
-M. G. Sriram

    Feelings have become reduced to jumbled words on a Facebook status... Facebook and the Internet is really a desert wasteland of lazy desires and wishes.

    Wish someone a happy birthday on Facebook is nice...like dribbling inside the bowl when shaking off. But I prefer to hear the voice of a living person who made the effort to call me. The tenor of a person's voice who is happy to speak to you is worth more than all of the demands on this planet.

    My Grandpa never emailed me, yet I can still hear his voice...

Author's note: *As a writer, you want people to read what you have to say. Facebook is an immediate outlet, but it's almost worthless...if not a bit satisfying. It's better to create something that the world can see instead of spinning gears online. I'm guilty of both.*

-or-

Drunken writer logic: An immediate outlet that no one reads is almost as good as a permanent one that everyone will.

Facebook is a colossal waste of time. Life is too short to be bombarded with braggarts and mediocre bullshit that irritates. Facebook feeds into the rampant societal problem of Narcissism...where you don't exist unless you take a Selfie.

I will use the dismal experience of being on Facebook to create a superior social media site that has actual Meaning.

36. 31 day Deadline

My body is scuffed up from fornicating in my father-in-law's lap pool for two straight days in 115-degree heat. He's been away on holiday while I've been making frequent deposits of organic yogurt into the chlorinated water. Whitesnake should make a song about it.

A book can take years to write, but a strict deadline is necessary: the type of set in stone deal that causes assholes to pucker and hemorrhoids to burst.

Batten down the hatches. It's August 1st, 2013 and only 31 days left to complete a readable rough draft. Stock the fridge with cold cheap suds. Lock the office doors. No more social life. Time to fall off the planet and Write. The days of pool parties and casino jaunts are finito.

Pack on the blubber and plant the buttocks at the computer until deep vein thrombosis pulses throughout my lower body. The only lean muscle required is the cerebral cortex. Everything else is extra baggage.

Eat once a day and shower after every other meal. There are no beauty prizes for writing. You can tell someone's a writer by the gouty quality of his or her typing hands.

The Buddha may have walked across hot coals, but I'm shittin' out peach pits of pure knowledge.

Pain mixed with pleasure. I may never write another book, so this one better be good. So, until September, *Selah*.

"I'm slow to finish, but I'm quick to start."
-Red Hot Chili Peppers

August 31, 2013

Finishing the rough draft of my book late late tonight or early early tomorrow. Then I'm taking a day off to rest the jets. Let the afterburners cool a bit.

There are worse things in the world than Deadlines, but I just can't think of any right now. Don't cry for me, Argentina. My fridge is stocked with leftover bbq, Bud Lights, and raspberry Jell-O shots. Plus there's coffee, Jameson, energy drinks, and my R2D2 Pez Dispenser is loaded with No Doz. In light of my imbibing habits I anticipate Jameson's quarterly earnings to increase by 2-3%.

My Mom told me that I lost my tolerance to alcohol but I disagree vehemently. I tolerate it just find. I think my wife lost her tolerance to it.

I have other thoughts; I just can't think of them right now...this book has turned my mind into mush. Writing a book is the opposite of watching television: I turn my mind to slush to strengthen the reader's. A transmission of brain matter. I should have a statue erected in my honor in front of every library & liquor store in America for my sacrifice.

The carbuncles in my lower butt cheeks need to be drained of pus, but I don't have time for such luxuries. There's a book to be written and a society to be saved. I only hope it won't be too late...

Sometime early September morning

Staring at the computer screen and realized I wrote 67 chapters. I used to be a hack that could barely complete a 90-page script...now I have a hard time stopping at 300 pages. I need a crazed Catholic nun bent out of her habit on angel dust to smack my knuckles with sharp metal rulers to stop these fingers from typing more chapters. My natural inclination is to write everyday, but I have to shift gears and shape what has already been written. This book could go on forever, but it's time to finish a final draft.

Most of the book was fun to write, but some of it was really tough. Gazing a stone-cold objective eye at the truth of our history & present was disconcerting at times. And parts will be just as tough to digest & read as it was to write. A morass of feelings and a web of uncertainty is the only way I can describe the writing process. The consolation is that we control our future. The New Generation, or the Now Generation, could be the best, or the worst generation in United States history. I lean towards the former. And so I shuffle to the fridge to grab a cold one so I can refine what you're reading right now...

Sandtown births Champions. Land was the #1 draft pick so it's only right that I write a classic book. Possess an attitude that if you're gonna do something then do it better than everyone else. So I stay up all night sculpting chapters. My book is going to be an equal opportunity offender, which is precisely the point.

After much trial & error, I've discovered the perfect writing system: Since I don't sleep much, I primarily write from 10pm - 4am...though I sporadically scribble throughout the day also...notes and bits & pieces of random info to make sense of later. Best of both worlds: Get the book done and spunk the spouse. What more can a man ask for? is my last thought as I conk out at 4:21am...I sleep when I have to, but I don't like to.

My bionic fortitude doesn't allow me to slumber for long. Up early, chipping away, despite drinking 24 some odd beers the night before. And I find it odd that I have neither hangover nor headache. A reason to celebrate. It's such a beautiful day in Vegas that I grill a half-dozen steaks just for the hell of it. Fry up a carton of eggs on a skillet and make a bountiful feast. Why not?

I heard of the tune "Tequila Sunrise", but what about Rum Afternoon? There is an obvious void in the auditory soundscape of pop culture and I aim to fill it with an original song while the Weber chimney starter works its magic...

Carving a freshly-grilled steak in a sunny backyard on a glorious Monday makes a man feel like a man. Each medium-well morsel is scrumptious; dripping honey BBQ & Ansaldo's hot chimichurri sauce.

Love Comes Over You

Eric Clapton's unplugged album sounds great on a surround sound system. Drifting outside, serenading the neighborhood. We all have the same senses: sight, hearing, touch, smell, and thought...and Love.

Life is Love. The combination of all the senses. Appreciation. If your Monday is not Awesome, then what are you waiting for? We only get one life. Many decades from now I will look back on this "ordinary" day with the fondest memories.

I enjoy the moment until some half-wit clod tries to buzz-kill me by asking the insipid question, "What happens if you never make it?"

I reply, "Make it? I'm alive. I've already made it." Then I smacked the asinine asswipe with stainless steel tongs.

As he ran away, I screamed, "I many not be great, but I'm pretty good, and so long as I continue using honesty then I hold the potential for greatness."

Great or not, I believe the journey is worth it. And regardless of success, I'm going to make the journey fun. How many people can define their life that way?

My aspiration is nobbers and for people to say many decades from now that He wrote a very good book in a mediocre time. I'd like to direct several thought-provoking movies also. The main thought to provoke is to be Yourself. What that is...I don't know...it is for us all to find out...just don't act like a cunt on the way. Speaking of...my book is becoming a polemical essay that keeps growing like pubic hair at a Woodstock concert. I should be shaving it instead of giving it a perm.

There are a lot of books out there about writing, but I model my wordplay on Eric Clapton guitar solos. Art is art, and if you hold master craftspeople in high esteem then you will hold yourself to high standards. My fingers typing on a keyboard hold the same artistic potential as an artist jamming a Fender. Language is music to the mind.

Writers are risky moths -- we like to fly too close to the truth 'til it burns. Cut us some slack. Whether it's too much drinking or a high page count because of rambling like this, please appreciate the effort. I have a tendency "to go there." And it's what I want to write...but it's not easy to write. Because truth is painful...and can make you feel like the only person on the planet with any sense. And I'd rather be embraced then ostracized; yet I can only write the truth as I see it. As a writer it's important to be liked by the right people and loathed by the wrong ones.

The aspect I love most about writing is that rare moment you get in a groove then look up at the clock and realize two hours passed, yet it only felt like two minutes. This is what alien abductees call "they time." These moments happen with a higher consistency the more you write. It's that simple. Even though it is anything but.

As the final draft winds down I feel like I'm starting to suffer from a slight case of appendicitis while passing a few kidney stones. These may be imagined ailments...merely the nervous knot-twisted twitchings of intestines that consistently shuffle around every half hour. The psychosomatic spasms could be a reaction to the fact that my book is almost finished. My life will never be the same...for the better. The last time I felt this way was decades ago when my lil' sister was a born a month premature in a Hershey, PA hospital. That turned out well, so at least I have a bit of hope to cling to.

Through the accumulation of weariness & failures, I thought it a good idea to start a bonfire in the backyard and burn my old screenplays one page at a time, because that's what they did to me. Instead, I walk to a bar and leave a trail of PBR cans so I can find my way back home. Tomorrow's another day.

[There's a low throbbing pulse humming through my body. No doubt the result of Fat Tires, caffeine, and vodka shots disguised as Jell-O. But my body should know better. I've trained it. All this meandering sunplay of the eyes is nonsense. My body has a pronounced tolerance for alcohol. The very thought of it makes my lip quiver in disgust. Anyone who sips even the minutest amount of Devil's Dew should be whiplashed back into basics. A man stands on his own. No crutch is needed, especially that of distilled grains sifted through Satan's lower intestine.]
-My discombulated thoughts upon waking up.

And so I find a way to get out of bed, hung-over, and finish the Final Draft...And now you read my scrambled thoughts of the past five years. I hope you enjoy them...I'm either crazy and the world is normal, or I'm wise and the world is crazy.

Writers should recognize the insanity that surrounds them. At least we have made progress and I'm free to write a book like this...a man was once persecuted because he thought the Earth was round. If my writing is criticized as pedantic, then so be it. Pedantic is a word pseudo-intellectuals invented to label people bold enough to hold opinions. I've been told that I possess a talent of cutting through the layers of bullshit and getting to the shiny kernel of truth. I embrace being a pedant because I possess a brain that flourishes. Unfortunately, Pfizer hasn't created a blue pill to give lame brains pedantic thoughts, so my book is the cure.

I'm not scared of failing; I'm scared of succeeding. That means change. But...isn't it time we all did? Evolution is necessary, and a bit overdue...

Author's note: *I think my kidneys have expanded to the size of Nerf footballs. They're the Dwayne Johnson of the kidney world. If someone gave me a kidney shot right now they would break their hand. My blood type is OE with a blood pressure of 800 over 40. This better be the last book I write, otherwise I'll be grave robbing organs like Mary Shelley.*

37.
Time...

...the most precious commodity anyone will ever possess. The great equalizer.

Money can be made and lost (especially if you're a Vegas gambler), but time can never be gained. It is constantly running out. The rate it runs can vary depending on a person's lifestyle. At the very least there is a constant Slippage of time for everyone. Even when we sleep. Especially when we sleep.

Being an aspiring filmmaker the slippage of time is more pronounced. It is a tangible phenomenon that gnaws away my conscience. Even when I'm getting a haircut, or going to the grocery store, there is a recognition that time is slipping away and that this time could be better spent working on a script or movie.

A metaphor to better explain the slippage:

Imagine yourself in the middle of an ocean. There is no boat, and you're bobbing in the sea amongst 10-foot waves. You're not wearing a life jacket. It's a dark grey overcast day and rain is pouring. Lightning streaks in the background. You desperately try to stay afloat, treading water with all your might.

This is the life of an aspirant. And most don't make it because they can't tread water long enough. Constant rejection drowns the weak...

Five miles away you can barely glimpse an island. The Promised Land. Upon this island are movie cameras, film stock, actors, sets, and editing bays. Maybe even a Steadicam or two.

But it is not possible to swim all the way to this island. You need an "opportunity" to get closer. Fortunately for you the sea is teeming with them. Dolphins, whales, and other things with fins. You just have to grab hold of one. Unfortunately, the grasp is slippery and almost impossible to catch. Imagine how hard it would be to grasp a slippery wet dolphin in the sea and ride it to that island. Or an enormous sperm whale where there is nothing to hold on to. The prospect is so daunting that most aspiring filmmakers give up and drown into a mediocre life that will always have a bitter aftertaste.

I've been wading in that treacherous sea for years now and that island has slowly gotten closer, but now is the time where I'm going to sink my claws into one of those passing dolphin's fins and ride that sucker all the way to the Promised Land.

I can tread water forever, but I have bigger plans.

    That island isn't going to come to me. It's sink or swim. The most valuable commodity I'll ever possess is my time on this Earth, and I don't plan on spending it at the bottom of the sea.

    My only concern: what happens when I make it to the island only to find it infested with cannibals?

Sunset

The most beautiful green vegetation resembles black claws,
pawing their way through the breeze,

reaching for something...

something better or worse

Leaves and branches silhouetted against the sunset.

Bas-relief

Charcoal bacteria
against the sea,
the only thing that calms me.

38.
Epitaphic

People rather be common than honest. It's easier that way...
If what I write makes you mad then that means there's some truth in my statement.

Shit, I'm a writer, I'm supposed to make you mad...or amuse you...but I accomplish both by doing one thing -- document the truth through my perception. No book worth reading reinforces your stupidity. A good book must not only amuse the mind, but inspire and elevate it as well. My book is a state of the union address by a brilliant someone who has no ulterior motives.

Writing is merely intellectual masturbation. I find it fun...but do it too often and it can become painful. Alcohol eases the pain like WD40 on a squeaky door hinge. When I write sober I feel a modicum of panic, paranoia, and pain, and that's on a good day, where euphoria peeks its beautiful head out in the occasional well-written sentence. There's a reason why masturbate rhymes with procrastinate. But then again, the very act of living is procrastinating...putting off the inevitable: dying.
  Ansel Adams' photography is an inspiration. His photos were art. I look at one of his black & white mountainscapes and see a metaphor for life: the twisting river is the journey we take -- a journey to get past those mountains, which can be obstacles or opportunities, and beyond those mountains is the goal. But the weather behind those mountains is a bit ambiguous -- is the sun rising out of the clouds? Or is a storm coming?
  I believe that the "weather" will be determined by how that individual conducted himself upon the journey. And like any belief, it's usually proven wrong by the chaotic realities of life. Regardless of the outcome, a person needs to stay strong and not succumb to the scumbag opportunities that soil the soul. The Right Path has many directions, and temptation can sometimes be okay so long as no one gets hurt. In fact, temptation can be a virtue if it feels good and makes you stronger. And benefits those around you. Just remember the all-important caveat: Unlike chances, you only get one soul. Don't waste it.

Which leads to a philosophy: A goal should only be obtained by honorable means.

In a letter to Dorothea Lange, Ansel Adams wrote, "What we really need is a revival of the Walt Whitman spirit -- the acceptance of the Whole of Humanity."

Now I admire that spirit, but as a writer, I'm conflicted. I try to embrace optimism, but it slips through like a lubricated pug. And yes, even the drool of optimism is gross...sometimes.

But, I embrace that conflict, because without it, I'd have nothing important to write about...though I could make a killing writing brainless comedy scripts...which is an idea. In case this writing thing doesn't work out, my back-up plan is to be a pimp with a stable full of midget hoes. Bitches betta not come up short!

It's widely known that degenerates pay double for the cripples in motorized scooters. Gnomes are in vogue. For an additional twenty spot, the perverted customer can work the chair throttle back and forth while receiving a standing nobber. A hobgoblin is head on wheels.

These sorts of business transactions are done everyday by resourceful entrepreneurs...or desperate men possessing bad credit and morally aloof women with bad genetics. A trip to the Tenderloin can yield a treasure trove of guilty pleasures. One society's trash is another man's meal ticket.

I'm working on a higher plane for everyone's benefit. Be it knowledge or enjoyment, it is important for a man to sacrifice only for the greater good. And I'm in a good place right now. I'm not young. I'm not old. All I have is my dreams, and regardless of the results, the important thing is that I have them. Dreams are more precious than diamonds. They sparkle in your mind.

Around 4:31 AM this morning a burst of energy bolted into my arms...letting me know that it was time to either write or jerk off. So I passed up temporary pleasure for posterity. A permanence of proclamations. Here are my skills:

I compare the writing process to using a water pump.

Some days, the writer will barely pump and a flood of ideas springs forth.

Other days, the writer will pump and pump and pump, and barely get a trickle. That's it.

And only the good writers pump everyday, regardless. Not because they want to...because they have to. I like to think that creative people have a never-ending supply of creativity. But what if that well dries up?

If a person involves themselves with life and people, cares about both -- really cares -- then that creativity will always be there. Creativity is synonymous with feelings. Once a person goes numb, there's nothing left to say.

A writer sacrifices for their craft

I'm sacrificing more organs than a thuggee cult high priest. At least 1 kidney, 1/3 liver, a sliver of the frontal lobe, and not a bit of pride. But my heart is still beating. I'm a biological anomaly with a cast-iron constitution capable of drinking twenty Hammer Ales in one sitting and not be hung over the next day. When I'm sober I'm mildly interesting, when I'm drinking I'm almost brilliant. So I chose the latter approach for this book.

I'm treating my book like a John Waters movie. I want to offend the reader with the first sentence. These asinine asswipes in our country need to be offended. You may have even been one before you read this book. Shit's been too comfortable: Cable TV, Dennys, Disney, Colitis, and Global Warming. Colitis? How does Colitis fit into the equation? The country has a disease and can't help but to foul its own pants...leaving the next generation to clean the shitbag.

Our generation needs a bitch-slap and my book will do that...I hope. Disrupt the destructive complacency...

I must have an overbite, 'cause I always bite off more than I can chew. Some writers are competent, but they lack soul...a purpose. Wasting away their mediocre gifts. Yeah, they might get paid for it, but so do prostitutes. Just because you can get paid to screw doesn't mean you should brag about it.

"Albert Einstein was a ladies man."

Writing this book is sort of like wallpapering a grand dining room: Trying to match all the beautiful snippets of thought into a coherent whole...just so people can glance at them while picking at their food.

Writing a book is fun, but there are moments of doubt that arise from conflict. It is an inherent human need to be liked. Only a sociopath loves to be loathed. But my book will meet intense resistance, ensuring that I will not be liked by a lot of people. The need to seek truth conflicts with this.

The only thing that matters is History. In a hundred years, will my book be prescient and Right?

Tangents of Honesty

I've started to use my own weaknesses as a person to make me a stronger writer. A technique I use is called Honesty.

I have to stay constantly busy; otherwise I have a tendency to veer off into two disparate paths. The first and most common is the debauched hedonistic bender variety where I turn into a tornado of impropriety.

Or...succumb to a minor case of existential angst...which forces me to wash away the blues with heavy doses of alcohol, sex, and writing. (and not the kind of writing that will benefit my career like screenwriting, but the kind of writing like Bukowski's *Ham on Rye*, only that no one will read my ham on whole wheat because I'm not as good as Bukowski)

Both paths end at the same place: me bouncing around the house like a sloth on speed. So stay busy. It's a good thing that getting Heattwave Productions off the ground is a tremendous amount of work.

Norman Mailer once wrote, "...it is inevitable that a bad fall comes to the strong-willed man who is not strong enough to reach his own peak."

I've set high goals for myself and the only way to avoid the bad fall is to never give up.

Trying to achieve one's dreams keeps a person full of hope. And that's a good thing to have. I've seen what happens to people when they lose it. Their eyes lose the sparkles. Their words no longer matter. The only thing they wake up to is a bottle and that's only so they can go back to sleep.

Probably the most admirable thing a man can do is not to do something -- and that's give up. Some weird or faulty logic that a writer likes to create with self-righteous word play.

The truth is: A writer who neglects their subconscious is a wingless bird.

And the only real way to get in touch with the subconscious is to grow wings. Beer, wine, and OE 800 are just a few feathers. This sort of writing style should be exercised with a bit of moderation, but only if you care more about your body than your reader. A sober writer is about as interesting as the father of Patty Hearst. Maybe the leakage will be exciting.

I don't think you can write a good book unless you're angry or curious...and if you're both then it should be great. Even then, a good writer is one in a million. Being there are over 300 million people in the United States means that over 300 people might be better, so I have to outwork them. Stay up 'til the sun rises. The body is a machine. Use it accordingly.

Perform Profane Rituals

Sitting half-naked in a Red Rock Casino room sipping Coors Light. Leg draped over a couch, glancing at the strip in the distance: a glittering magnet, the gold dust woman of dreams & nightmares. Down below me, in the casino, 99 people are losing, but 1 may have won. Side to side in the other rooms, people are fornicating in brief bouts of squeals. I can almost hear the sweat drip from the greasy bodies of the lazy swine. It's very rare in these obese days for a heavy bout of loud prolonged screwing to permeate the halls. The last time I heard such a thing was at some second-rate hotel by LAX. The room next door was occupied by some nymphomaniac stewardess who exclaimed her love for nine-inch black dildoes throughout the night. The more her friend sodomized her, the more she screamed & moaned. No such luck tonight in Fat City. Just as well, as I listen to Pink Floyd's "Money" in a junior suite custom-made for all types of deviate behavior. Writing this book qualifies. Might as well crank out some pages so I can convince my old lady that I deserve a nobber. Or I can just jerk it and skeet in the ice bucket for the next sucker who gets this room. Or maybe dribble in the dresser drawer. I like to put my stamp on a hotel room. I masturbate a minimum of two times a day in the bed sheets. Sometimes on the furniture, carpet, and walls also. I mark my territory in a primal way. I've probably performed this profane ritual in about 25-30 different Red Rock rooms. But this time will be different. I'm here for a comped two night stay...meaning I should be able to shed my DNA all over this suite in a dozen different places. Be sure to bring a black light if you ever stay at Red Rock...that way you can see my mark. I skeet in a frenzied zigzag pattern. Call me the Zorro of bodily fluids.

 Just so we're clear on this: You just spent 2 minutes reading about my masturbation habits in hotel rooms. You're welcome.

 That maniacal naked man in the Red Rock window flogging his mongoose is me. Surprised I haven't ended up on YouTube yet. Maybe if I get "caught" then I could get my own reality show. Why not? My penis has more personality than most people on these shows. TV is basically one big nut-busting barrage of seminal ads spaced between imbecilic fluids. *Selah.*

 Strange times when RIPD commercials break up the news updates of the Martin/Zimmerman case. A week after Newtown, the TV advertised such family friendly fare like *Bullet in the Head* and *Gangster Squad*. Now Gabby Giffords is shooting guns at the range. Everything officially means nothing. Pigs haven't grown wings yet, but they're sure as hell shittin' feathers. Life has become something you destroy in a video game. A time to be frittered away in a passive state of aggression. Clap at its loss in an action flick. Bullets & $ are intertwined and ingrained so deep in our culture can they ever be pried out?

 Just saw a *Jack Reacher* commercial. I want to buy that DVD because he's so much tougher than me. Mr. Reacher is the man I wish I were. And there you have the mind state of the people who pay for that shit.

I turn off the TV before I have a brain embolism brought on by the constant stream of bull manure. Then I manage to get a couple winks and wake up to see a smoggy haze hanging over the strip. A mixture of exhaust fumes, forest fire smoke, and methane gas emitted from buffet enthusiasts. A good day to stay inside Red Rock and play bingo. It's cheap and I can usually score 3-4 free beers a session. Me, and old women & men with the faces of catcher mitts, all chasing the elusive American Dream with a dauber. It's easy work...just wait for your number to be called. Bingo or not, that is how most people spend their life, whether they want to or not. We're a culture ingrained with Christian guilt. We're not supposed to do this, or that, especially that which makes us happy. Work 9-5 and spend the rest of the time watching television. But what if I don't want to watch TV? Or if I prefer to work 9pm - 5am? What if all the cacophonous pop culture cunt shit makes me feel alone? The only way to escape the monotony is to be awake while others are asleep, sheep resting for the next day's slow death. I don't want to die today, or tonight. This little piece of solitude I have of doing something I want to do is enough. It makes me feel alive. I am my own boss. My own maker. What I write means something...if only to myself, and that's all that matter because it's *right*. So many people try to please other people, but the only path to happiness is to please one's self. My writing is like a vibrator for the mind. And so I play with it all day instead of going to bingo...

Mani Motivation

Growing up in Sandtown I'd run into the local Sack n Save and shoplift the biggest bottle of Manischewitz wine they had. Then guzzle it outside in the parking lot -- savoring the sweet warm nectar.

Until one day I drank too much and barfed everywhere -- a scarlet stream of puke that painted the sidewalks a gory yet festive shade.

I may be older now, but the Mani still causes me to spew on things...it may as well be on your brain.

Thank your 2nd-grade reading teacher for what you're about to try and comprehend:

Make a Hater eat shit like a John Waters flick,
slaughter it
Never write a watered-down flick,

Spy vs. Spy, Why drive when I can fly?
like Blake Griffin, there is no competition
As long as I'm alive,

Dunk from the 3 point line with every word I write,
Up 'til 3AM every night tryin' to get this script tight,

Feels like I die every time I close my eyes,
Here today, Gone tomorrow, can't get any cash singin' lullabies,

My office light on longer than the Luxor light,
I won't say goodnight until the Eastern Sky gets bright,

You sleep, I write
You eat, I write
Your dreams, My life
My eyes open on the prize

    Just blowing off some steam in a Mani-induced haze...I'm not an egomaniac, but after writing for a twelve hour stretch it feels *good* to just blow out some hip-hop poetry.
    Finished my spy script...an idea that's been bouncing around inside my mind for a decade...and it's taken me a minute to get it down in screenplay form. Now I may discard it just as quick. Too much gunplay in real life, do we need another violent action movie?
    A job is tough, but I don't think anything's tougher than staring at a white page or computer screen and have to create something magical upon it...and I've had damn near 50 jobs...none's tougher than writing...but nothing's better.
    So allow me to talk some shit...I've been screenwriting for a while...and I've learned this:
-It never gets easier
-But you become a better writer (I can't even read some of my old scripts)

    It's hard work...and that's fine...I watched *The Social Network* and realized that I will never be "the smartest guy in the room", but I will be the hardest working man in the room!
    Any writer worth his weight has some doubts...questions if they are any good...and so every now & then a Mani-inspired self-esteem boost is vital to beat the odds.

I can say this:
-If you write every day, you are a writer.
-10 years...unless you're Zoroaster, then you need 10 years of steady writing to do anything good.
And progress, get better, revise, and Believe in yourself.

Author's note: *Writing is playing the guitar with the mind, using words instead of guitar picks. An Eric Clapton riff is the aim...at least one a chapter.*

39.
Bitch-Slap List

Every book should end with a bitch-slap list...a reader's guide to the contemporary bogeyman lurking in their society. Shine a light on the swine. Pigs prefer to rut in darkness. These Porkupines can be cunts or corporations, which, according to the Supreme Court, can be the same thing. The best way to bitch-slap a corporation is to boycott their services and products. The best way to bitch-slap a celebrity or politician is to boycott their movies or vote against them. The best way to bitch-slap a person is to rake an open hand against their deserving face.

The official *Teaching Snapping Turtles* bitch-slap list:

-**Banks** that gouge the consumer – Wells Fargo, **Citibank**, Sallie Mae, Chase, Bank of America, Capital One, and the worst one of all, federal government student loans. Exploiting college kids who can least afford it is a multi-billion dollar scam. Avoid student loans at all cost -- they are designed to enslave the populace and turn the middle-class into indentured servants.

-**NRA** - terrorists. I'll bitchslap any member before they can pull their piece.

-**Halliburton** - A physical manifestation of Satan.

-**Shell Oil** - Google 'Shell and Nigeria'.

-**Kock Brothers** – The Koch Bros may be the worst scum in the world who continually profit from pollution and corruption. They have bought more politicians and Supreme Court judges than Tammany Hall, and dream of one day completely controlling a ruined Earth from a cryogenic state safely ensconced on the moon so they can still delude themselves into thinking that the world revolves around them.

-**BP** - Obvious choice unless you've been comatose for the past few years, and if that's the case then you're probably not reading this book. Maybe one of your intelligent relatives bought the audiobook version for you and is playing it right now for your enjoyment. Thank them when you wake up.

-**Tea Party** Politicians - Some of the most dangerous people in the United States. Palinites keep spitting hatred all through the media. If only 5% of their followers are crazy then that's a concern because they've already infiltrated our society and more than likely armed because of our nation's lax gun laws. Don't Tread On Me is now a terroristic flag draped on dead police officer thanks to the hatred that Tea Party people spew.

-**Monsanto** - Used to make Agent Orange and now they sell genetically engineered herbicide & seeds to farmers. Their Roundup contributes to autism and pollution. Their seeds contaminate our nation's integrity. Obama & the FDA not only turn a blind eye, but also protect the company.

-**Walmart** - Pays its employees peanuts even though the Waltons are billionaires. Employees are forced to drain away taxpayers' dollars on food stamps & welfare. Anyone who shops at Walmart deserves a bitchslap also.

-**LeBron James** - Read the *Whore of Akron*. Scott Raab writes with a vulnerable honesty that most modern day writers shy away from. A refreshing read in our age of self-promotion. My favorite excerpt from the book: "What another sees in you will reveal that person. What you see in another reveals yourself. We are -- each of us and all of us -- mirrors." Which reminds me of a line from Marquis de Sade's novel *Justine*: "The mirror sees the man as beautiful, the mirror loves the man; another mirror sees the man as frightful and hates him; and it is always the same being who produces the impressions." My impression of James has always been the same: someone who desperately needs a bitchslap. His behavior is a trait of American corporate culture: Corrupt. No Loyalty. Exploits the expectations of his consumers and employees. And breeds disappointment. On the other hand, can I really criticize an Ohio dude who prefers a warm climate to the harsh winters of Lake Erie? Miami, Cleveland. Take a pick.

-**Rob Zombie** – Remakes a horror classic like *Halloween* and ruins it with his white-trash aesthetic.

-Anyone who says anything negative about **Bela Lugosi** -- don't disrespect a legend.

-Anyone who boos **BB King** at a concert is a dick that deserves a bitch-slap with both hands. I'm looking at you, St. Louis.

-**Bryan Singer** - Made that wack-ass *Superman* movie. Back when I lived in Fairborn, I drove to Cincy to see it, and paid extra for 3D. Singer also tried to make Nazis heroic in the lame *Valkyrie*.

-**John Boehner** - The boner from Ohio who constantly squeezes out tears like a hack actress during a Merchant-Ivory audition. Helped shut down the United States government for a couple weeks to show his disapproval for Universal Health Care. He believes sick people deserve to die, and (Sam Jackson voice) he hopes they burn in Hell!

-**Joe Eszterhas** - The raspy born-again ball licker who wrote *Showgirls* yet called me disgusting when I met him in Cleveland. I gave him a pass because his grandson was with him...but the crusty cunt still deserves to be bitch-slapped with an AARP card. The scumbag attends some snooty Christian church in Cleveland and trudges down the aisle carrying a big cross. Maybe not a scumbag because scumbags are human, but he's insectile like a roach. He wrote like a nihilist when it was profitable then changed to a god-fearing conservative because of self-inflicted throat cancer. Slime-infested maggot shite are his new stories of choice. He aims to write a Jewish epic starring Mel Gibson.

-**Mr. Albert** - The horsemouthed 7th grade choir teacher in Sandusky, Ohio. He bopped my head against my buddy's head because we were talking during choir practice. No warning, just a bop that sounded like a cue ball break. Choir practice -- the same thing as douching...no reason to make a big deal of it. And certainly not reason enough to smack skulls. So the next time I see that ugly shovel-tooth fuck, I'm gonna bop his head against something, and I hope it's when he's eating out with his wife. That type of disturbing experience would shake him the rest of his days. To sit down to a nice comfortable dinner only to have some unknown man walk over and coconut-crack your head so hard against your wife's head that her dentures fly across the table for no apparent reason. That would be it. Game over. Donkeyface would develop a sudden unshakable case of agoraphobia, and the last thing he would hear years later when his brain aneurism bursts causing him to fall face first into a pile of mashed potatoes and suffocate would be the Pop!

-**BYU** - This institution is enraptured by a religion that dictates sodomy a sin. I can't subscribe to any theology that frowns upon anal sex. God created that orifice for a reason and I hate to think it's only for poop.
These pious cretins have an "Honor Code". Basically, it says they're against drinking alcohol and coffee, having sex before marriage, beards and shaggy hair, foul filthy cuss words, and homosexual behavior. What aren't they against? Oh

yeah, a boring bigoted life! Any Mormon who comes ringing my doorbell is getting bitch-slapped. I find BYU's honor code ironic, as there is no honor in being homophobic.

-Misc **Cunts**- American Chemistry Council, Weinberg Group, Exxon Mobil, Joey Heck, and the Blackstone Group.

-**Carlyle Group** - American global asset management firm aka War Profiteer. An inbred conglomerate of corporate hacks & political whores who made a fortune on the Iraq war. Made a half billion advising a Saudi investment in Citigroup...aided a Prince who financially supports Palestinian terrorists even though Carlyle exec David Rubenstein is Jewish...proving that Carlyle has no ethics or conscience. They also defaulted on over $16 billion of mortgage debt.

Boycott/Bitch-Slap these restaurants -- their greedy CEOs or Franchise Owners want to disenfranchise their employees by not providing health care...so they fire workers or cut their hours to part-time:

-**Dennys** (this grease spoon has a sordid history ranging from racism to despising Obamacare)
-**Papa Johns** (crappy pizzas that clog arteries. John is a rich cunt who supported Romney and gripes about Obamacare -- echoes of "Damn that Darky" cascade down the empty halls of his mansion)
-**Applebee's** (my vote for blandest restaurant in America. If you want to be surrounded by douchebags with no taste then this is the spiz-zot)
-**Wendys** (big girl cut employee hours to avoid Obamacare)
-**Olive Garden** (fake Italian slop...if you want Mudbutt, eat here)
-**Red Lobster** (overpriced garbage...they only hire part-time workers now)
-**Five Guys Burgers** (if you want to resemble a matzo ball, eat here)
-**Cheesecake Factory** (for the prices they charge, you'd think they could pay their employees)
-**McDonalds** (refuses to pay workers a decent wage, advises employees to stop complaining and to take two vacations a year...destination of choice: skid row)
-**Whole Foods** (CEO compared Obamacare to fascism -- Holocaust survivors disagree. To make matter worse, some of their beef was recalled due to Mad Cow fears…proving that the CEO's beef was misplaced.)

These purveyors of slop all despise Obamacare and do not want to provide employees with health insurance. They'll cut hours and fire employees even though the profits keep coming in. It's ironic; most of the businesses against

Obamacare are the main contributors to health problems.

There are plenty of good alternatives in every city and town. The local mom and pop restaurants are smart picks. Or hit up my TripAdvisor recommendations. Even better, cook at home!

And there it is...

If you find yourself on this list, don't fret; it's just a bitch-slap. Your face may sting and be red for several hours, but eventually it will go away. And no, you can't worm your way off the list until you've been smacked. The only way to stay off this list is to not act like a bitch, which for some is an impossibility. At least now, there are consequences. So stop acting like a bitch before you get slapped...

40.
Prognosis

There is darkness at the end of the tunnel. Shadows swirling. Soft sounds of trepidation scuttling down the track. An unlit fuse runs through. No matches anywhere. How to light it?

"An era can be said to end when its basic illusions are exhausted."
-A quote by Arthur Miller that Brad Meltzer used in his comic *Identity Crisis*.

   This quote sums up the era we live in. A blind gluttonous populace clings to illusions of greatness while reality pokes holes in those Swiss cheese slices every single day. And so our country is experiencing an identity Crisis. We are taught that America is the best country in the world, and we believe it even though we do nothing to prove it. Paying taxes and eating Taco Bell is not making America the best. Reveling in ignorance and hiding behind the flag actually degrades the symbol you use to hide your stupidity. Adhering to the current status quo only contributes to America being a Bully Nation composed of pococurante pricks.
   The generation in power is a lost cause. Old people prefer to flounder in ignorance...their inadequate response to Newtown proved that. It's up to the young people to make changes. Maybe this book can be the small spark that ignites a much-needed evolution. And maybe we can work together and begin a new era of trying to fulfill the promise of a great America.
   People *can* change. I changed. We all can. It's possible.

   Just because it's possible doesn't mean it will happen. Some people refuse to change. They'd rather our country crumble before they let go of their outdated superstitions & guns...which are usually one and the same. Teaching a snapping turtle how to chew bubble gum is an impossible task. Wisdom is wasted on the weak-minded. This book is for the next generation who I sincerely hope will be better than mine was. Anything is possible...is true...but for any worthy change or endeavor to happen requires work from every single person. A populace *willing* to change can accomplish anything. And this populace has to want to do it for the right reason. Not for personal gain or money, but for a sense of purpose and accomplishment. There is no greater feeling in the world than doing something that is Right that benefits other people.

Some people refuse to change because they feel an overwhelming sense of helplessness. The obstacles are many...and in some communities, progressive thought is drowned out by ignorant conformity. Mob mentality can be a powerful deterrent, especially when your family and friends are the mob. You can't choose your family, but you can choose your friends. And if your friends are ignorant then it's time to make new ones. And if your family is ignorant, then maybe it's time to start a new one. One person can change the world, but it's important that one person surrounds themself with the right people. Start a civic group based on a social movement is just one easy way to foment change in any community.

Rx

The most important change that needs to happen before any other is our mind state. We can no longer be a reluctant pessimist whose refusal to change is based on fear. Heroes do the right thing in the face of overwhelming odds. There will always be evil in the world. History has proven that, and contemporary violence continues to reinforce the point. But are we to let evil rule us? Should we stand idly by while our collective ignorance slowly kills the country we profess to love? Even if we don't win, at least we fought the good fight. History judges the real winners and losers anyway.

I put off finishing this book for five years. This is the sort of book an author with any sense of self-preservation would publish posthumously, yet it's my first. Sometimes, in the rarest moments of frustration, I wish I were dumb so I wouldn't think about our society and the world. Instead: My brain *never* quits thinking, and maybe I would be a bit happier if it did. Is ignorance bliss?

Maybe not, maybe the reason I love life so much is *because* I never quit thinking. I realize the true temporal beauty of our existence is so important that we need to make the best of it. Heaven is here on this Earth, and so is Hell. Without good people trying to make a difference then the balance gets thrown further out of whack, to the detriment of Humanity. My aim is to relegate the notion of Hell to mythology and everyone on this Earth can live a life worthy of respect. It is possible to enjoy the pleasures of life and to make society better. When a person engages in both to equal proportions, the two facets become indistinguishable.

For the most part, America is a decent place to live, but there's an undercurrent of violence that runs below the thin veneer of civilization and it pokes its evil head out on a daily basis to disrupt the monotony of consumption. And the people are left in the lowlands to fend for themselves while the politicians are safely ensconced atop their ideological mountainsides of greed. So the system becomes rusty, clanking, gears clicking. Progress on a pulley, being lifted with as much efficiency as building a pyramid in the desert. And when it's all done, and the original workers are all gone, the progress they initially strived for is nothing but a lie. This is where we are in American History.

   I love America, that's why I want to make it better. To me, this country is not a commodity to be exploited, nor are its citizens. The American Dream is the ability to say there is no American Dream. Freedom of Speech. That's it. Not a Cadillac and a white picket fence, but the ability to change the government to make it a more sustainable and equitable government for all...just by speaking, or writing. That is my dream.

   I'm the living, breathing embodiment of the American Dream: an average man with average skills, with a small to medium penis (depending on wind speed and temperature), no definable talents or motivation, yet possessing a spirit that never quits. Over-achieving is our national past-time.

"The most terrifying fact about the universe is not that it is hostile, but that it is indifferent. If we can come to terms with this indifference and accept the challenges of life within the boundaries of death, our existence as a species can have genuine meaning and fulfillment.

However vast the darkness, we must supply our own light."
-Stanley Kubrick

We are the spark.

Project Pissbag

supplement

You know heavy business is on the horizon when you wake up humming the "War Hymn of the Republic". Past the point of no return lies freedom. I don't always say the right thing. I may not always write the right thing. But I try to do the right thing. Action defines Character. It is time for everyone to be the amazing people of change they were born to be.

The 1% extremely Rich do not care about the American People. They do not respect the political process…it's just another tool to be bought. And they are mildly amused by Occupy protests. Just another buzzing mosquito to be swatted by the hired help sporting riot gear. The Rich continue to accumulate massive amounts of wealth, poison the Earth with their companies, and avoid taxes like a bulimic in a dodgeball game. It's time to change the game and send these heathens packing. They hide their money in foreign places like Sweden, Ireland, and the Caymans; it's time we make life so uncomfortable for these exploiters in America that they flee to live with their money.

30 MPH winds gusting through the Las Vegas valley forced me indoors to celebrate Earth Day this year, and the best way I knew how was to write this supplement to my book *Teaching Snapping Turtles How To Chew Bubblegum*. Mother Nature must be mad, blowing away everything, trashcans and scorpions all. Except: the human form of scorpions inhabiting boardrooms still roams freely. Project Pissbag is my answer. A brief guide to Evolution based upon the idea of Nonviolent Fear. Corporate scum has been too comfortable too long. Time to take the fight to them. Protests and petitions are too weak when faced with the overwhelming all-consuming machinations of Capitalism. We have to make them fear the people using nonviolent means. Psychological warfare is the only answer.

Project Pissbag's tenets will be dictated by instilling Fear in corporate assholes, having a sense of humor, and most of all, displaying that there is a consequence for immoral corporate actions. We will become the true people's court. The common man's Batman. No more hiding behind the cloak of the Supreme Court, it is time to hold the corporate CEO's accountable for their actions and make it undesirable to work for cunt companies. Working for a cunt company will not only be morally reprehensible, but socially unacceptable.

If a corporate democrap doesn't protect the people then the people must protect themselves. Wait for a snail to move through a polluted river to change it doesn't make sense. The People must protect themselves. Sabotage may be the only answer.

The first few potential projects:

1: Increase cyber vandalism in conjunction with Anonymous.

2: Start a drone program to constantly prank & soil & defile CEO's houses that run companies that soil the environment. The initial prank of choice: Urine safely secured in sandwiched bags. Seems innocuous until a drone drops a gross (a dozen dozen) of them on the roof of a home. They piss on us. Let's piss back. First up: Rex Tillerson.

3: Utilize the restless youth (high school & college students) to relentlessly prank an offensive CEO's company. Sheldon Adelson's & Steve Wynn's casinos would be prime targets due to their reluctance on not properly financing Clark County Schools.

4: Financial Anarchy: Let us all brilliantly "game the system" like the oligarchs and their banker tops do. Get a credit card, max it out with no intentions of paying it back, then hide behind consumer laws. It's time to fight dirty. If the Federal Government bails out the targeted financial institution then tax boycotts should be implemented in a strategic manner along with widespread pissing on federal property so no grass grows unaffected. A small vegetative sacrifice to make

Mother Earth better. It's better to piss on a lilac than pollute an aquifer. Our enemies engage in Machiavellian financial schemes, so should we.

5. Organize with traditional protest organizations. They have the supporters, financial means, and know the prime targets. Though we will need an environmentally conscious Bruce Wayne supporter.

Every project will be conceived with the philosophy of nonviolence. Project Pissbag is an assault on corporate tyranny using devious means of Fear and Humor…two things that the Rich are unaccustomed to. The overall aim is to drive them out of our great country before they wreck it. Not everything will be legal. What the corporations do when they pollute our lands isn't either. So anonymity is a must. Nationwide.

Fear is a useful tactic. Try to coax decency out of an indecent pig is like trying to pluck feathers off a snake. There is none to be had. They feel nothing but greed and fear. It's fight or flight, and we outnumber them so it's time to send them packing using whatever nonviolent nefarious means we can. The 1% lives in our country. Not the other way around. We don't live to serve them. They're not gonna stop Fracking, Polluting, Mining, Exploiting our country unless we stop them. The time is now or subsequent generations will suffer the adverse effects of Global Warming and income inequality.

Cyber Vandalism

This is the one area where young savvy eco-conscious computer programmers would be invaluable members of the revolution. Anonymous is one such entity, but other ones could be formed…with the intention to not criminally do financial damage to online companies or corporate websites, but to deface them with cyber graffiti on a regular basis until they change their ways. Hack their systems and make their hyperlinks transport the clicker to bestiality porn. Or Mister Rogers videos. Same thing. And post righteous anger on their homepage. And to constantly barrage social media websites with examples of their corporate cunt transgressions until people wake up or delete you.

The entire Internet is like an interconnected mirage: gleaming pools of half-truths a mile ahead while you sweat it out in the desert of reality. Pull the plug out of their heads, and their ass will follow. Truth isn't a pill, but the courage to communicate it.

Drone Delivery

Faygo soda or Pabst Blue Ribbon is the fuel. The considerate do-gooder consumes the liquid then recycles it, aims straight into the outstretched samwhich bag. Fills it up. Seals it. Then throws it in the direction of evil.

A rich sweat-hog who pollutes other communities with legal impunity shouldn't be allowed to hide behind gated communities in leisure. Ironically, thanks to the technology of the Establishment, drones are a viable delivery system of Fear-inducing pissbags. Rex Tillerson, the CEO of Exxon, oversees an exploitation program of fracking nationwide and believes in this clean technology so much he is suing another fracking company for fracking his backyard. Well, frack that! A month-long strafing of his house with pissbags and buckets of oil should prove a point. The CEO of Shell should get their monthly dose also, considering the decades they polluted Nigeria. These heels need to understand what it means to open your front door and see pollution. Let's give it to them.

Another worthy recipient is Ira Rennert, the king of pollution and building mansions. One of his favorite places to hide is his 100 million dollar mansion in the Hamptons. I'm sure we could easily initiate a bodily fluid drone campaign with the surreptitious help of helicopter-weary neighbors. This is just a temporary, yet satisfying, diversion, as Global Warming will wash away his architecture of ego in a hundred years. Virus Ira will be long gone, so it's imperative to provide the Fear to him now…the sort of sudden ecological disdain his companies provided to so many other communities over the years. A virus values companies over

Community. So let's provide these bastards with company. Ira's companies poisoned communities from Missouri to Peru, it's only right we poison his with excrement. Though human shit probably smells just like the offender smelling it.

Wall Street bankers and banks that are exempt from criminal prosecution should be provided company also. It seems we live in a country where only Companies count, so it is our patriotic duty to provide impolite company when the situation necessitates itself. Maybe this sort of impolite public response is not civil, but neither are its targets. These reptiles sun themselves on the warmest rocks, domestic or foreign, never worrying about the insects underneath those rocks. 99 insects can overwhelm 1 reptile.

Youth

Young people have an excess of energy, but no direction. Protests seem boring. Books take too long to read. Youth have misplaced passions...see: every pop culture fad. But that misplaced passion can be redirected into nonviolent fear campaigns. Utilize their mischievous spirit in useful ways. Turn the lucrative demographic of corporations into their main source of opposition. Have kids make daily walk-thrus of certain casinos strategically dropping stink bombs inside and outside. Strategically place ready to be hatched python eggs around the Encore casino. Reptile egg incubation services are easy to find on Craigslist. Note to Wynn & Adelson: Increase school taxes or suffer.

Pranks can be the gateway venue to political activism. The main weakness of contemporary liberal movements is engaging the youth in meaningful change. The main thing we forget is that young people are in a perpetual sea of confusion being led by the tides of consumption of acceptance. They really don't know any better until we paddle a progressive surfboard out onto the currents of Capitalism and show them something fun and meaningful. Sure, pranks can result in the expulsion from a casino, but so what? Good riddance to bad rubbish.

Young people have been bombarded with advertisements of enticement since they were old enough to open their eyes. And now they have smartphones and Internet. Crackheads are easier to reform. And I'm not in the reformation business. Show the truth to the youth, and then appeal to their vitality. Point it in the right direction. Something I wish I could've shown my teenage self years ago. The 60+ students in Teaneck, New Jersey who vandalized a high school as a senior prank are prime recruits. Turn pranks into progress.

A gelatinous tide of consumption sucks us all in then retreats, leaving us sprawled out on the beach of life like quivering clams. No bodies, just hard yapping shells that need to be fed and picked on a regular basis. The only sustenance is the protein tongue. A muscle cuz it never stops wagging. While the brain resembles a thimble. The tongue outgrew it. Lapping at the water fed to it. Even if the water is poisoned. It doesn't matter. The tongue is thirsty.

And so we're sold truth in twenty ounce bottles of high-fructose syrup. And you must be 21 years old to drink something beneficial. By then, you're indoctrinated into a Walt Disney fascist fantasy. The good guy gets the girl. The good girl gets the broom. And the bad people get shit. Wipe your ass and make room. Or…

Put down the smart phone and be a smart person. Instead of texting, do something that a writer may one day commit to text. lol: the reactions of old rich men to impressionable young people's obsession with Fashion/Fascism.

Maybe our country is just one great big chunk of land where a never-ending battle is waged between greedy opportunists and democratic idealists. And so it is up to us idealists who share the wit and wisdom of the founding fathers to protect against the imperialistic infection that runs through the veins of America like Mercury in a thermometer. Tories don't sell redcoats anymore, but coats with corporate logos made by young Bangladeshi women crushed in bad conditions forced to drink dye-polluted waters. Our freedom is not just ours, but everyone's. Our dollar pays for the enslavement of others unless we stay vigil.

Abe Lincoln died for what he believed in. So did MLK. The least we could do is live for what we believe in.

Not what we can buy.

Money can't buy love. Or Identity. Or writing ability...or musical ability. And definitely not beauty. (Discounting plasticized monstrosities with electric eel lips and scud missile silicone tits...these sperm hoovers need beauty like Michael J Fox needs to play ping-pong.)

Bad Humor doesn't preclude me from insightful examination of the American psyche. Do unto your neighbor before he undoes you. The bigger the car, the bigger you are. Greener the lawn, the better chemicals. You are what you appear to be.

Image is everything to a young person. But the only image that matters is the one we assign to our self. Anyone can wear a nice shirt, but only a real person performs a good deed. Say something nice to someone: contributes to Humankind.

Wear something expensive: contributes to rich dicks. Exploits poor people.

So go to retail stores with mouthfuls of grape juice and surreptitiously spit on every bullshit shirt you see.

Discover Card Anarchy

Immediately get a Discover Card soon as you turn 18 then max it out on stereo equipment, shoes, clothes, beer, and escorts. Buy beers and laugh at their stupidity...then chop up the card whilst screaming in an inebriated rage. Make sure to point two middle fingers at the sky. Wait five years, and this transgression will be erased.

Repeat at age 24 with as many credit cards you can get your hands on. At least 10-12 credit cards should suffice. Use these cards for groceries & beer (one and the same), online sports gambling, online sports gambling, and did I mention, online sports gambling? Deposit the cards' max into your online sports gambling accounts. Make sensible bets and win. Extract your winnings via Fed Ex checks. And fuck the credit cards!

These dickless banks deserve to be exploited. Max out the cards on misc hedonistic enterprises. Check state laws, avoid contacts, and then sit back with the assurances of time-barred debts. Statute of Limitations is garlic to these financial vampires. Roll up obscene bills on these bastards, and play the game. Why not? They travel first-class; we can enjoy happy hours and surround sound. A couple of these pissbombs in the face of banks and we can start evening the score. If all else fails, declare bankruptcy like a corporation.

Student Loans are the Jaws swallowing limbs and souls with impunity. Loans are federal insurance. Big sums of money insuring the populace behave. After the 60's & 70's the Establishment made it a priority to make college unaffordable to the lower & middle classes without loans. And the shylock guv gives us people a pass with the sole condition: Conform.

Pretend. Smile. Take the admission. Learn the game. And attend for a semester and cause trouble. Get a grant; spend it on an escort or weed. Get a Stafford Loan, spend it on an escort or weed…then bounce. These cathedrals of Capitalism are built brick by brick by the dollars of poor students too bright-eyed to know that they are being pimped.

Colleges like UNLV swear up and down they are hurting for money and need to cut employees and/or academic programs yet pony up extravagant amounts of money for mediocre coaches in football and basketball. The biggest scam going around. Boycott these bitches, and the female dogs residing in your own academic community. Probably the best thing you can do as a student with a conscience is travel down to Blue Diamond with a few buddies, especially ones that own a truck, and find a burro. Entice that burro into the cab with a few carrots and a mush made from gravy, Valium, corn, and liquid lithium.

Transport the snoring burro to the backyard of the nearest AD, and lay the beast at the screen door. Gently stick a blackcat firecracker into the poopchute of the poor beast and light a match.

The savage sounds of panic are almost worth the psychic costs of witnessing mankind at its worst. Sometimes I think we'd all be better off with a firecracker exploding in our own tight asscracks from time to time. Or maybe 2Pac had the right idea: that the poor and rich should alternate lifestyles from time to time. Say every year?

Sounds too much like an 80's comedy movie like *Trading Places*. Instead, how about a society that is fair to everyone?

It would be interesting if everyone just made a deal to abstain from Banks and Casinos for a year. Could we do it? I'm ready...

Benefactor

Bunch of rich guys out there admiring their social profiles in cigar smoke circles reflected on the clouds their factories keep spewing. Maybe there is a guy or gal out there who believes and wants to contribute money to the cause. Cool. Let's set it up. They can control the drone if they want to. Crash it, fine, but hook us up with another one. I'll supply the pissbag munitions. PBR provides.

The donations to our cause are a special kind, the first of its kind. A couple bucks to a renegade cause that results in fear & laughter is unheard of...something Benjamin Franklin would think of with a remote controlled kite in a lightning storm.

Have some fun and give money to the cause. Drop well-deserved bodily fluids on the true villains of the 21st century, and pay some fearless daredevil to run through a CEO's yard with 500 yards of twine…naked.

Che Guevara promoted revolutionary ideas that may seem palatable in another 50 years if Climate Change continues unabated. His ideas, not mine, will become a reality in the next century unless things change…immediately.

I wish life were just about nobbers and music. Until then…

The asshole companies will not stop to Frack. Pollute. Mine. us til' it's too late. A "Corporation Mind" is made up. It's not a matter of if? It's a matter of when. A cruel game of leaping through toxic hoops wearing ankle bells. Lift your legs in the air and let the bells ring. Sing. A Chevron tune is a happy thing.

I can buy a bottle of Red Rooster wine for 5 bucks and the quality is comparable to the finest wines Roman emperors drank. And my spice rack would be the envy of kings. We live like royalty. But at the cost of others. Americans are the 1% compared to the rest of the world. So the top 1% of American wealth is the malevolent viral strain that causes inequality and it spreads like Ebola.

Where it goes, who knows? We are all infected. With what? Humanity? Or Capitalism?

What do you want to buy?

Or

Who do you want to hug?

Author's Last Note:

The Queen's English is for the Aristocracy.
My English is for the people.

The Chicago Manual of Style promotes all these superfluous petty rules that distorts Writing into an elusive source of awe and authority. Fuck that. Anyone can write so long as they possess intelligence and a point of view worth paying attention to.

[Oh, I know where to correctly place a comma so that makes me more qualified to communicate than a person with benevolent ideas to better society. Stay in your place while the petty people practice proper grammar.]

"May I pollute your aquifer in exchange for pennies?"
That's proper grammar.

About the Author:

Jonathan has a BA in bs from Nomadic Life University. A man with a conscience and a buzz in equal parts, depending on the day. If you seek any additional info then re-read the book.

"The meek shall inherit the Earth.
Maybe so
But that's only because the Bold inhabit the stars!"

If the meek inherit the Earth then I'm moving to Mars.
-JH

www.ingramcontent.com/pod-product-compliance
Lightning Source LLC
Chambersburg PA
CBHW022004220426
43663CB00007B/956